IMAGES
of America

GRAY
MAINE

IMAGES
of America

GRAY
MAINE

Louise M. Knapp
and the Gray Historical Society

ARCADIA
PUBLISHING

ISBN 978-0-7385-8982-4

Published by Arcadia Publishing
Charleston, South Carolina

Printed in the United States of America

Library of Congress Catalog Card Number: 99-62639

For all general information contact Arcadia Publishing at:
Telephone 843-853-2070
Fax 843-853-0044
E-mail sales@arcadiapublishing.com
For customer service and orders:
Toll-Free 1-888-313-2665

Visit us on the Internet at www.arcadiapublishing.com

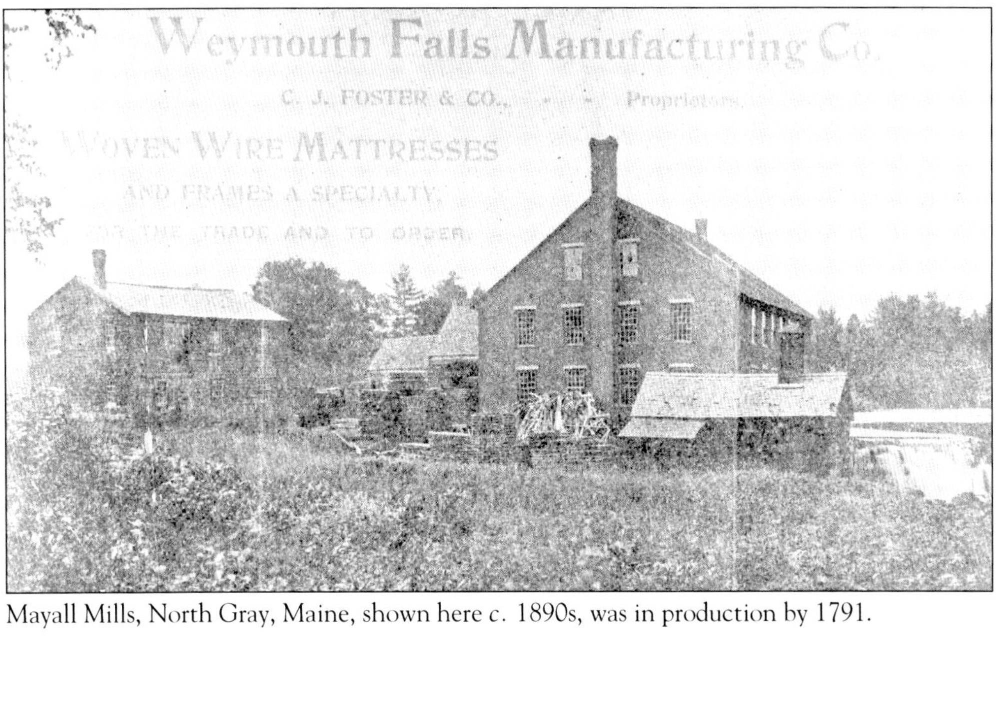

Mayall Mills, North Gray, Maine, shown here *c.* 1890s, was in production by 1791.

Contents

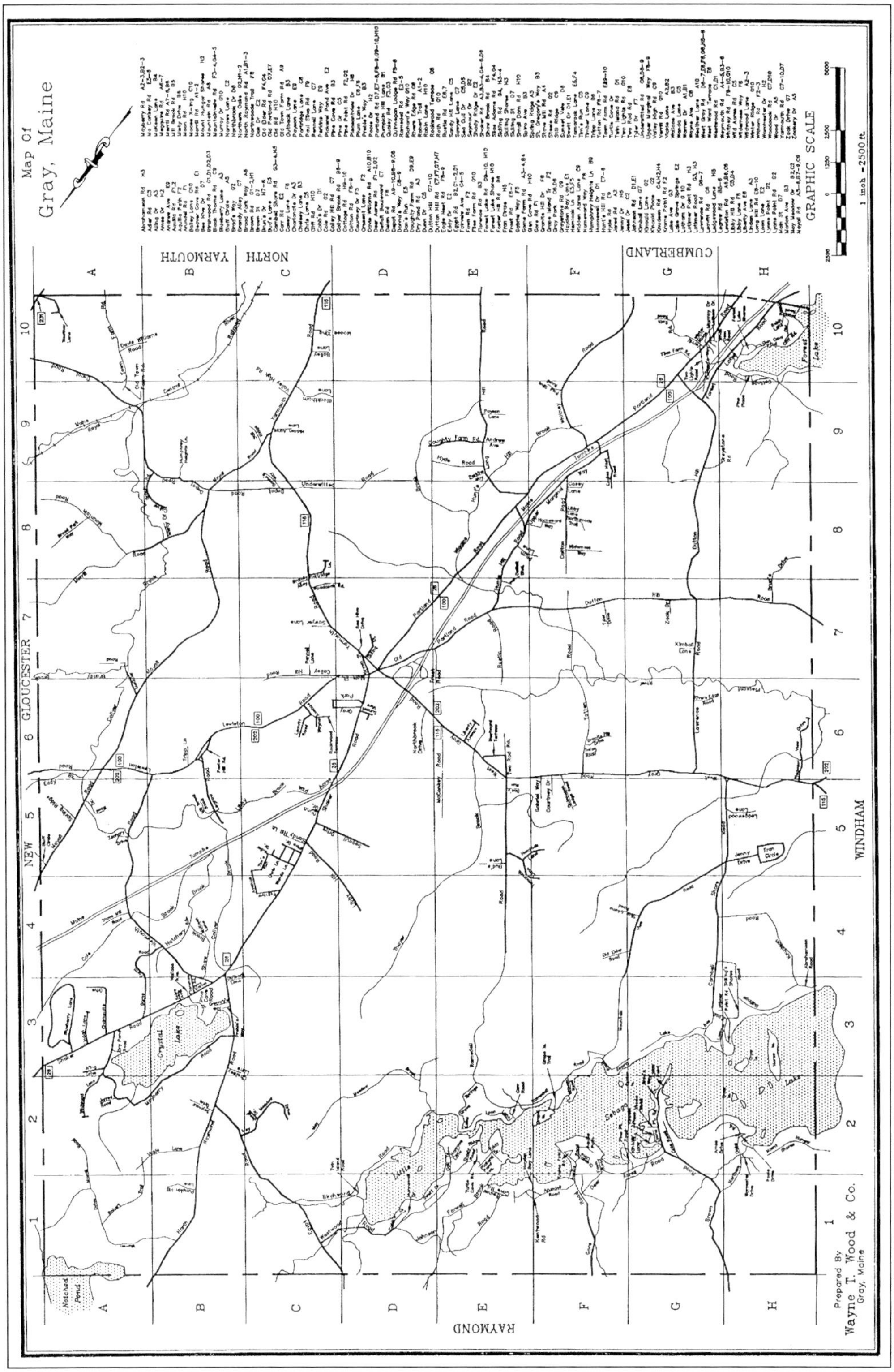
Map of Gray, Maine
GRAPHIC SCALE
1 inch =2500 ft.
Prepared By Wayne T. Wood & Co. Gray, Maine
NEW GLOUCESTER
NORTH YARMOUTH
CUMBERLAND
WINDHAM
RAYMOND

Introduction

Following a practice designed to encourage expansion in unsettled territory, reap the benefits of natural resources, strengthen claims on long disputed areas, and contribute to their defense, 60 men petitioned the General Court of Massachusetts Bay in 1735 to build homes, clear the land, build a meetinghouse and a church, clear a lot for a school, and have 60 families under such rules and regulations as the General Court shall direct. In 1736, the General Court voted that this petition be granted; that the petitioners lay out a township of 6 square miles; and that they return a plan for this area to the Court within 12 months. These conditions were met and the settlers authorized the formation of a group of "proprietors" from Massachusetts to oversee the establishment of public and private plots of land to form the necessary town properties.

By the early 1740s most of the public and private residences were completed and the town was nearing completion. In the spring of 1745, the new settlement was attacked by Native Americans, and all of the town structures and bridges were burned. The town was rebuilt by 1751 with the proper public and private 10-acre lots, shortly before the French and Indian War ignited and the town was once again wiped out. During the early 1760s, after the war had subsided, settlers began returning to the township and clearing the land, and the "proprietors" found it necessary to keep the original grant of land valid. The current Massachusetts Legislature was then petitioned further by the settlers for instructions, regulations, and conditions for establishing the new settlement.

One of the first families consisted of Moses Twitchell, his wife and children, his father, Thomas, his brother Jeremiah, and a crew of men. The group arrived from the Falmouth area bringing with them teams of oxen, a cow, and some hens, and in 1762 they settled permanently in what is now the Dutton Hill area near the Old Portland Road. Moses established a King's Mast Yard, to obtain suitable timber to be used by the Royal Navy and others as masts for their larger vessels. The mast timbers were cut, hauled during the winter to the Pleasant River in Gray, then floated down the Fore River through Westbrook to Portland, where they were loaded for transportation to England and other destinations.

From the 1760s to 1777 the number of families increased enough until the town became eligible for incorporation. Several of the early settling families included Moses Twitchell and his extended family, William Webster, Jabez Matthews, John Jenks, William and Joel Stevens, Daniel Hunt, John Humphrey, and a Captain Jonas Stevens. Jabez Hatch and a Samuel Hawes (Hewes), who was one of the proprietors, came to the area as contractors hired by the proprietors about this same time. Many other people from all walks of life settled within the boundaries of "New Boston," until the population became large enough in 1777 for some of the early leaders of the community to consider incorporating the town and setting up rules and regulations for all to follow.

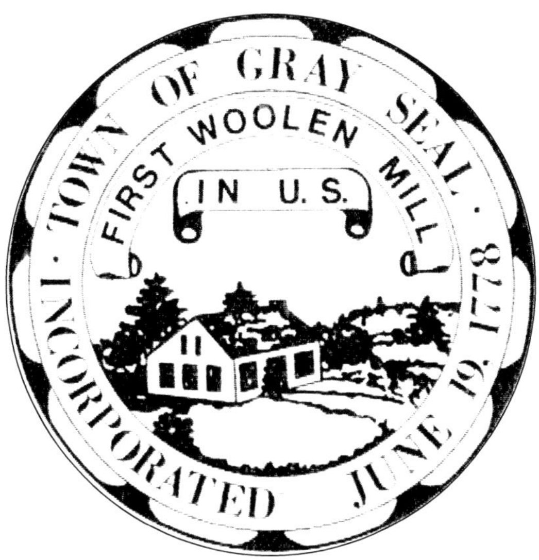

One

Watch Gray Grow

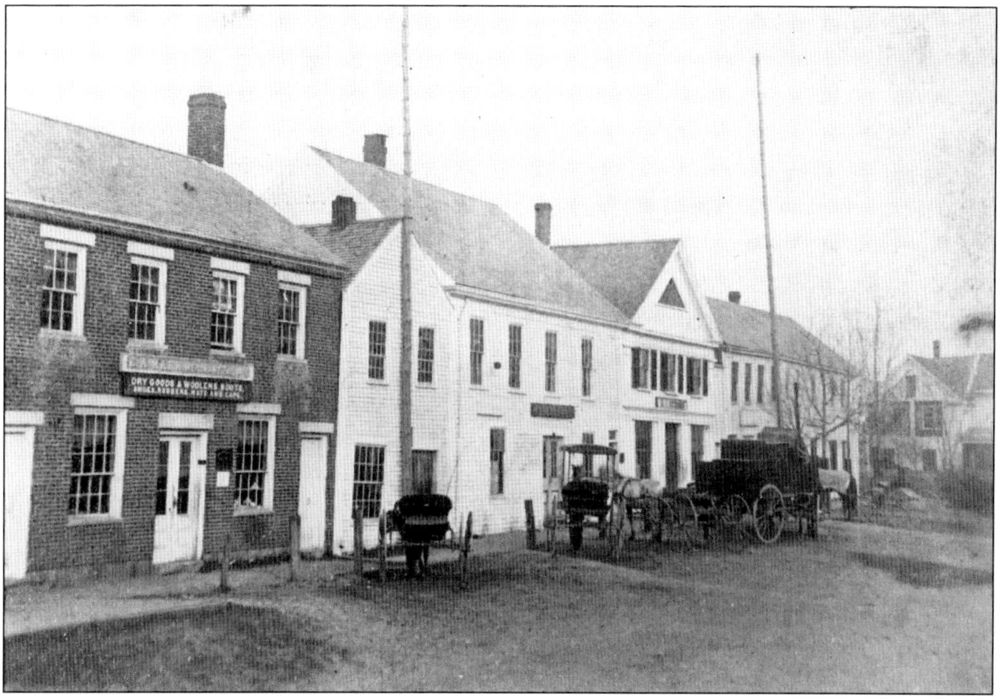

The west side of Gray Corner is shown here looking north, *c*. 1890s. The first building is the brick country general store, built in the 1840s. The narrow, wooden two-story building is the old harness shop, built in the 1830s and torn down in the 1880s for a new harness shop. Jim Small's store is the next building; by 1906 the second harness shop and Small's store had been replaced with a new building known as the Clark Block. The Latham Store is up next, followed by John Millikin's shop on the corner. To the far right is Osgood's Ice Cream Parlor.

Gray Corner was a great trade center, and the corner was busy with travelers from as far away as Vermont, many of them on their way to Portland to exchange their products. Hay, grain, food, and lodging were in great demand at this time in the life at Gray Corner.

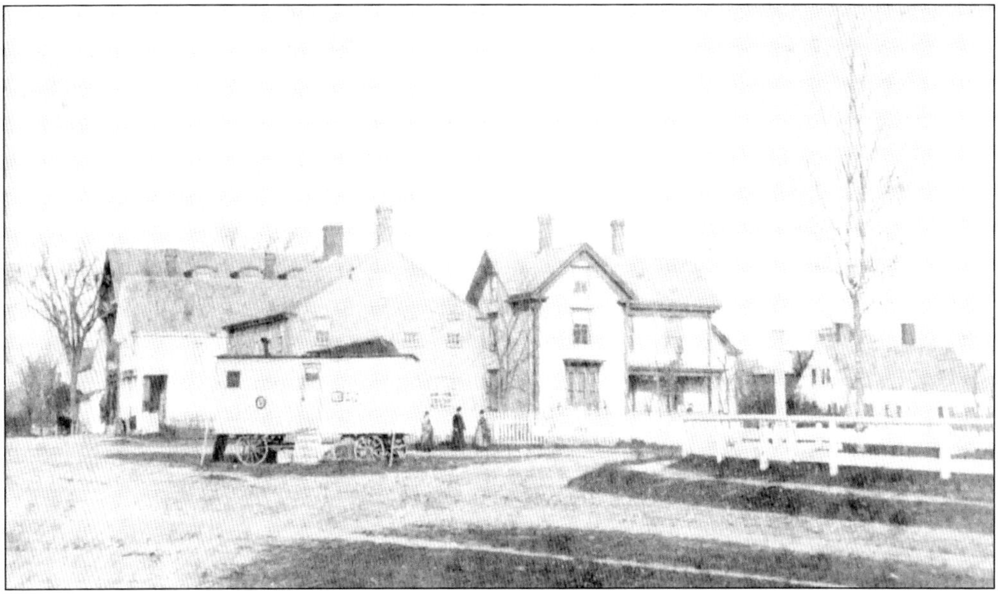

This *c*. 1880 photograph of Gray Center was taken looking northeast from Old Portland Road, where the "Centennial Elm Tree" was set in 1878 in commemoration of Gray's 100th anniversary. Later the new Civil War monument was placed here after removing the tree in 1911. Townspeople could have their picture taken by a traveling photographer who did his work from his wagon, located in the center of this picture. The first postmaster's house (to the far right) was the only building on this block that didn't burn in the 1921 fire. In the 1880s Gray had 90 dwellings built on 7 streets, and its population was 1,798.

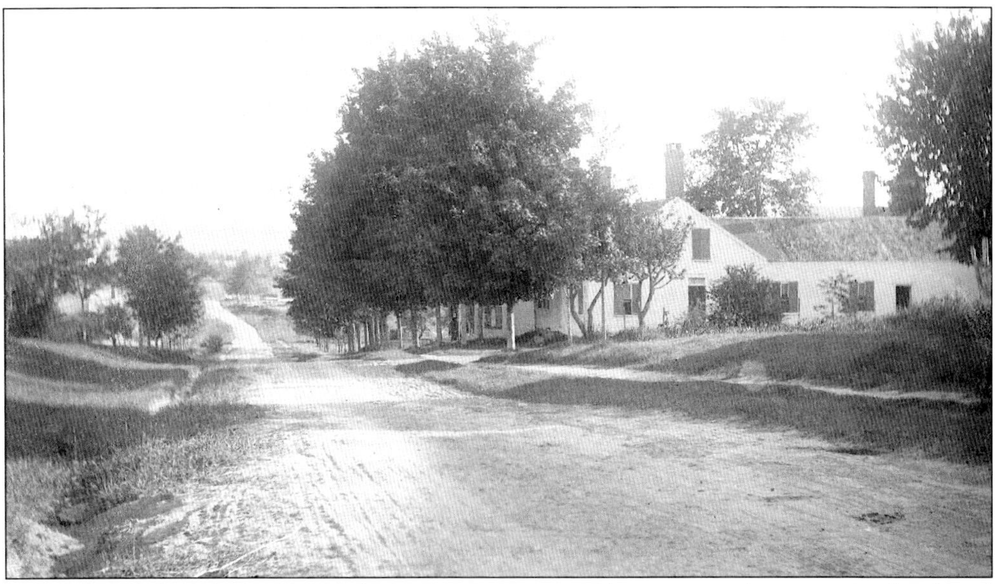

Old Portland Road, looking south from Gray Center, was the major road to get to Portland until 1829, when construction of the New Portland Road through Gray Meadows was completed. Gray Corner is located at the busy crossroads and was a convenient day's travel from Portland or Yarmouth for horse-drawn "buggies." At this time in Gray there were six stores and one hotel. The house belonged to Helen and Angie Frank.

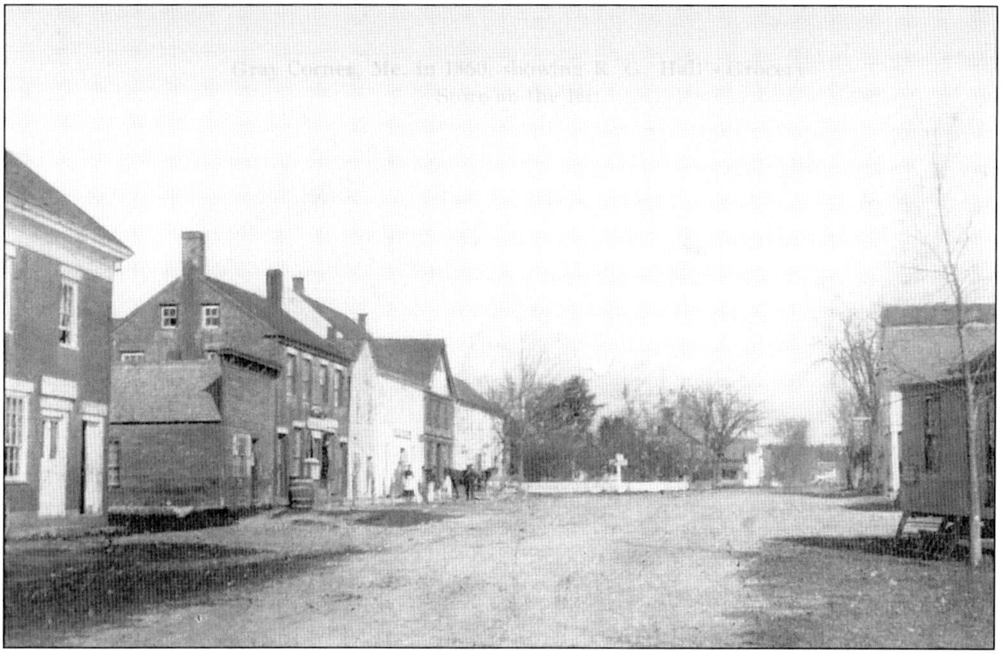

This view of the west side of Main Street was taken looking north, *c.* 1860s. The buildings, starting from the far left and moving right, are the town hall (built in 1836), the grain store (built in the 1820s), Daniel Hall's Brick Store (built after the 1830s), the harness shop (built in the 1830s), and Jim Small's store.

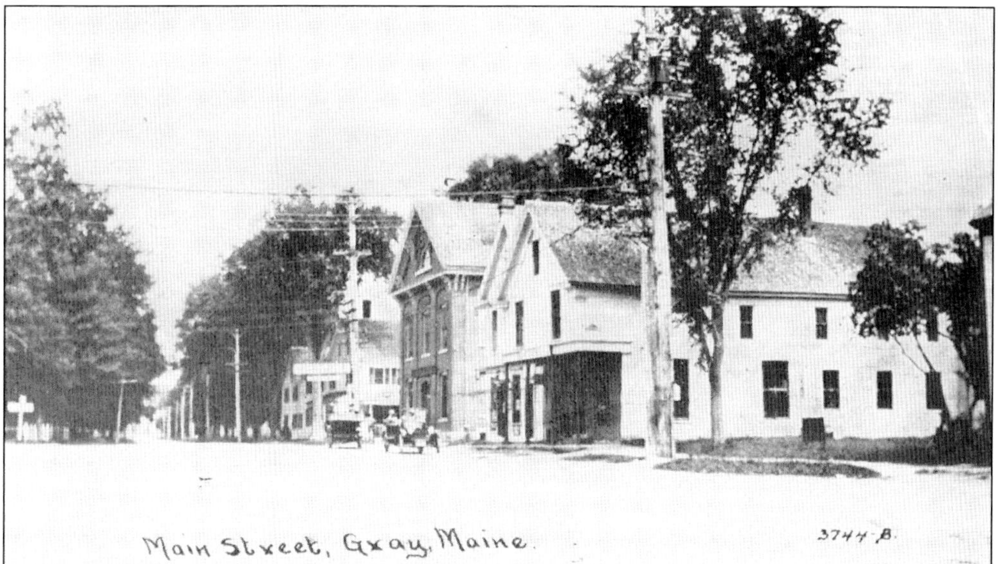

A corner of Cobb's Hall can be seen to the far right in this *c.* 1915 view of the east side of Main Street looking north. Following Cobb's Hall, moving from the foreground to the background, is a vacant lot, Stevens' Hardware Store, Antonio's store, and Hancock's store. It looked like this for almost 50 years until the fire of 1921.

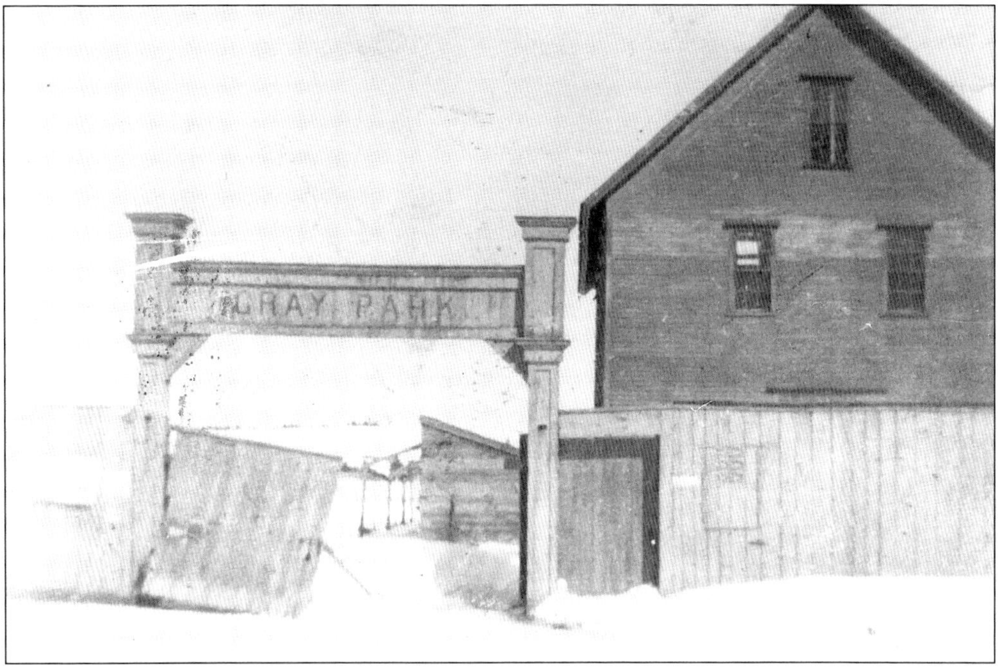

The entrance to the Gray Fairgrounds was once located on the east side of Shaker Road. A single admission to the grounds and the exhibition hall was 25¢, a ticket admitting exhibitors of livestock was 50¢, and exhibition hall exhibitors were charged 35¢.

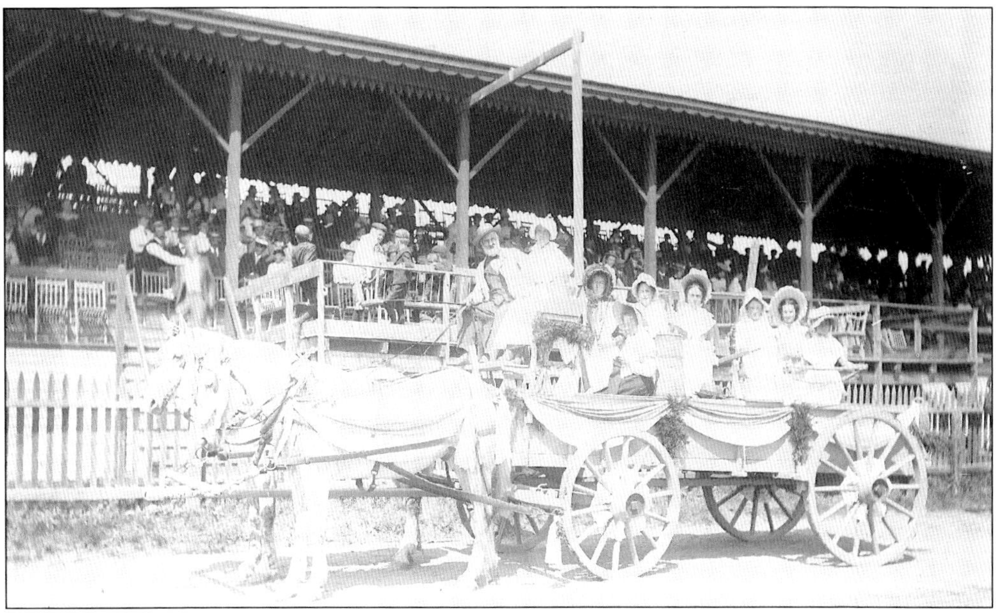

One of the decorated wagons parades around the track at the fairgrounds, *c.* 1890. The day's program consisted of baseball and many field events, including the 100-yard dash, one-half-mile run, broad jump, and pole vault. Horses, sheep, oxen, and steers were examined and judged for special premiums. Farm products, fruit, honey combs, jellies, preserves, and canned goods were also judged, and the most outstanding exhibits of house-hold manufactures such as quilts, rugs, worsted, and fancy articles were awarded special premiums.

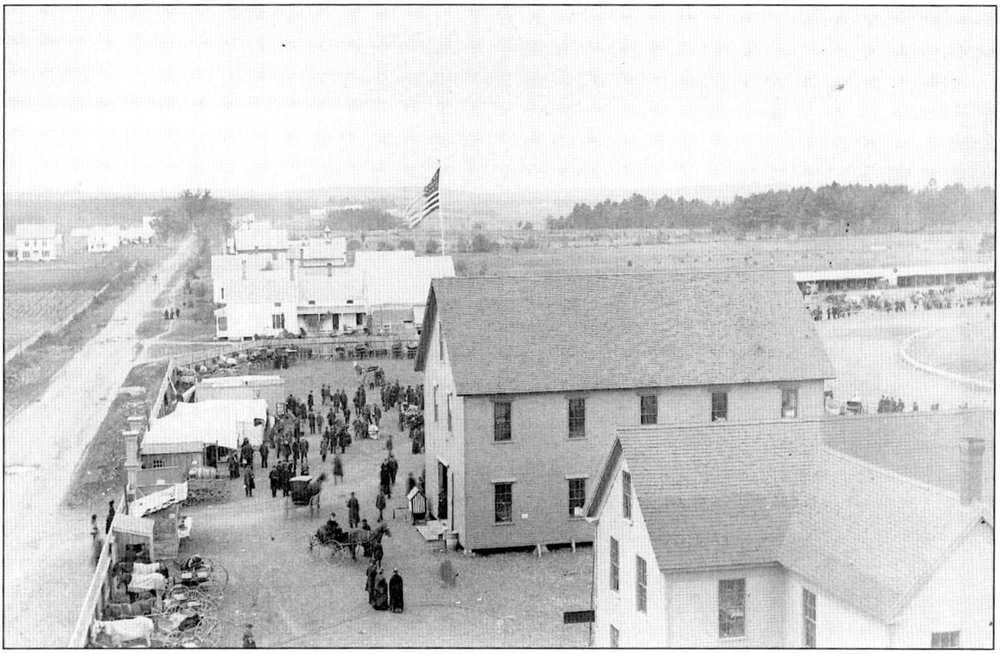

The exhibition hall and the dining hall of the Gray Fairgrounds are visible in this *c.* 1900 view of Route 26 looking north from Gray Village. The dining hall was originally located on the Portland Road; before being moved to the fairgrounds, it housed a business that manufactured marbleized mantels. After the fair was discontinued, the dining hall became the home of a local dentist, Dr. Cushing. The exhibition hall later housed the Gray Grange.

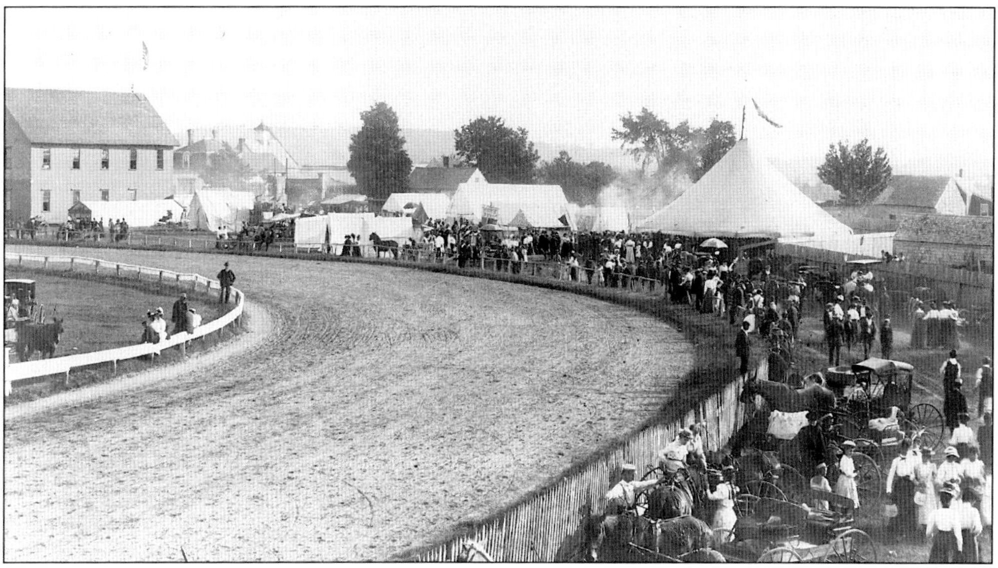

During the years 1884–1902, the Gray Fair Association operated an annual agricultural fair on the grounds, now roughly encompassing the Gray Park area. A half-mile horse race track, two-story exhibition hall, dining hall, and long sheds for animals were on the grounds. The association dissolved in 1902. The grandstand went to the New Gloucester Fair Grounds, and the dining hall was converted to a residence. Today, Gray Park is the site of many homes and the Russell Elementary School.

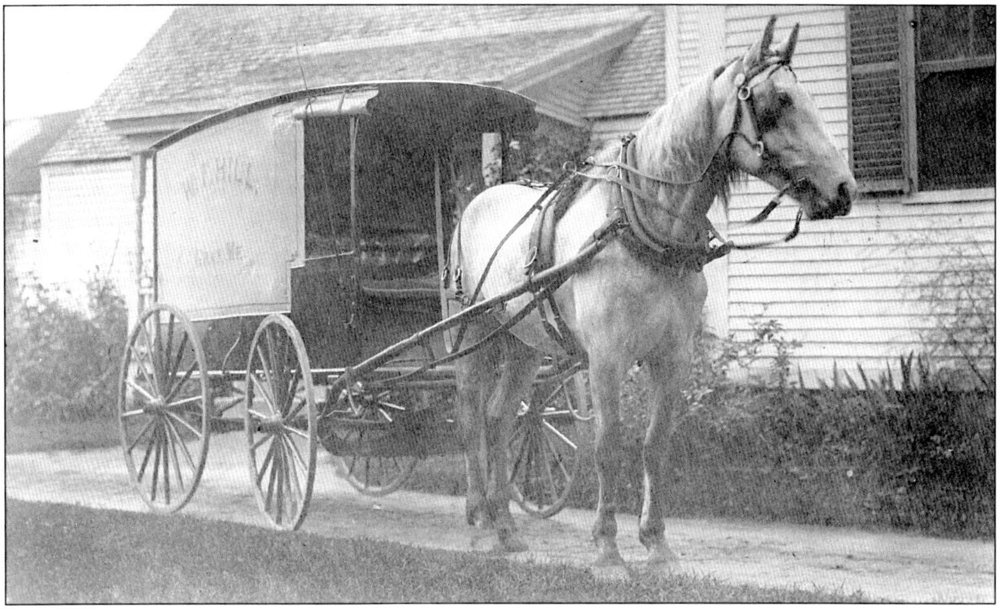

Will E. Hill lived in a residence on Greenleaf Street, built in the mid-1800s, that was once owned by Captain Charles H. Doughty. Hill sold meats from his wagon in the early 1900s.

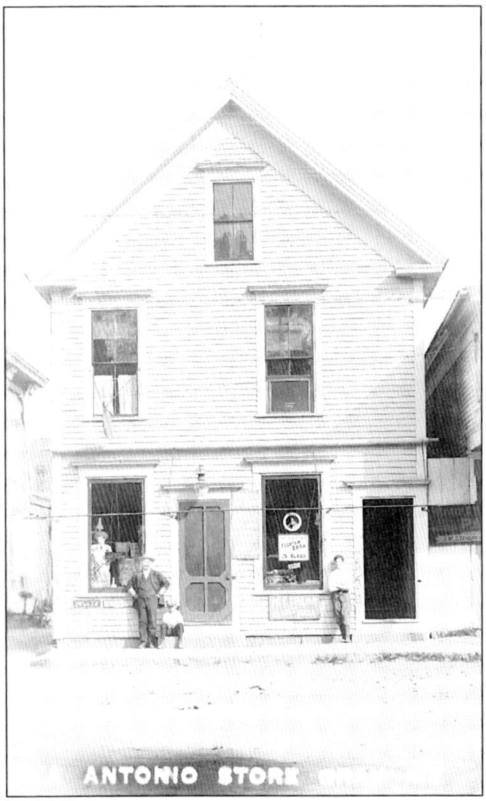

Antonio's store was located on the east side of Main Street next to Hancock's store, c. 1880s. To the rear of this building was a blacksmith shop. Antonio's store was built by John Newbegin and was used for a short time as a millinery shop. Over the next 14 years it housed many different businesses. In 1905 a confectionery and stationery was located on the first floor, while Antonio and his wife lived in an apartment on the second floor. The building burned in the 1921 fire.

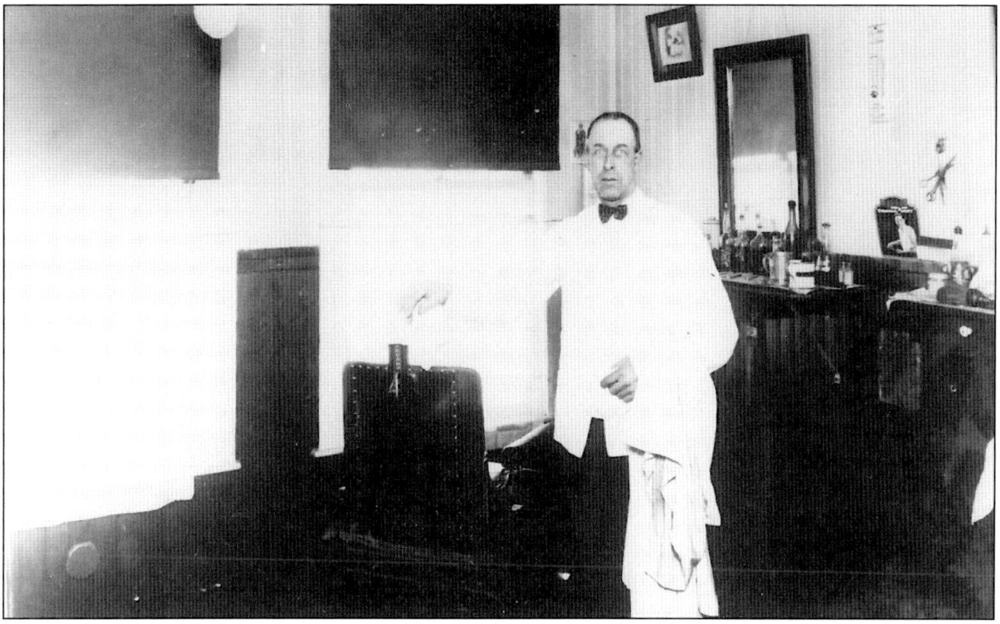

Andrew Antonio had a barber shop on the second floor of the building next to the harness shop, which was located on the west side of Main Street. In 1911, Mr. W.I. Whitney became the barber. He remained in business for 50 years.

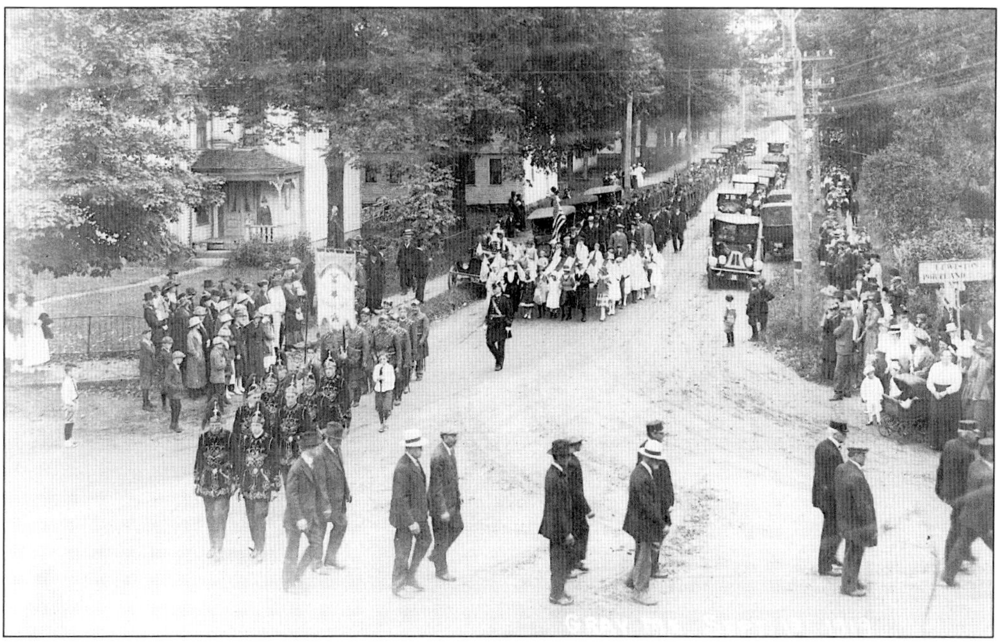

On September 1, 1919, a Welcome Home Day celebration was given by the Sons of Veterans Order of the town to honor all the people in Gray who had served their country during World War I. The parade is making a left turn from Shaker Road and traveling up Main Street to Pennell Institute, where a dinner was served. After Major John D. Anderson made a speech, the afternoon was filled with sporting events on the athletic field. The day closed with an evening dance at the town hall.

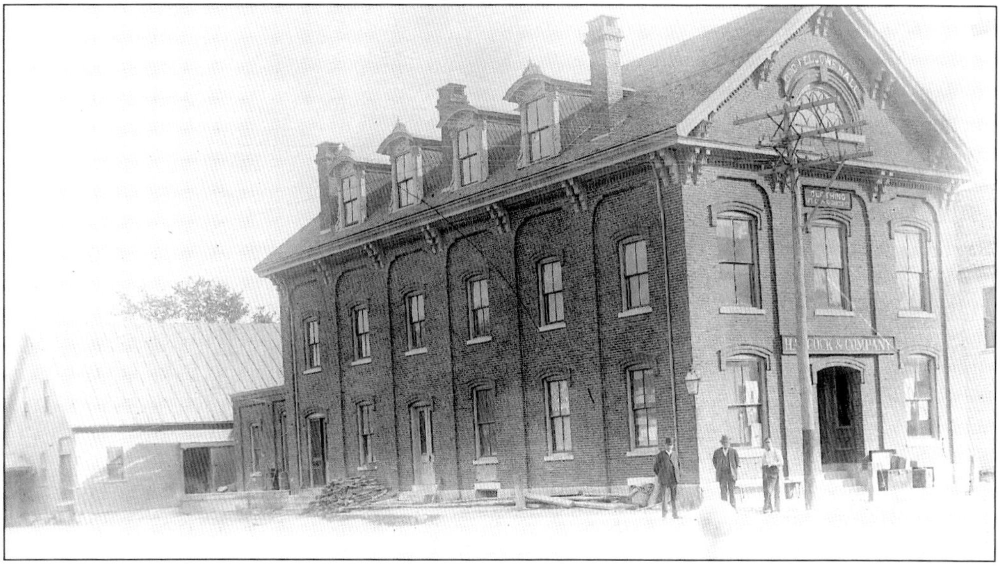

The Hancock & Company building was constructed in 1876 by Henry Goff out of bricks from his brickyard at East Gray. It was the town's largest merchandising store, and had a horse shed and a grain house. The third floor was used by the Odd Fellows Organization. Over the years many businesses have occupied the building. Today it still displays the architectural design it featured after being rebuilt following the fire of 1921.

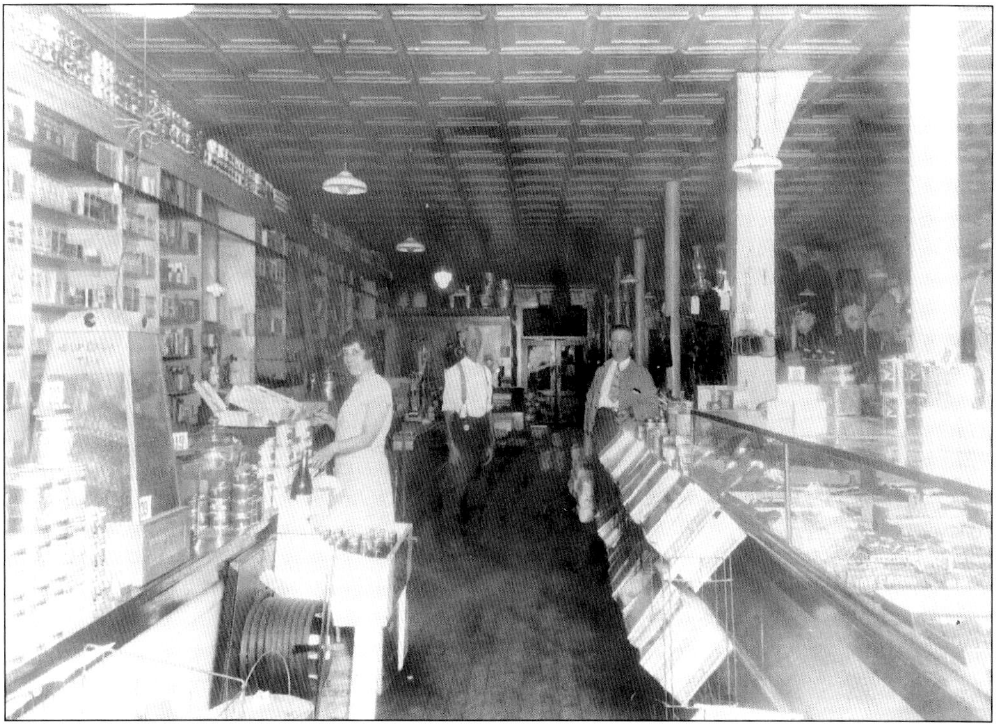

This is the interior of the Cole-Marsden Company at the Brick Store in the 1930s.

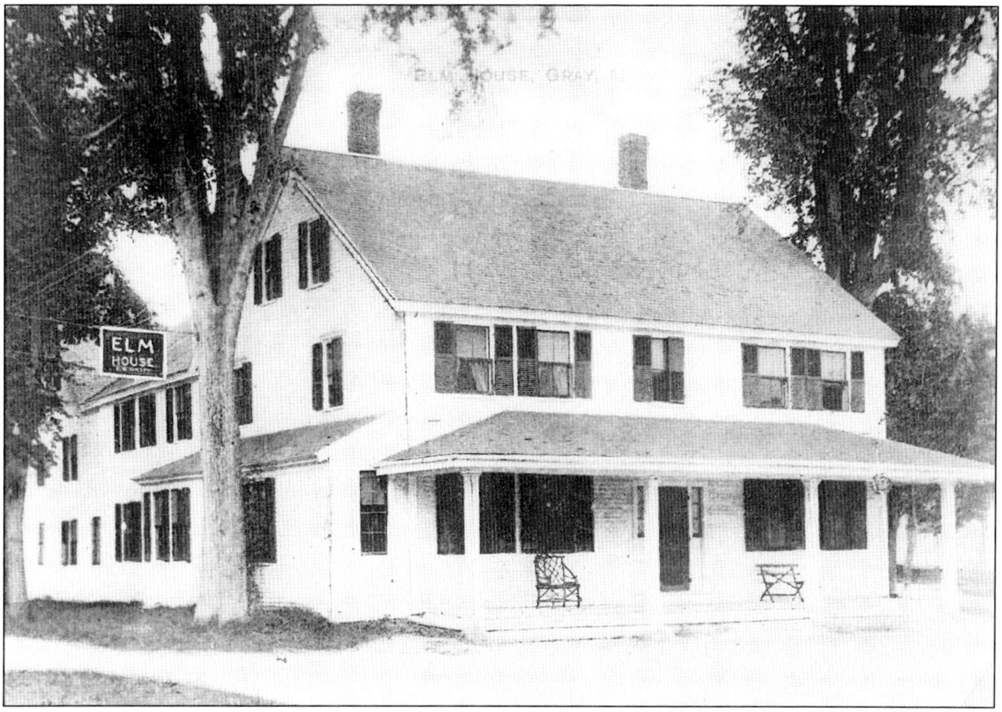

The Elm House was built in the 1700s by Daniel Hainey as the Eagle Tavern. The building remained standing until 1923 on the north corner of Lewiston Road and Brown Street. The Elm House was a place where people traveling through town could stop and rest, and also rest their horses in Colley's Stable, located at the rear of the inn.

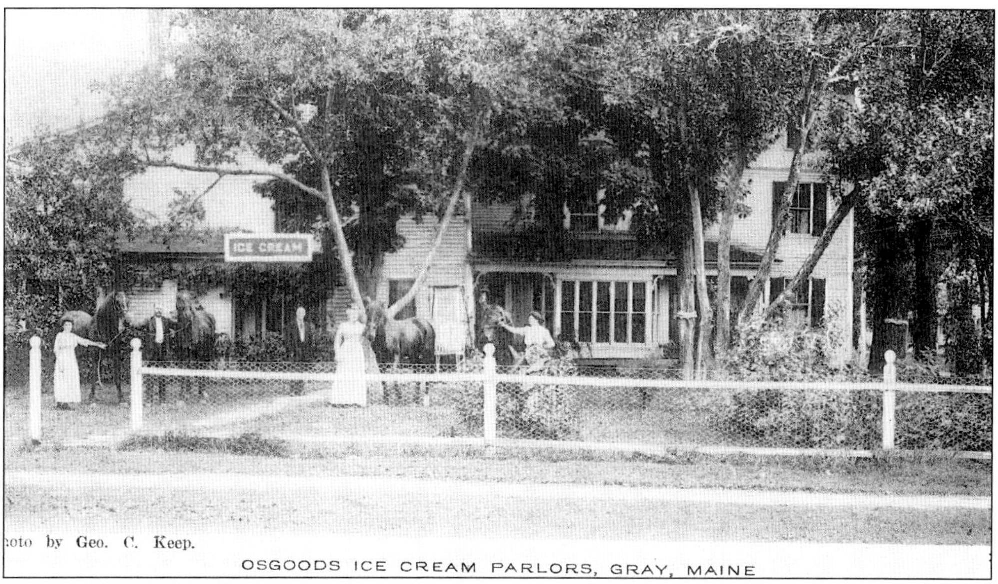

Osgoods Ice Cream Parlor was located at the corner of Shaker Road and Main Street. From 1890s to 1920s, Mrs. Lizzie Osgood sold homemade ice cream from her ice cream parlor and soda fountain in her home. In those days it was a rare treat for one to go to the ice cream parlor. The grounds around the parlor had many beautiful rose gardens.

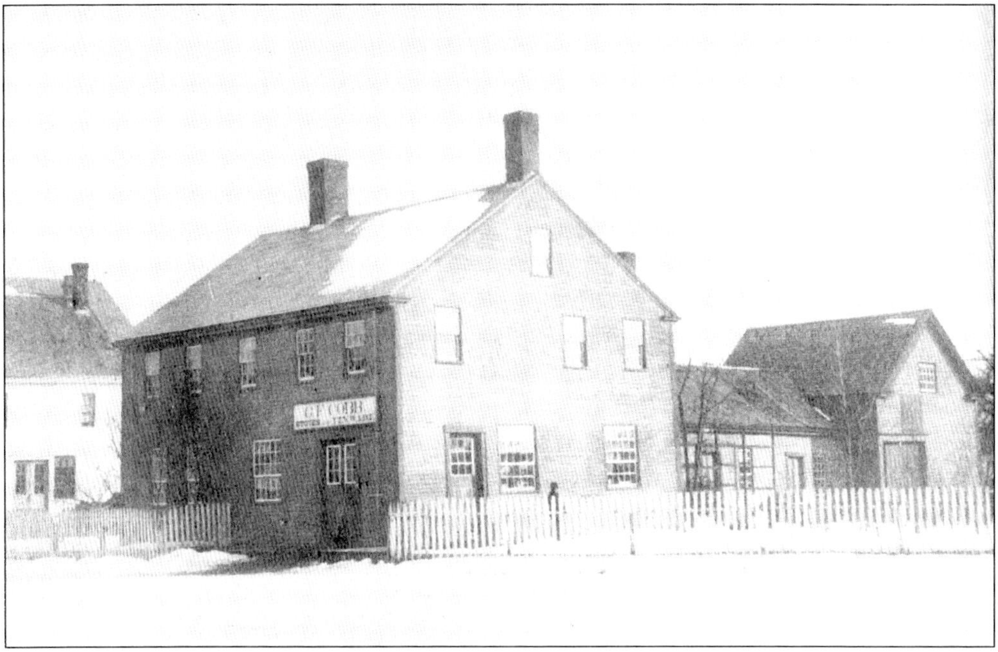

George F. Cobb was a tinsmith who established his residence and a hardware store in the building on the corner of Greenleaf Street and Main Street. In 1881 he sold tinware and stoves, but he later expanded his wares to include confections, fruits, school supplies, fancy goods, boots, and shoes. On the second floor there was a hall that was used for all sorts of social gatherings.

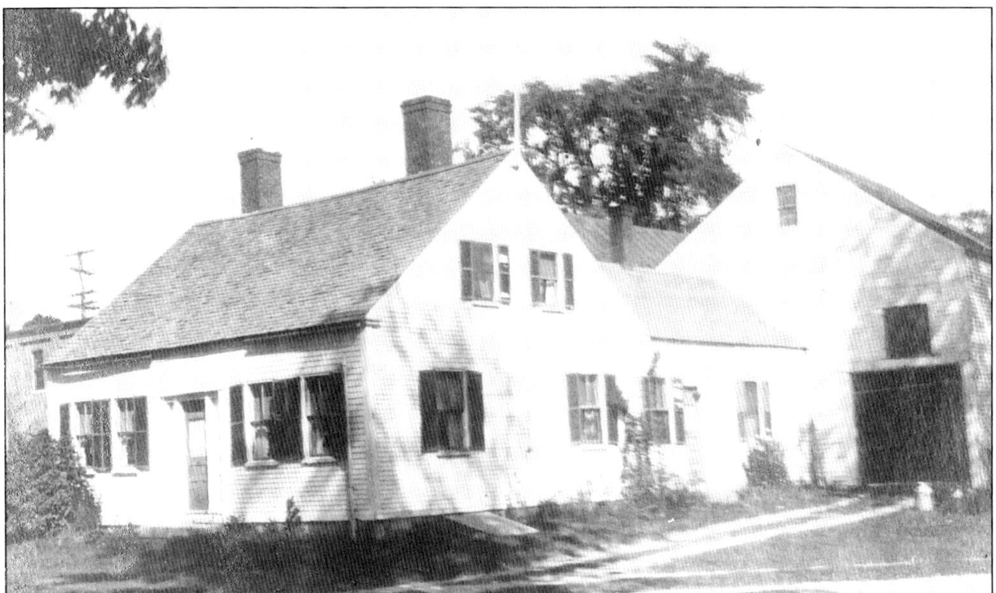

Joseph McLellan's Home was also the first post office. In 1795 Joseph McLellan was appointed as Gray's first postmaster, and a post office was established in his home on the north side of Greenleaf Street. Other post offices were established in various sections of the town. The rural free delivery routes started in 1915.

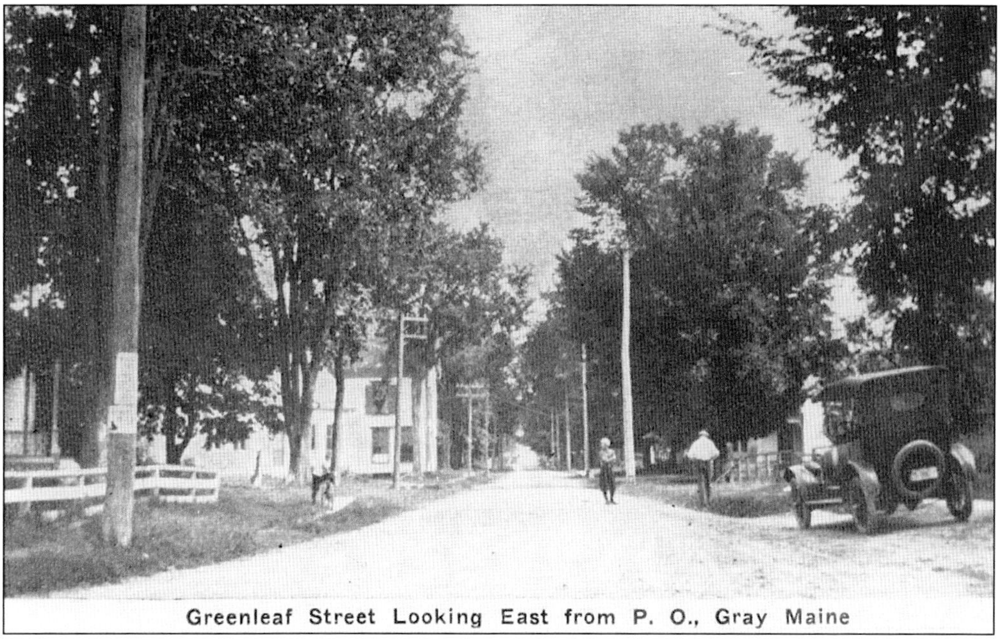

Greenleaf Street is shown here looking east from the post office, *c.* 1920s. As you look down the dirt road you can see the foot of Week's Hill on the Yarmouth Road.

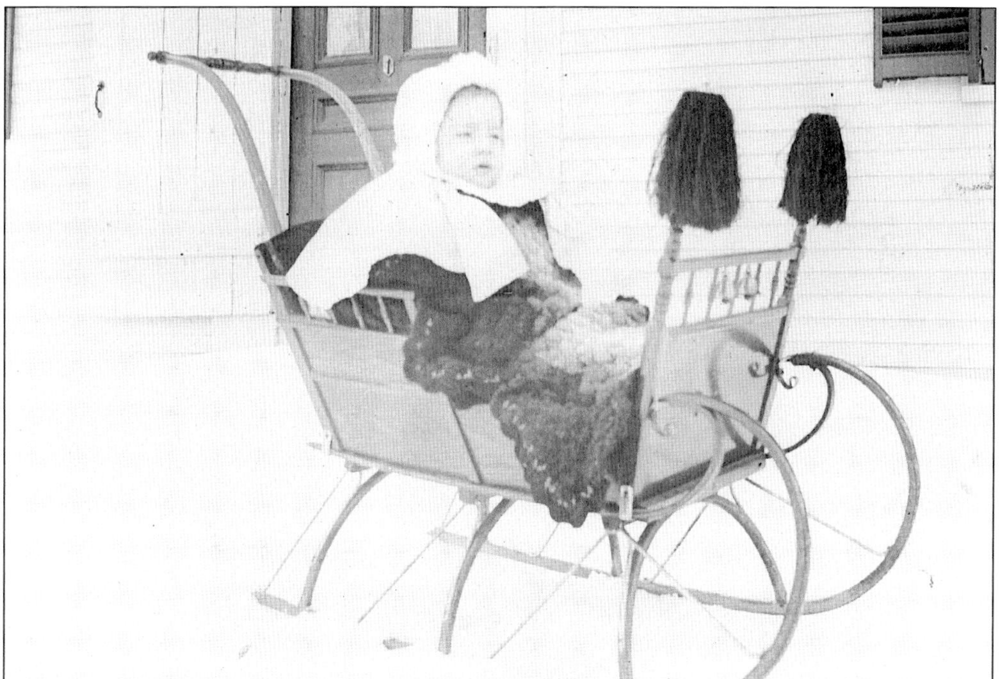

Fourteen-month-old John Tappan Doughty went out for a winter morning ride in his sleigh and stopped by the Hersey House, to see if anyone was home. This picture was taken March 15, 1900.

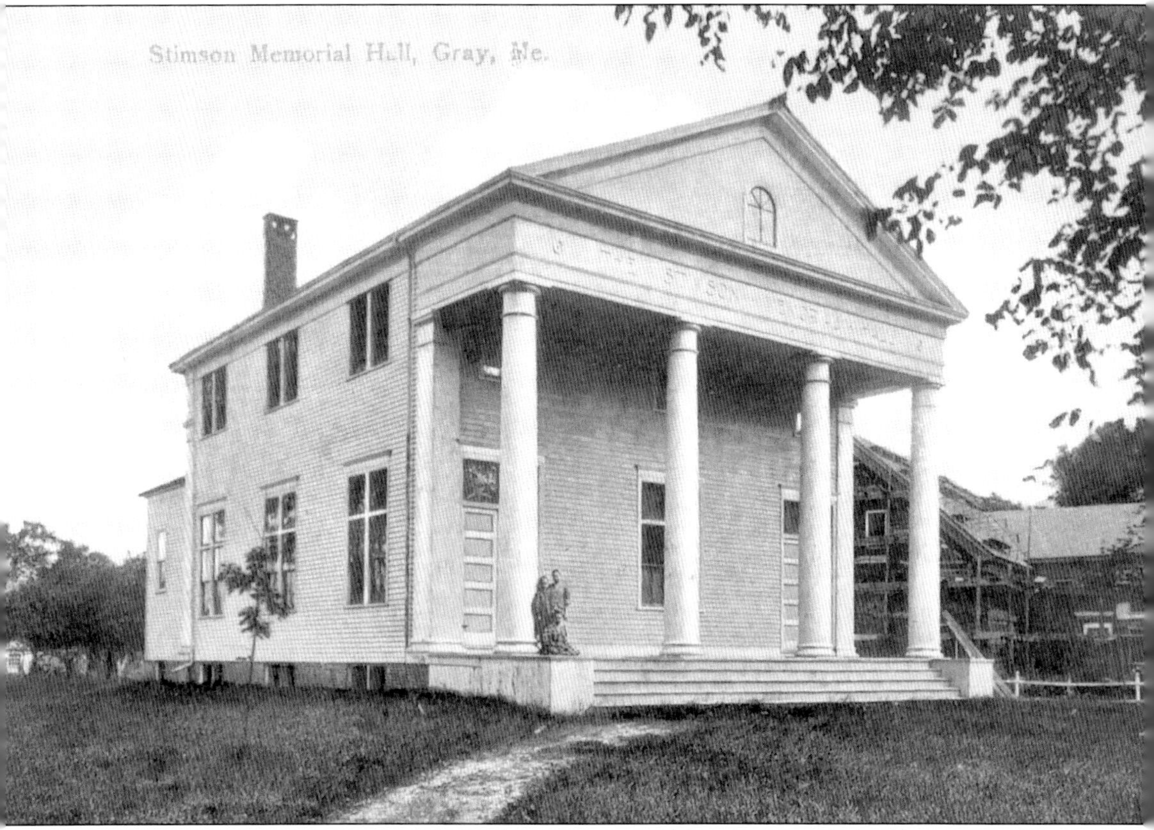

Stimson Memorial Hall was dedicated in 1900. The old Colonial-style building, copied from a model found in Europe, was a memorial to Captain Theophilus Stimson (1796–1872) and his wife, Mary Lawrence Stimson. Both of the Stimsons were natives of Gray. Captain Stimson was active in town affairs, the state militia (hence the title captain), and he was a representative to the state legislature in 1833–34. Theophilus and his brother Woodbury worked as iron workers for a long time, making farm implements and edged tools. It was through Captain Stimson's three sons and a daughter that the building was erected, at a cost of about $6,000.

On the first floor, beyond the vestibule, is a hall that seated three to four hundred people. A stage was equipped with a dressing room and a complete shift of scenery, which was painted by Edward Caswell of Gray. The upper floor contained a reading room and store room for the library, which opened in 1907 with 700 volumes on its shelves; that number soon increased to over 1,000 volumes. The hall featured yellow pine and white wood, hardwood floors finished in cypress wood, and gaslight fixtures. The Stimson name will be remembered for a long time by their impressive gift. Today, the hall is used for meetings by the town council and the community cable committee.

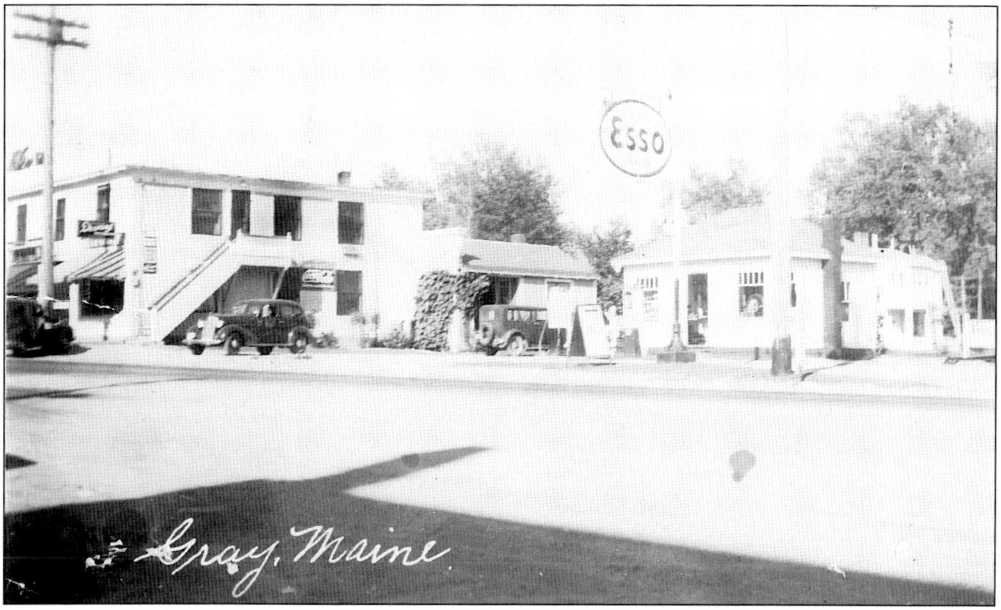

The east side of Main Street is shown here in the 1940s. The building to the left in the picture is Angie Frank's Drug Store. To the right side is the Esso Station, just one of the many gasoline stations that were located in Gray Corner to accommodate the traveling public. By this time the town had gone from oats, hay, and grain to gasoline and oil.

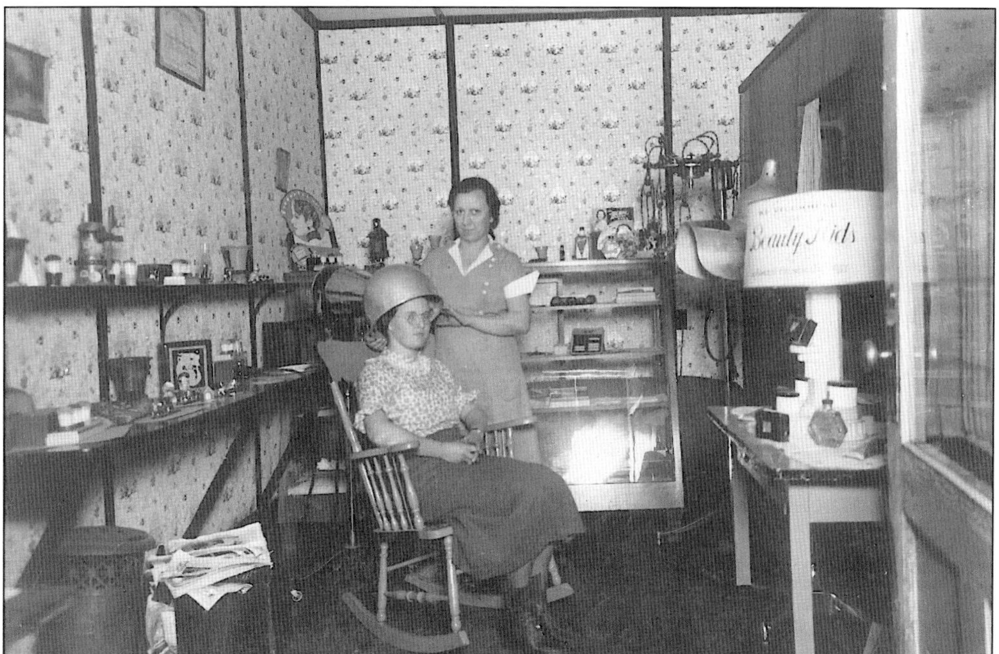

The Gray Beauty Shop was located on the second floor of Angie Frank's Drug Store. The outside stairway would take you to the beauty shop. Mildred Yeaton Austin was the beautician. Notice the up-to-date equipment to cut and perm your hair. Looks like one could be right in style with all the "Beauty Aids" that were available here!

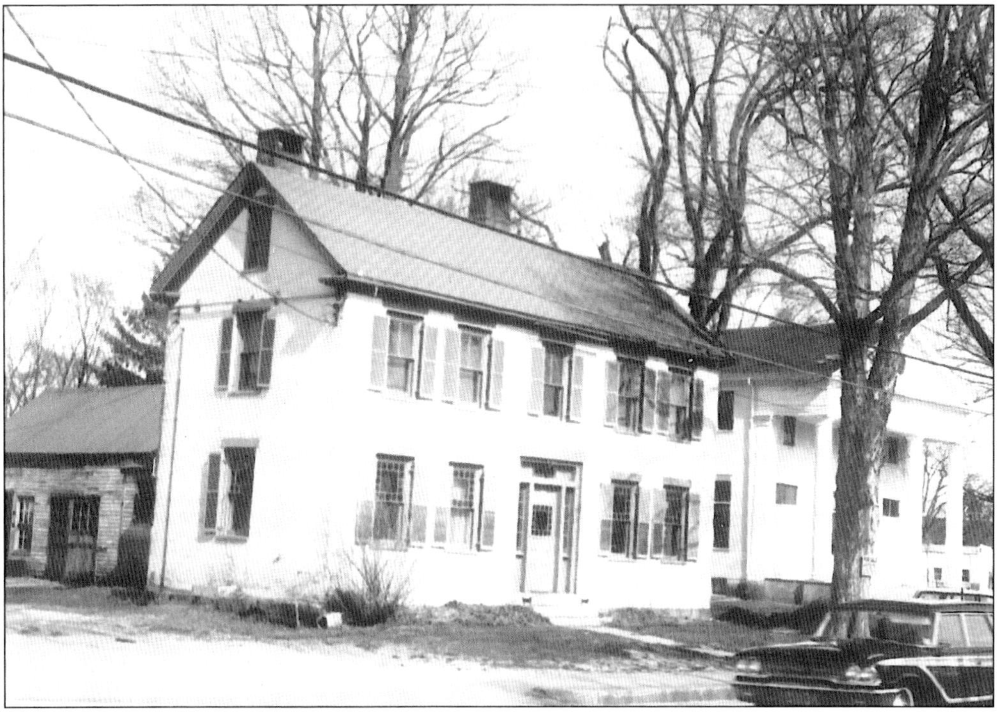

The Berry House was constructed of brick in the late 1700s. Merrill and Daniel Berry owned the house between 1815 and 1861. The Berrys were wheelwrights and had their shop in the western end of the old town hall, now occupied by the village fire station. After the Berrys, the house was owned by Reverend John Rice, William G. Latimer, and finally by Charles W. Berry and his heirs (no relation to the first Berrys). When electricity came to Gray, Charles Berry wired many buildings. The house was demolished in 1966.

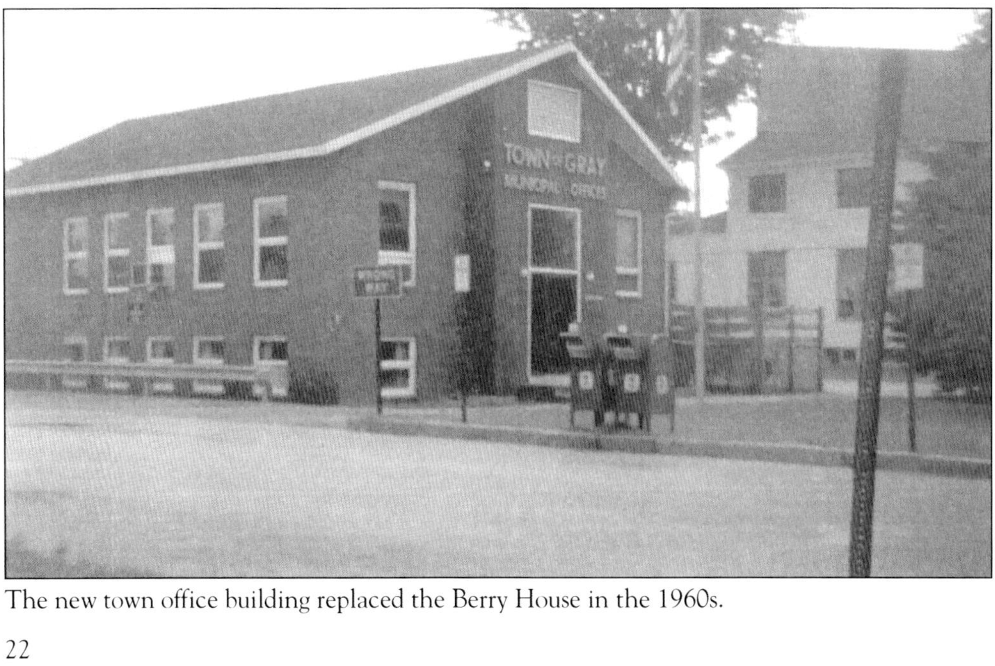

The new town office building replaced the Berry House in the 1960s.

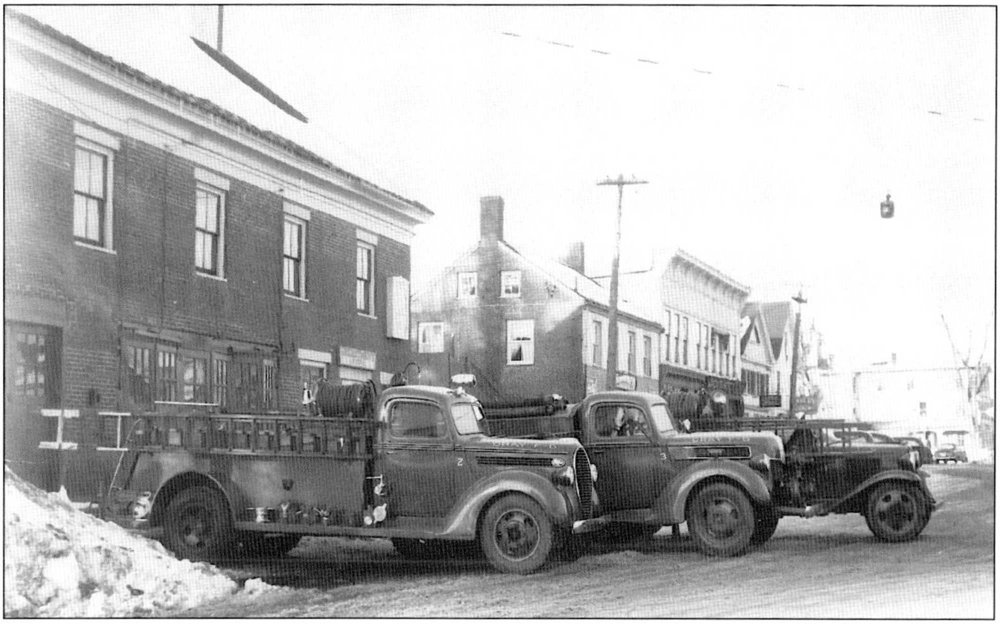

In 1880, a group of volunteer firemen was formed, calling themselves the Gray Fire Company. Prior to 1900, any equipment they had was stored in Hancock's stable. Later the equipment was permanently placed in the two-story brick building known as the town hall, which was located in the center of town. In 1915, the fire company's name was changed to the Gray Fire Department.

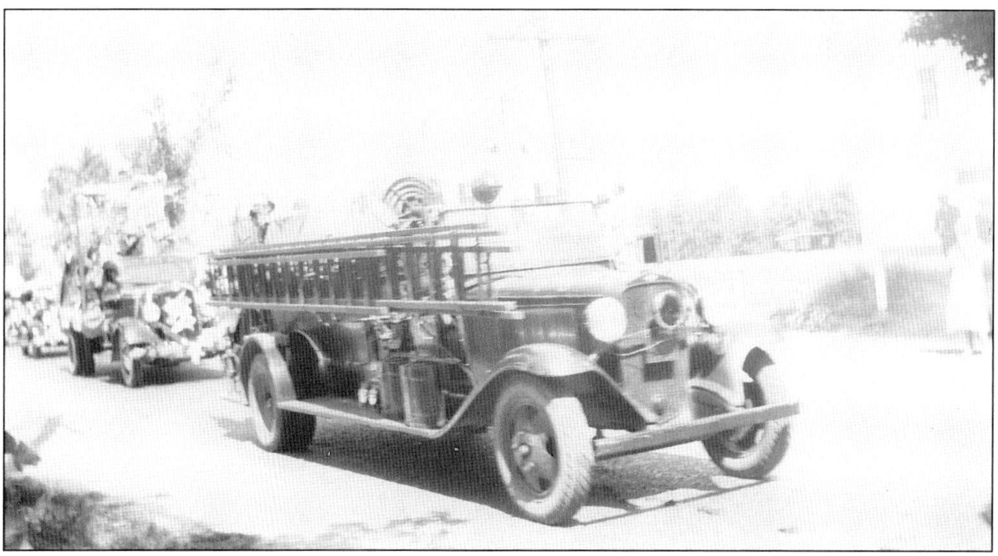

This old firetruck has been to many parades. It is shown here on Armistice Day in 1930.

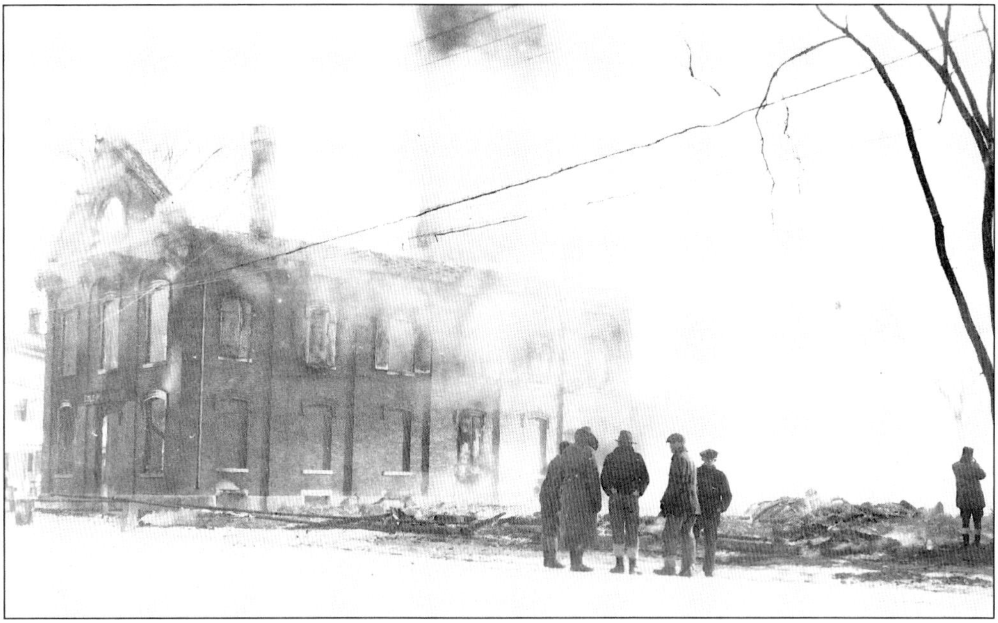

It was a bitter cold day on December 20, 1921, when a fire broke out in Stevens' Hardware Store. Bucket brigades were formed to get water from wells and homes. Gray's fire equipment proved entirely inadequate and seven buildings burned to the ground.

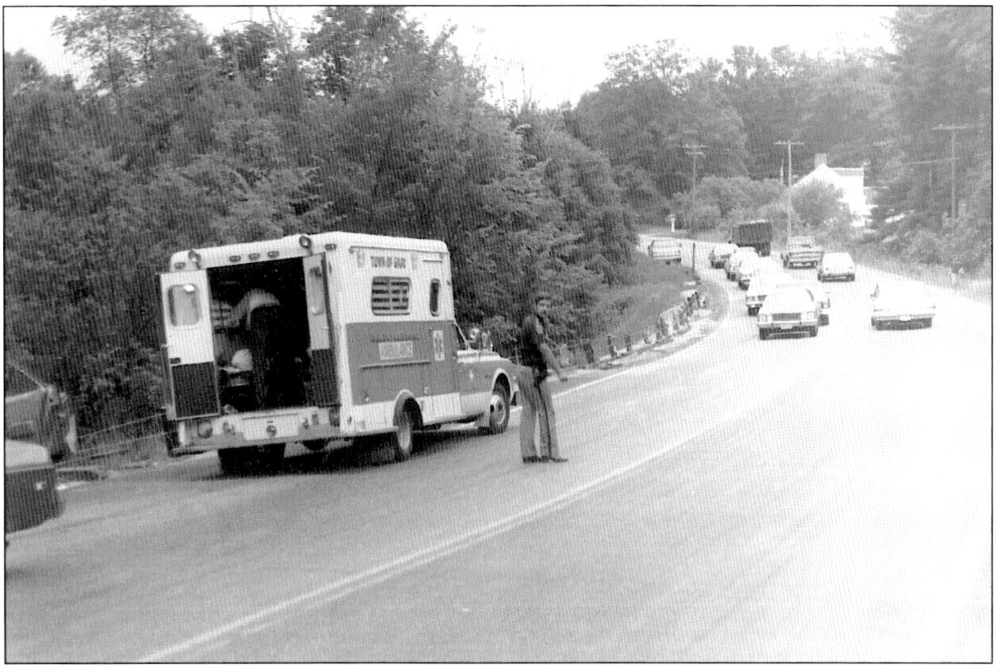

Gray's Rescue Unit, started in 1969, provides 24-hours-a-day medical emergency service to the town of Gray.

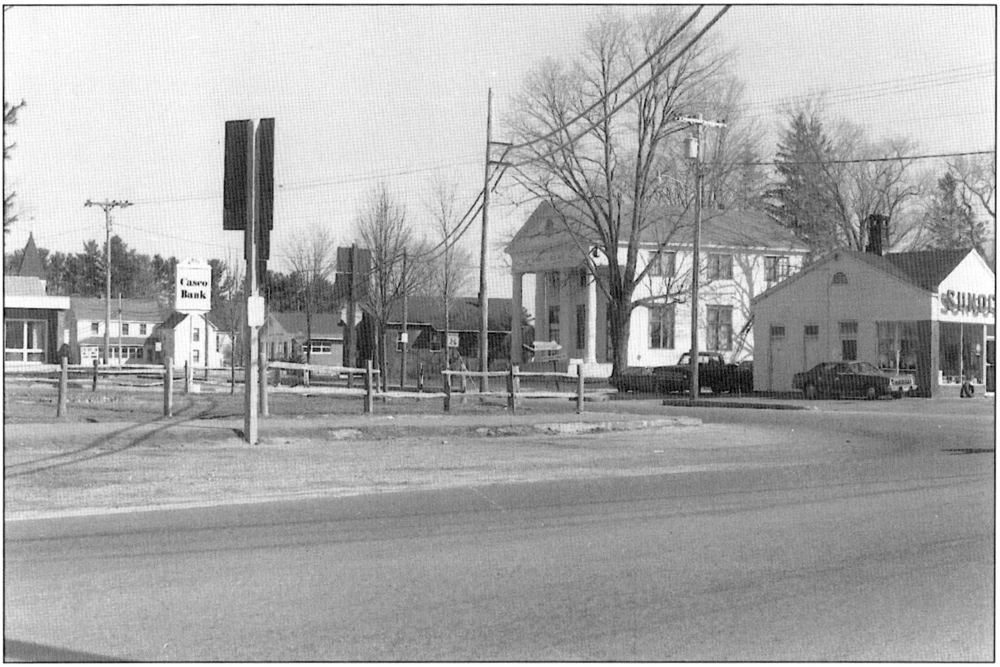

The corner of Main Street and Shaker Road is shown here in 1978. Stimson Memorial Hall remains the only historic building left from early Gray. It will always stand because it is listed on the National Register of Historic Places.

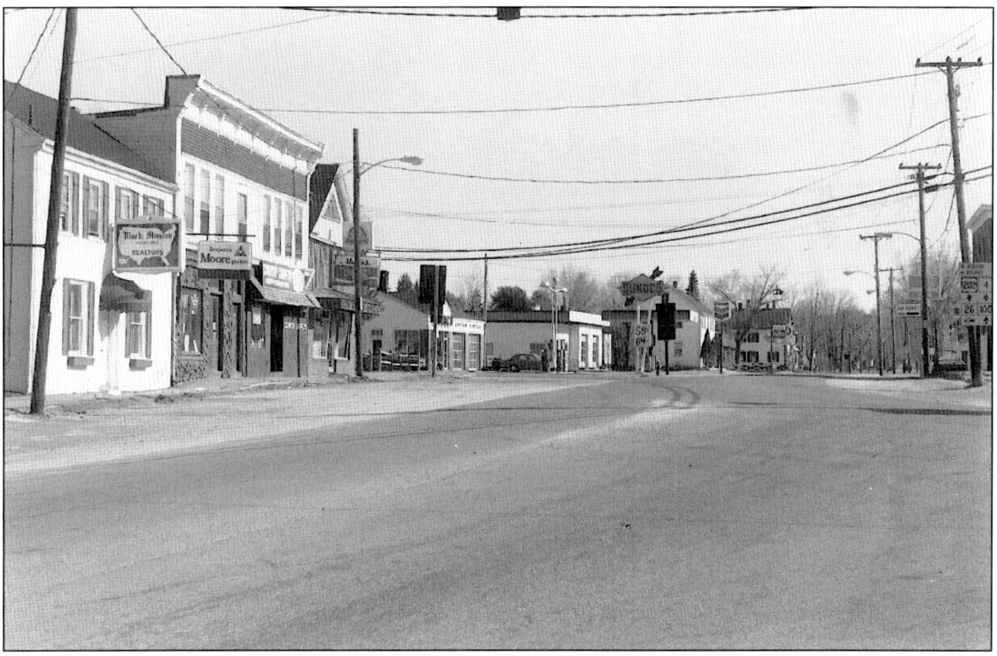

Gray Village grew from 1,189 people in 1930 to 4,344 in 1980, and the corner became busy enough to have a blinking light installed at the intersection of Routes 202 and 100. As evidenced by this 1978 photograph, many houses have been torn down and replaced by gasoline stations and convenience stores.

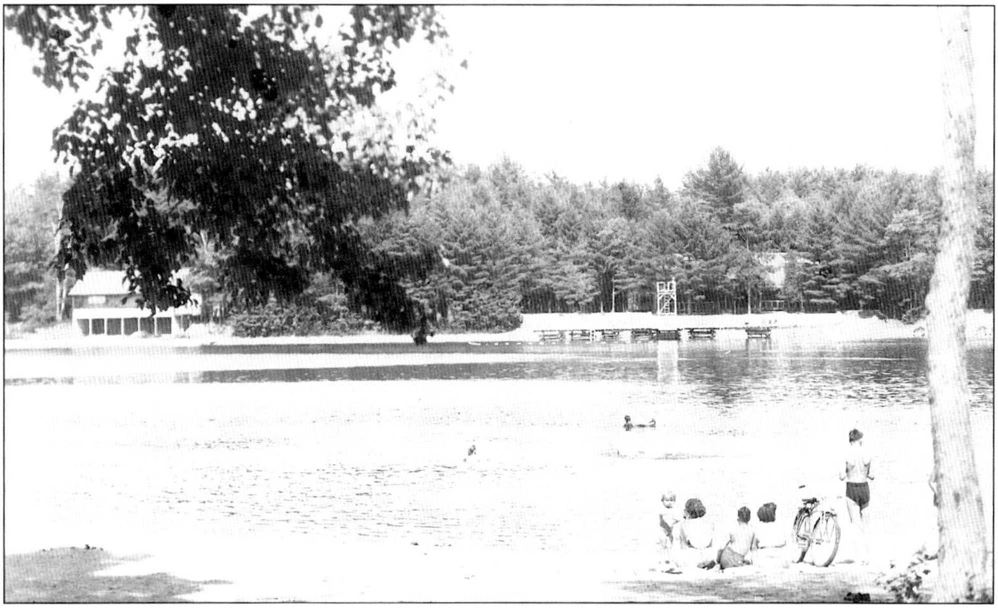

Dry Pond is known today as Crystal Lake. Legend has it that Native Americans referred to this mile-long, spring-fed lake as "always drinking and never full," for there is no visible outlet. The building of the first summer cottages on the lake in early 1900s ushered in a new era for Dry Mills. Many cottages and lots were developed along the shoreline. When the north end of the lake was built up in 1950s, the road was completed around the lake. Many year-round homes have since been constructed.

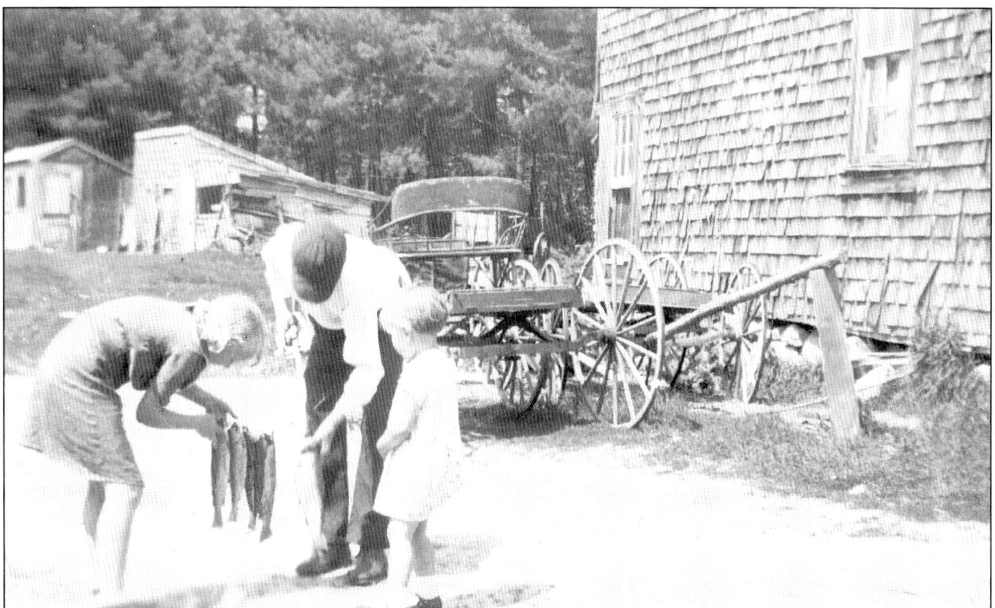

James shows off his catch of the day to his sisters, Edra (Wilkinson) and Beverly Maxwell (Prince). There are plenty of lakes and streams in Gray to enjoy fishing.

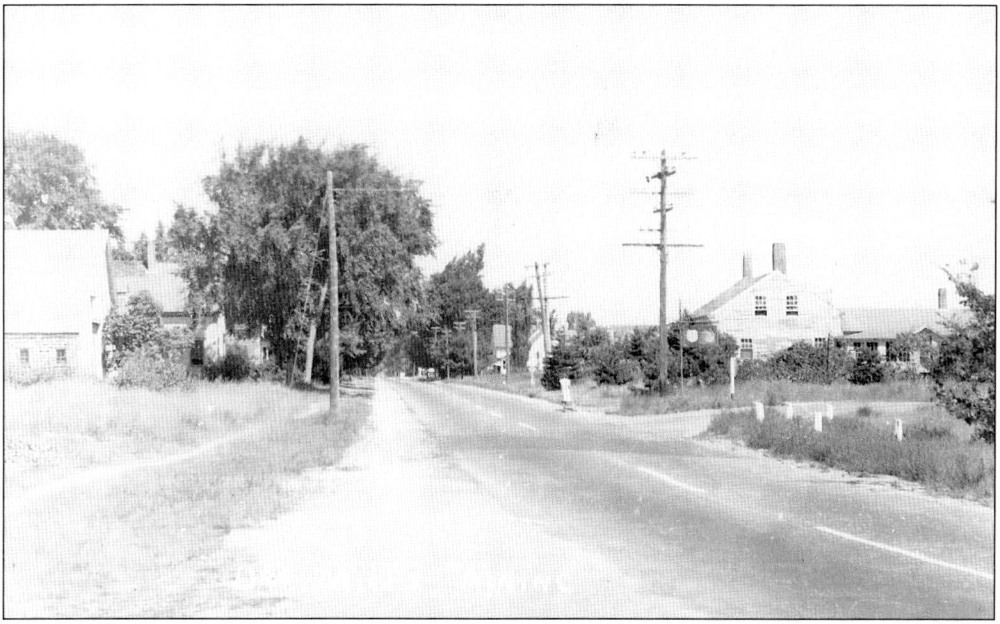

This photograph was taken looking north on Route 26 from the Dry Mills Store. The road that leads to the right has been known as Cross Road and Hatchery Road; today it is the Weymouth Road. The house on the corner belonged to the Reed family, and has since been torn down.

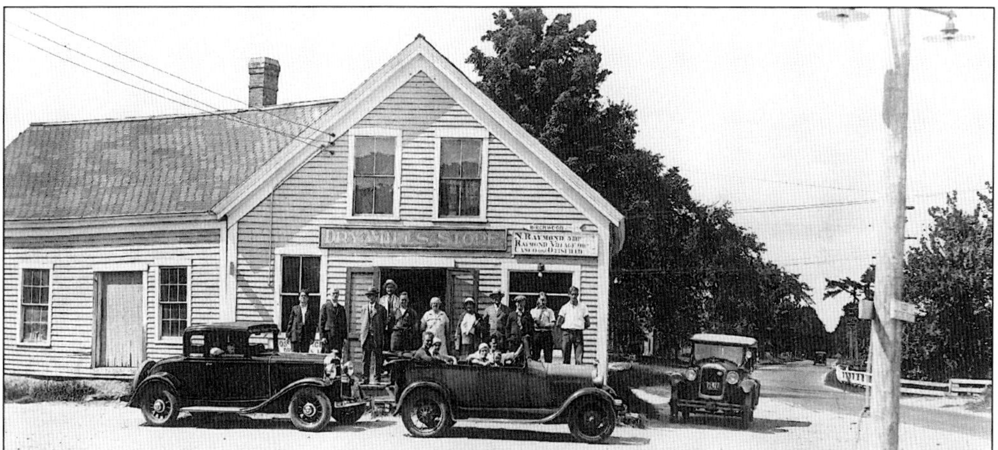

The Dry Mills Store was located at the intersection of the North Raymond Road and Route 26. This convenience store, which has served the community for over 125 years under many owners, also served as a post office until 1938, when the post office relocated across the street. As summer visitors and the traveling public came to this area, the store became a center of activity for goods and services. Today it remains very busy.

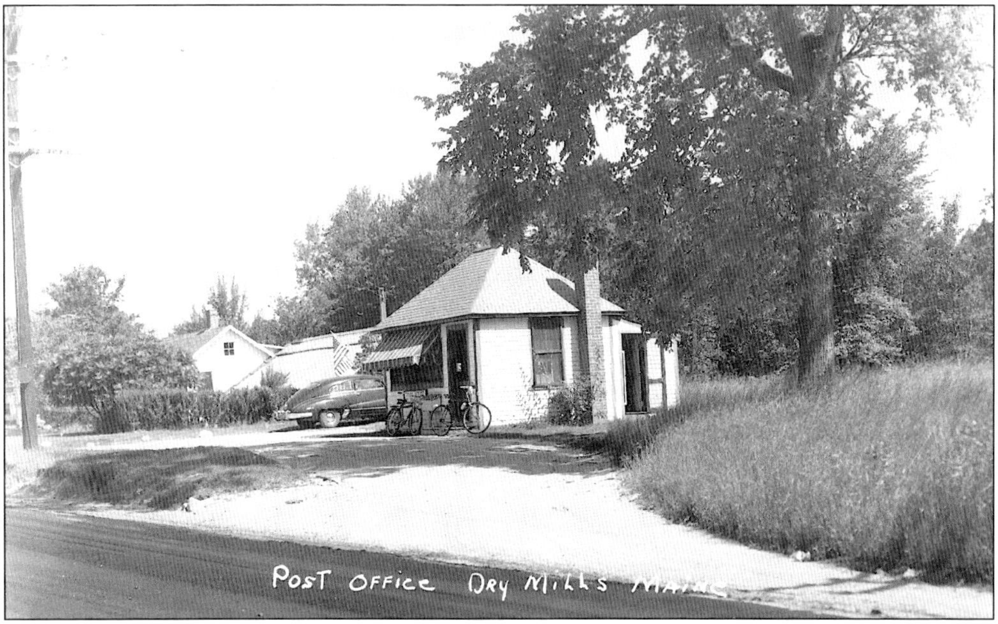

The Dry Mills Post Office, re-established in 1938 and closed in 1960, was frequently photographed and publicized as the "smallest post office in the state." It was a true local institution where customers could pass the time of day mending, sewing, chatting, and partaking of candy and soda pop. It now stands empty at the corner of North Raymond Road and Route 26.

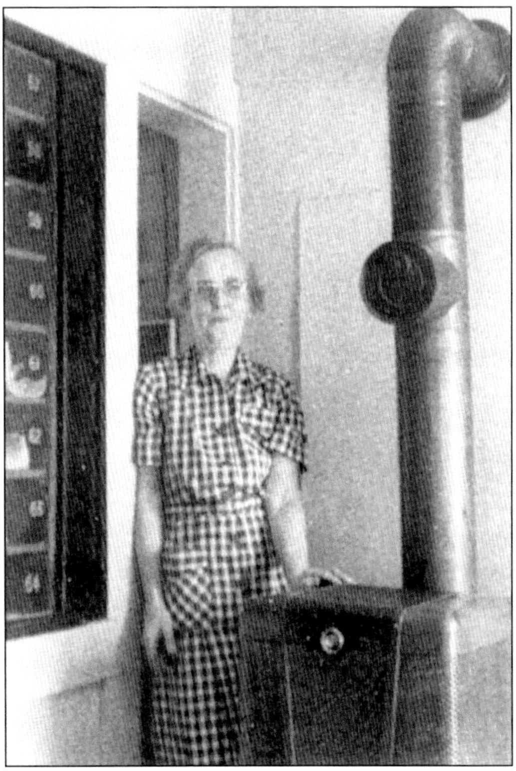

Postmaster Bernice Prince, who served from 1930 to 1960, poses in the Dry Mills Post Office by 64 wooden, gold-leafed, numbered mail boxes on September 24, 1957. In 1938 she asked to have the office moved across the Highway 26 into a small vacant building, once used as a tea room. She continued her duties as postmaster until the Dry Mills Post Office was closed in 1960.

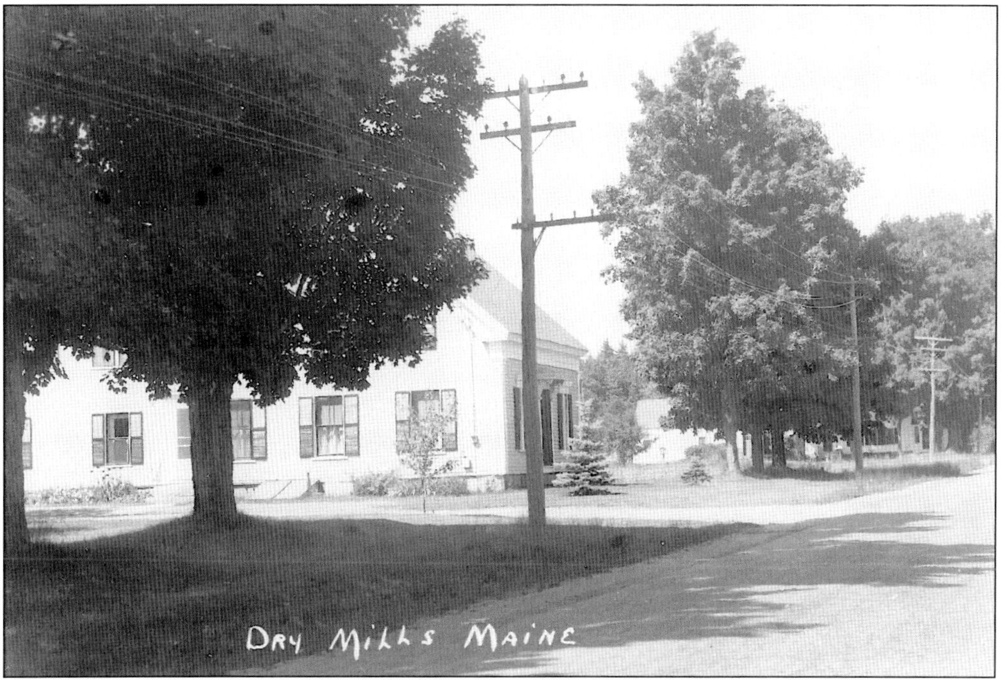

Bernice Prince, the last postmaster in Dry Mills, lived in this house on the south side of North Raymond Road. The building was constructed in 1870 by her grandparents, Mr. and Mrs. Richard Colley. It is now occupied by Bernice's daughter, Norma Liberty, and her husband, Robert.

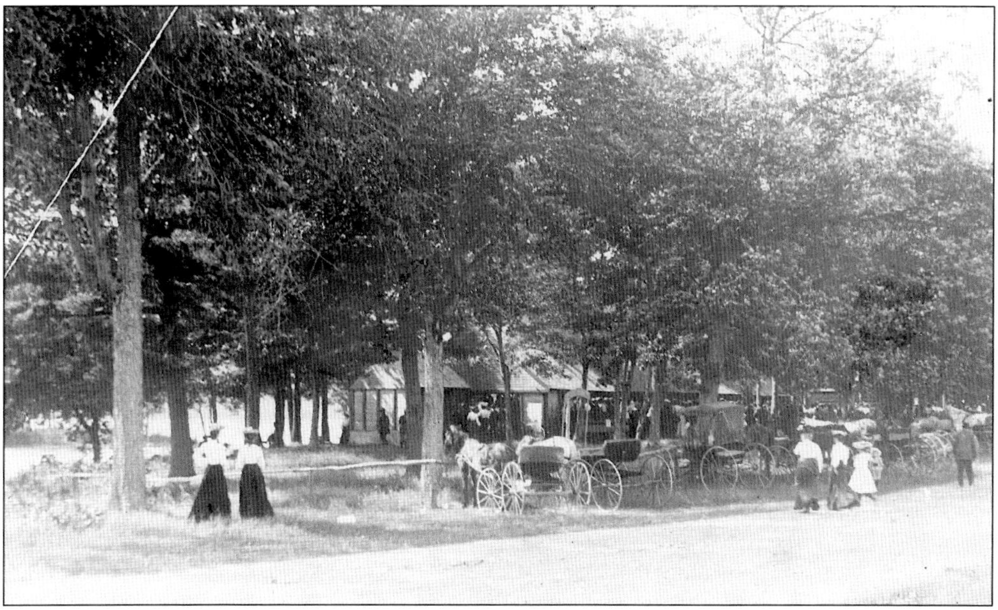

The Arthur Wilson's Open Air Dance Pavilion was located in Dry Mills, Route 26, on the shores of Crystal Lake. It stood on the present Jones Beach property for at least 50 years before succumbing in the 1920s to the public's demand for more sophisticated pleasures and entertainment.

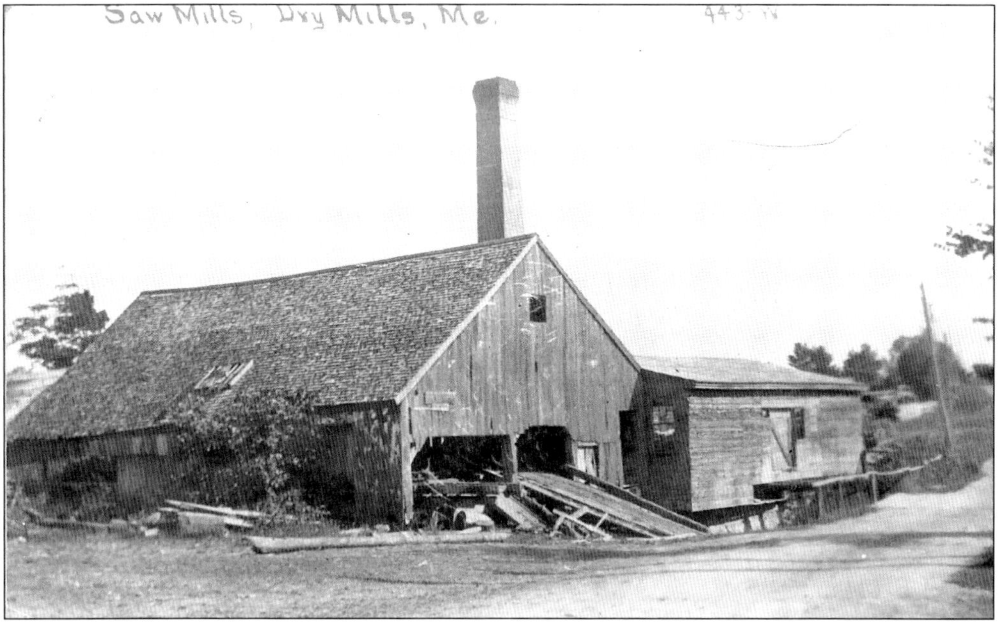

Around 1800, William Libby built the first sawmill at Dry Mills. Sawmills were the main industry for the settlement of Dry Mills. Three generations ran them, and they were expanded several times from 1800s to 1905. This mill was sold to the Merrill family and then the Goff family before closing in the 1940s.

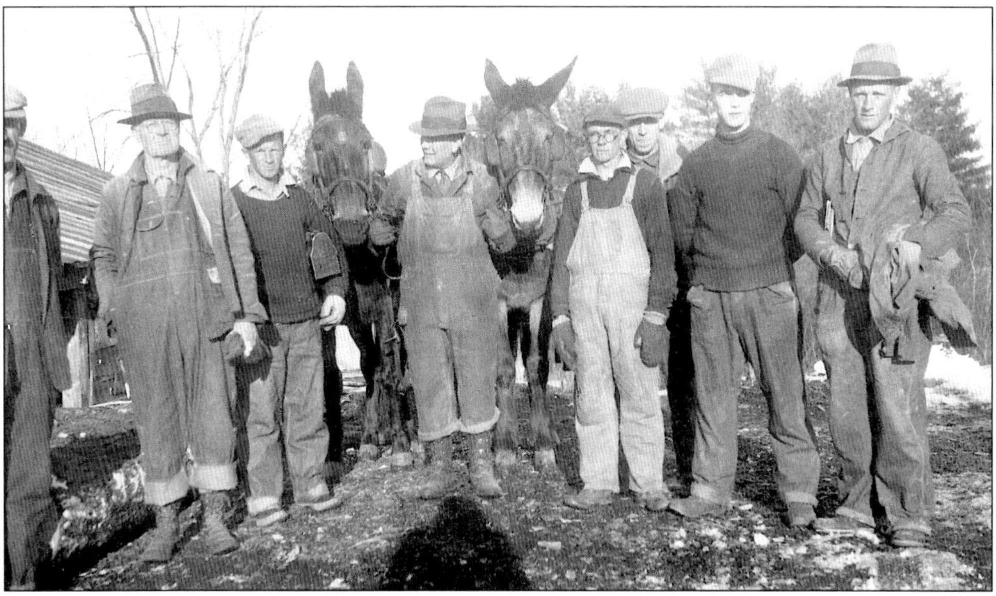

The mills provided employment for many people in the area. This Dry Mills sawmill work crew consists of, from left to right, Will Goff, Warren Flye, unknown, Bill McKenney, Norman Dolloff, Ernest Kimball, Silas Foster, and Roy Verrill.

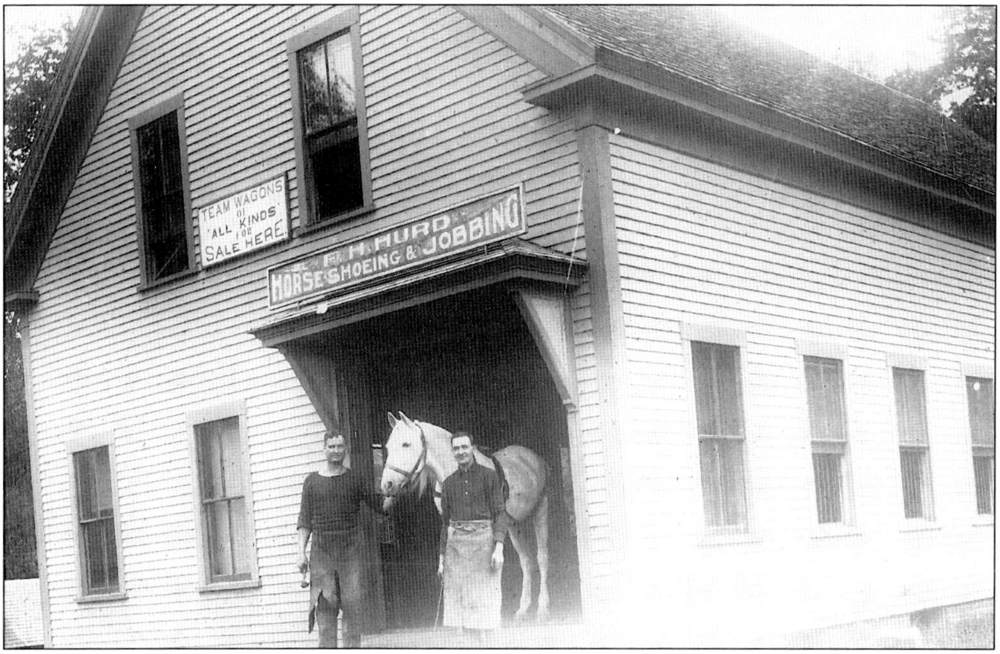

Hurd's Blacksmith Shop was located on the south side of North Raymond Road in Dry Mills. From 1913 to 1922 George Barrows had his blacksmith shop behind the Brick Store at Gray Corner. After the fire of 1921 he lost this shop, so he moved to Dry Mills, where he served customers from 1924 to 1930. Barrows is standing to the right of the horse in this photograph.

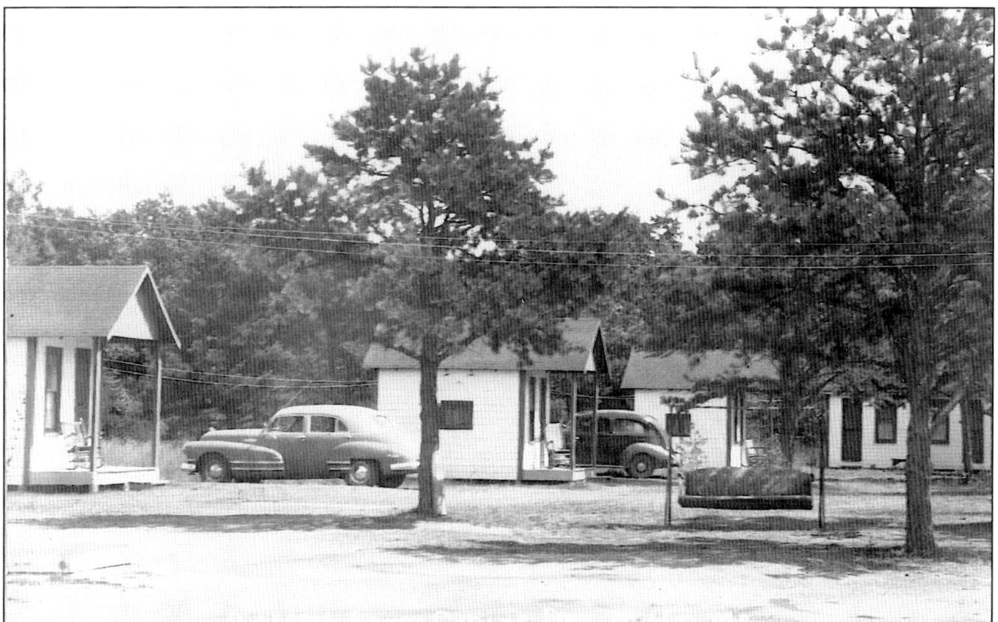

Overnight cabins began to spring up along the main roads in the 1920s as the tourist business began to develop. The Crystal Lake Cabins were located on Route 26 just one mile north of Dry Mills Corner, and Busy Bee Cabins were located in South Gray.

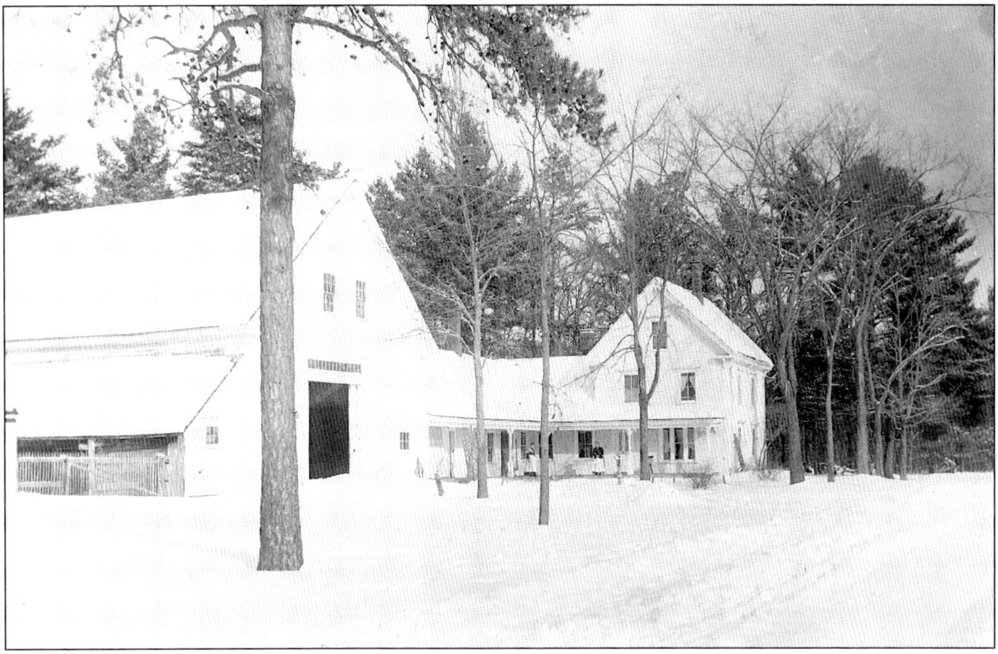

The home of Marshall and Maria (Foster) Morse was located in Dry Mills on the Weymouth Road, about where the home of David Finocchietti presently resides. During the 1920s the Morses took in summer boarders from out of state. The building burned in 1923 due to an overheated incubator in the ell.

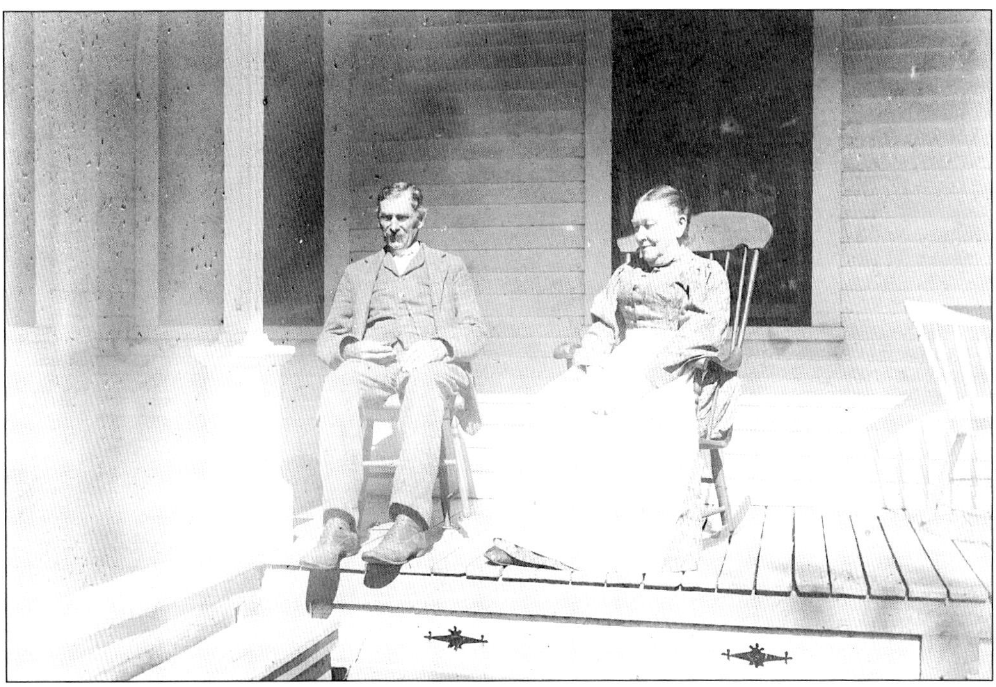

Marshall and Maria (Foster) Morse pose on the front porch of their home.

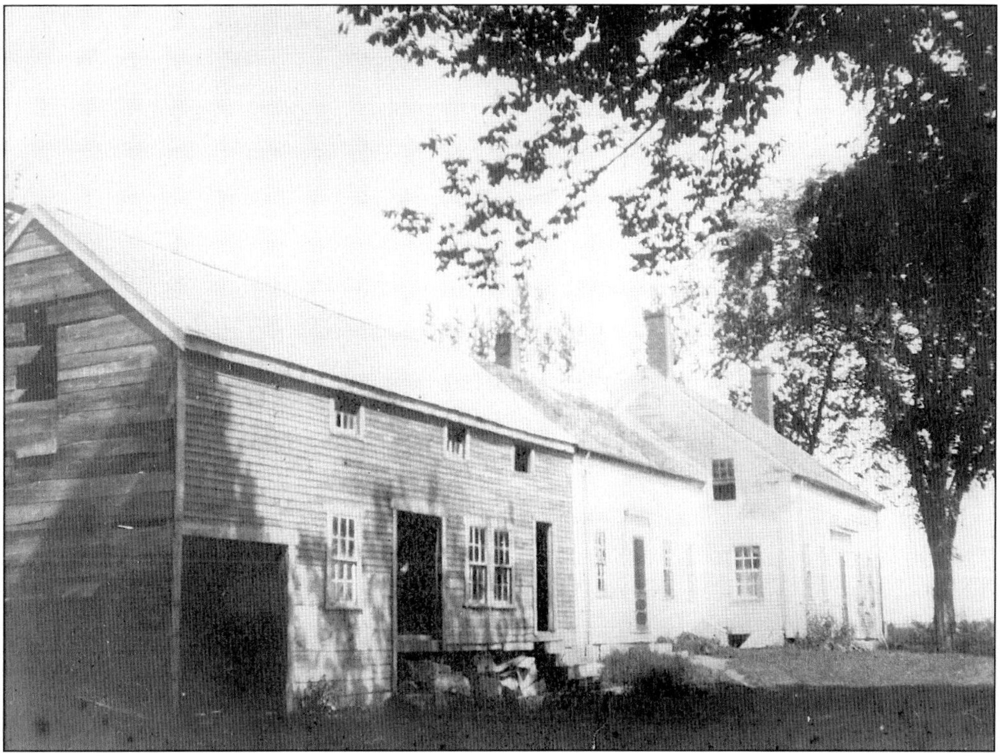

The original house of Victor and Inez Yeaton burned and was rebuilt about 1925. Victor was a tax collector from 1919 to 1933, earning $252.95 for the year and $15 for collecting dog taxes. Only the house stands today at the corner of the Weymouth Road and Lewiston Road.

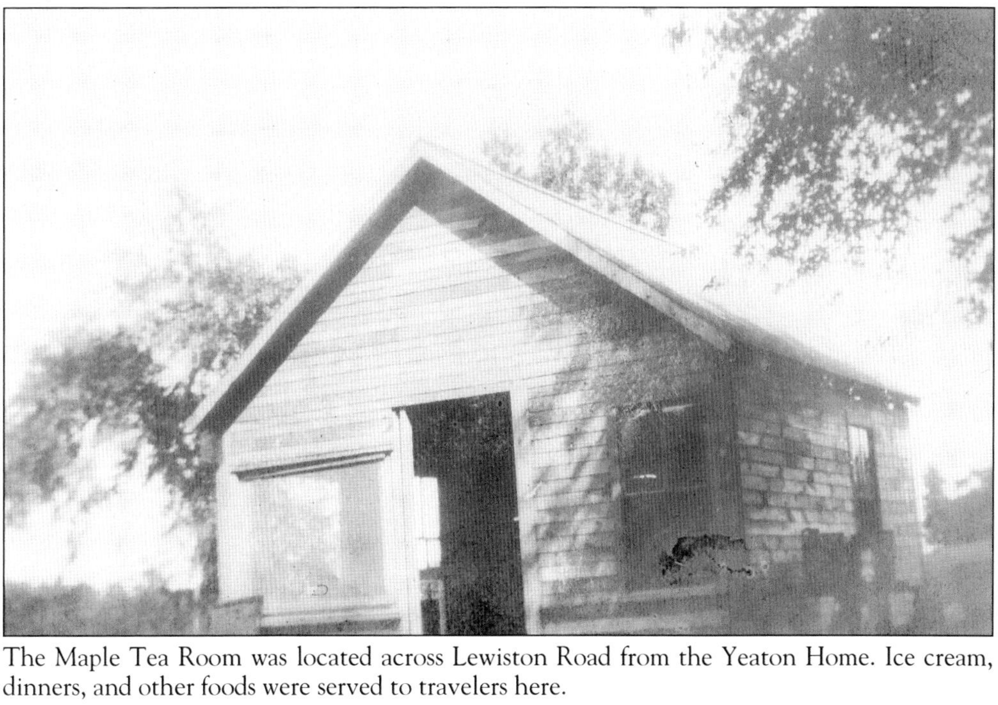

The Maple Tea Room was located across Lewiston Road from the Yeaton Home. Ice cream, dinners, and other foods were served to travelers here.

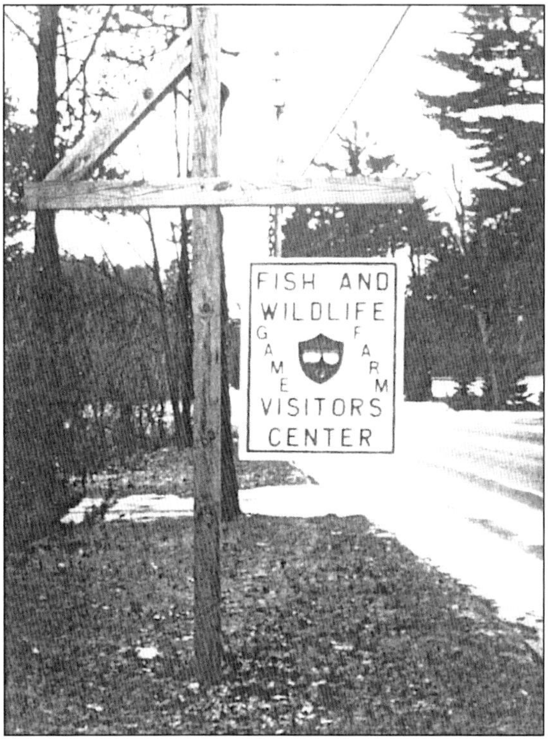

Hundreds of visitors enjoyed the state fish hatchery and the state game farm, where game, fish, and birds were hatched and raised for release in the hunting and fishing areas of the state. The collection of wild animals native to the state at the game farm also added to its popularity.

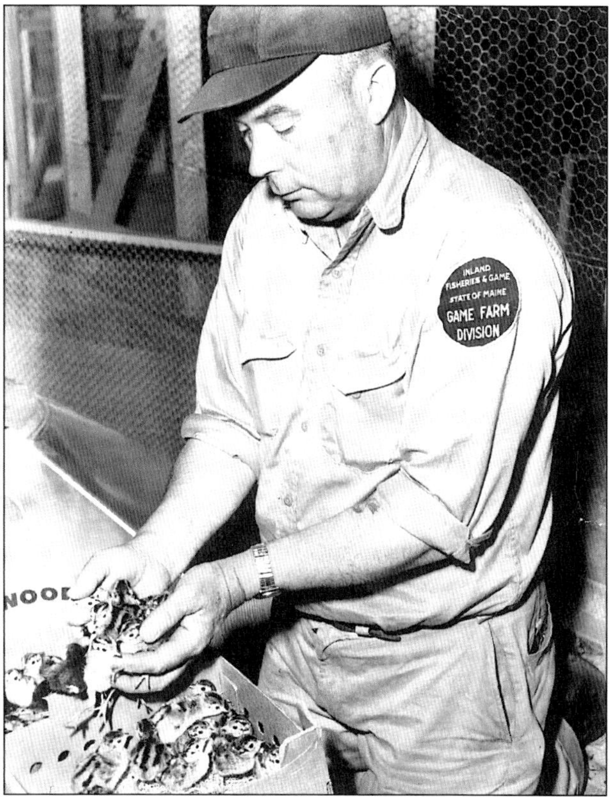

Approximately 30,000 pheasants were raised at the game farm, and with the help of sportsmen they were released prior to the fall hunting season. This picture shows William Wilkinson tending to the baby chick pheasants. The process of raising pheasants has been phased out by the state.

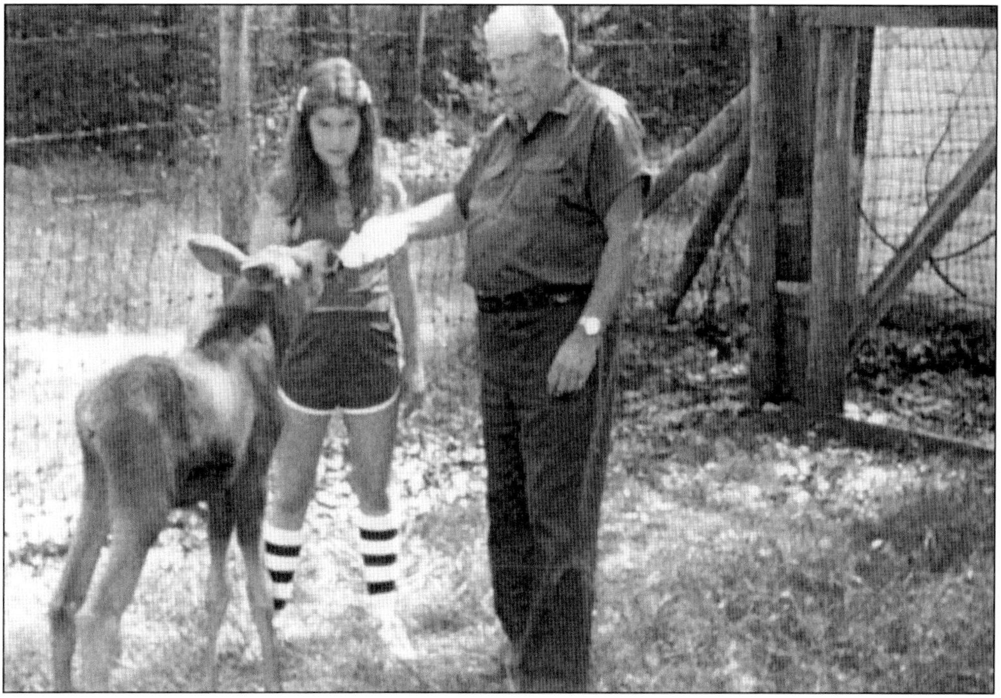

William Wilkinson, an employee of the game farm, and his granddaughter feed a baby moose that weighs about 100 pounds. The animal farm has many animals that are native to Maine. Moose and bears seem to get the most attention by the public.

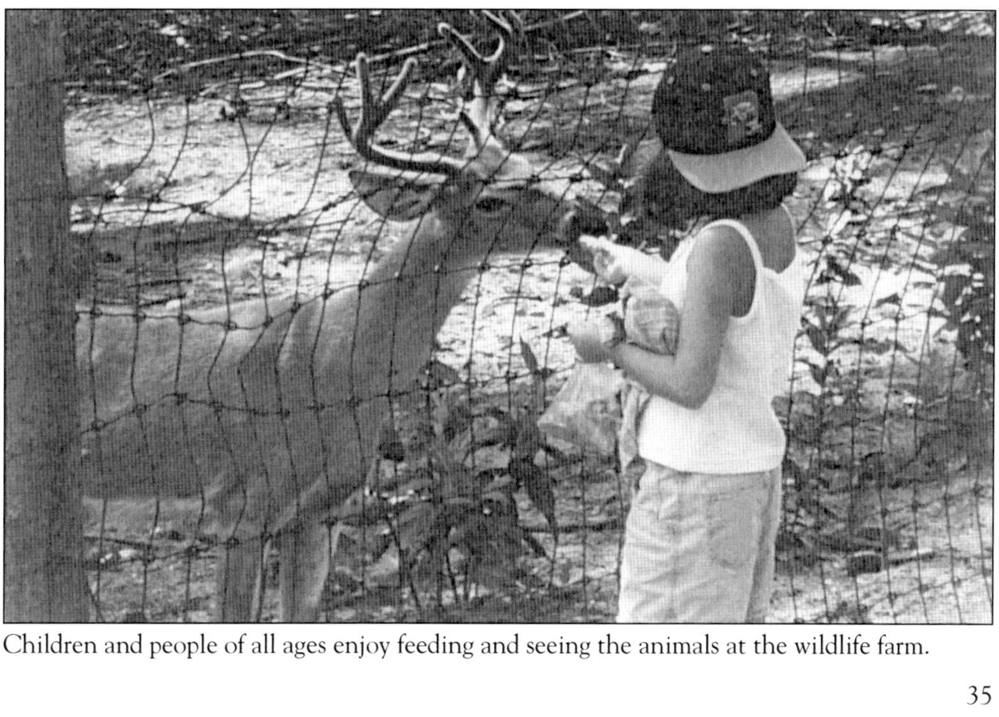

Children and people of all ages enjoy feeding and seeing the animals at the wildlife farm.

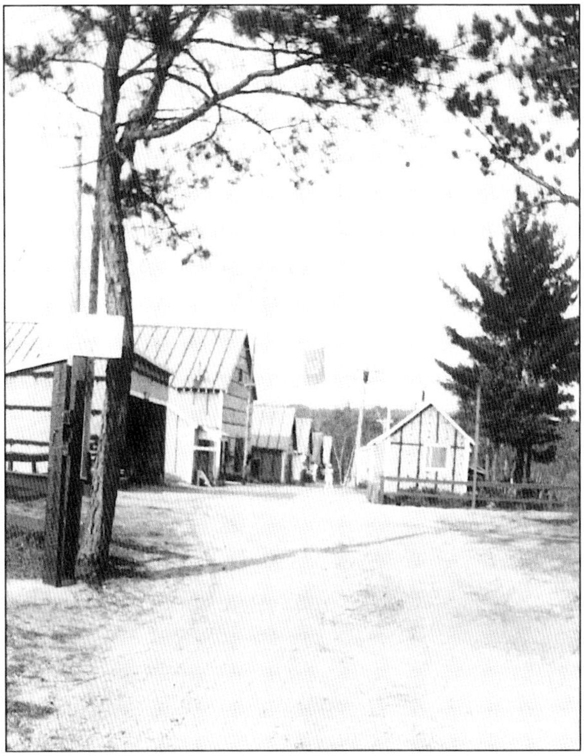

Federal Emergency Relief Administration transient camps helped supply the manpower to upgrade the Dry Mills Hatchery in 1935. George Maxwell got the contract with the FERA to help build the original main line of the pools. The work was all manual labor, which meant picks, shovels, wheelbarrows, and a strong back were needed. A steam shovel was the only heavy equipment used on the project.

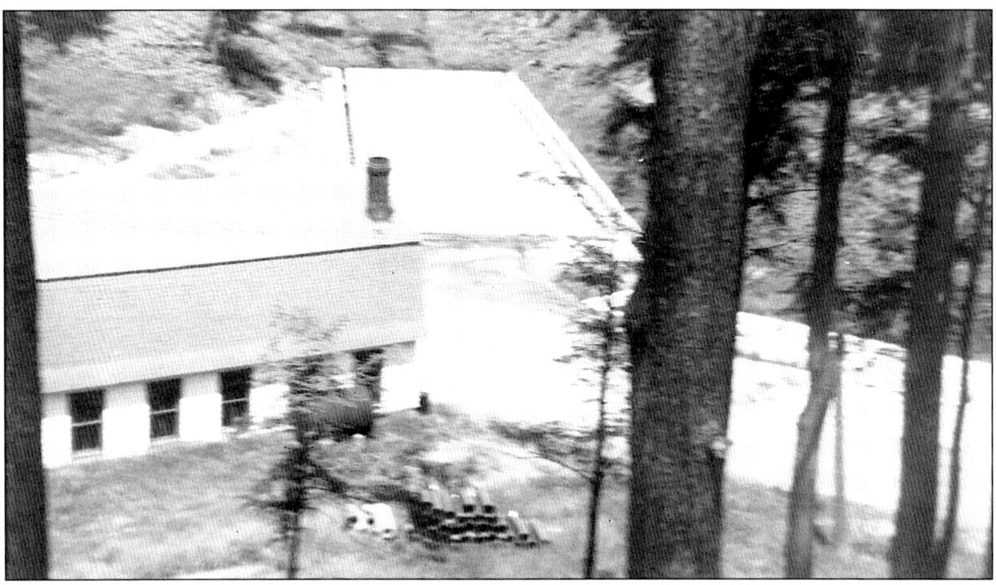

The original upper fish hatchery is shown here in the 1930s. This building is not visible to the general public, as it is located in a vast ravine to the left of the fish pool. The purpose of the hatchery was to supply other hatcheries with a healthy strain of fertilized brook trout eggs as well as other species of trout.

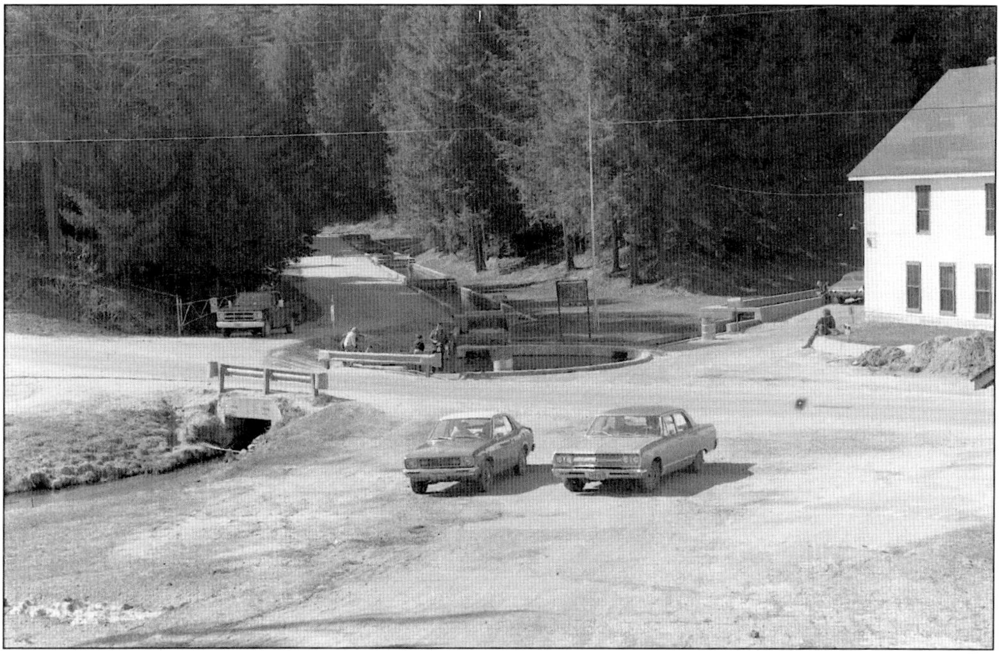

A concrete, circular, 30-foot-wide pool, located at the end of two lines of pools, shows off large brown and brook trout to the public. It is located right next to the Hatchery Road, which today is called the Weymouth Road.

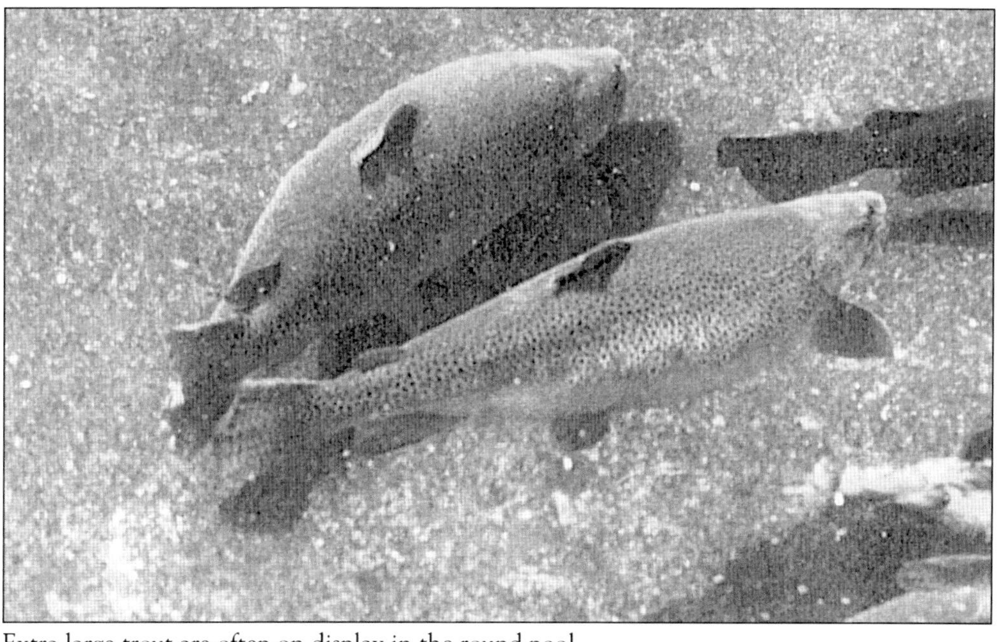

Extra large trout are often on display in the round pool.

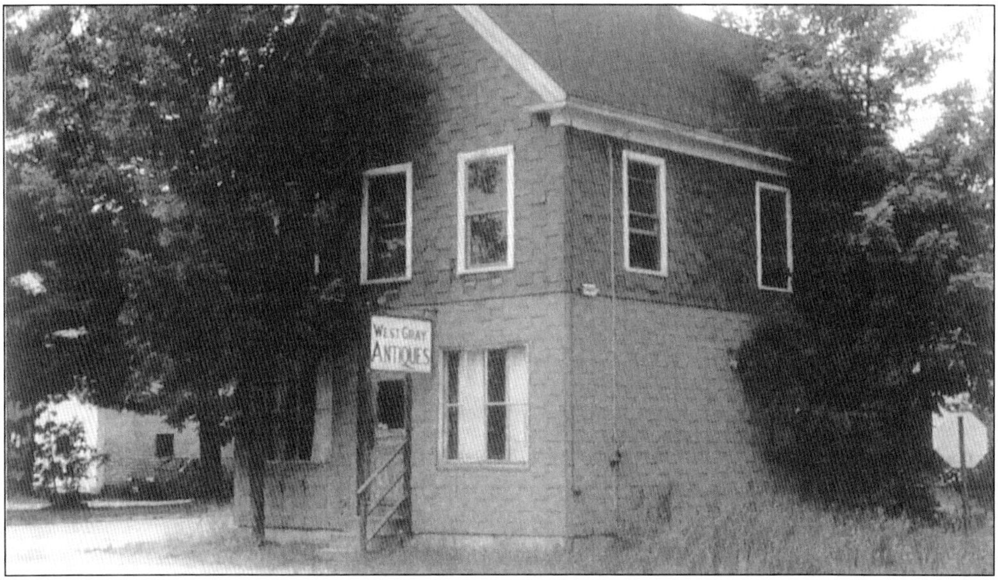

The West Gray Store was built in 1900 by Robert Allen. It has had several owners, including Clifford Barton, who ran it from 1918 to 1941. Groceries, grain, and kerosene were the important staples of the area. At the side of the store were hay scales, where farmers weighed their loads of hay, and a gasoline pump was eventually installed at the front of the store. The post office was located in the corner of the store; each family in the community had a box for mail, which was brought twice daily from Gray Depot.

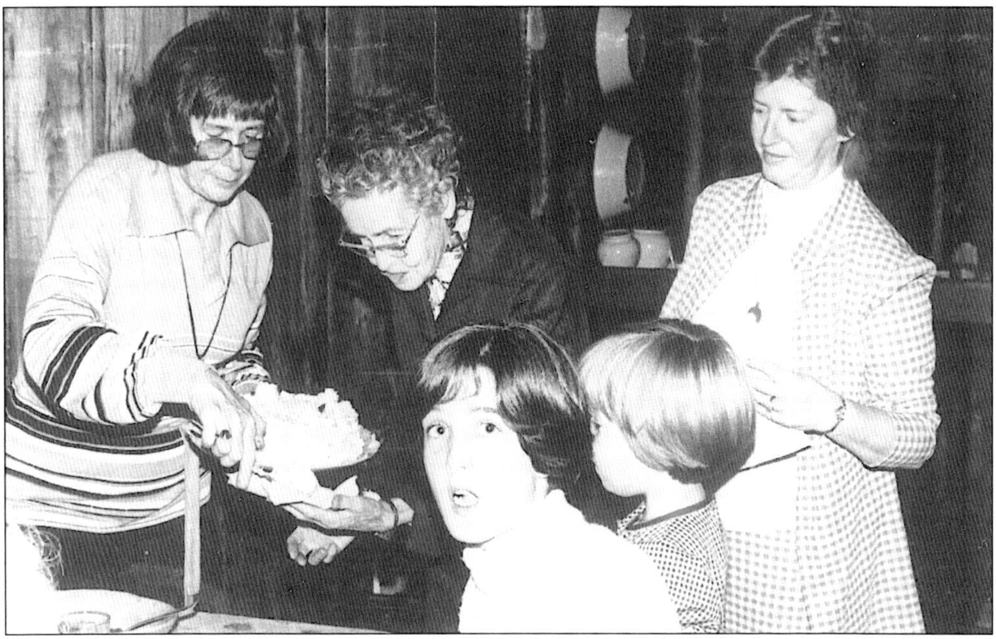

The second floor of Barton's store was used for many functions. Community pot luck suppers, sponsored by Myra and Cliff Barton, were held here every other Saturday. This event attracted people from miles around. Leftovers were auctioned off and the proceeds used to pay the utilities, wood, hot water, electricity, etc. After supper they might play cards, bingo, or show movies. Pictured from left to right are Mildred Pollard, Myra Barton, and Yvonne Wilkinson.

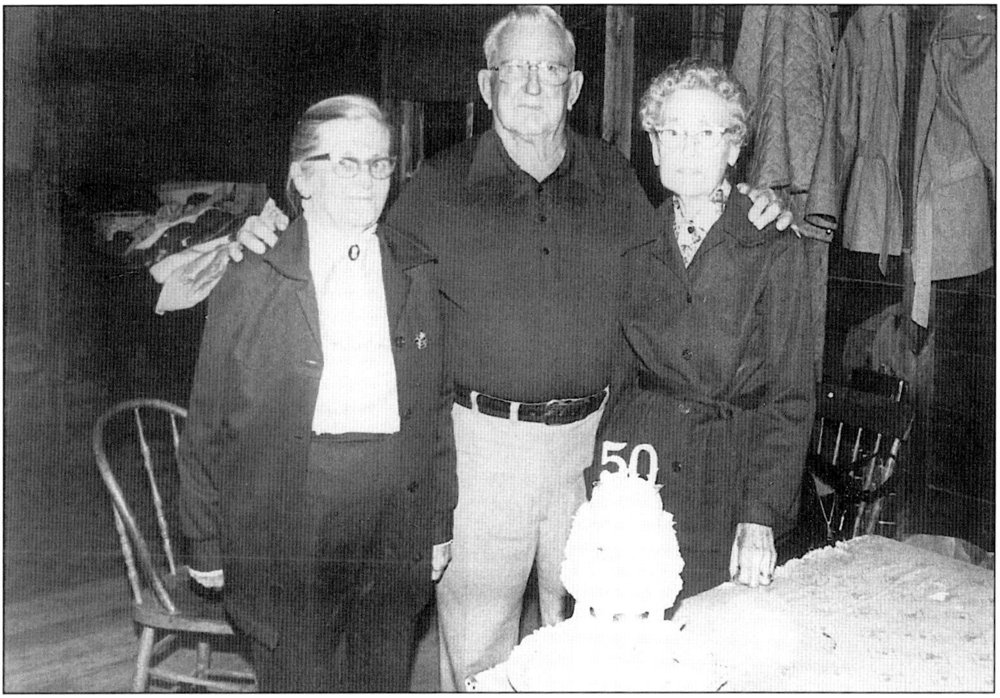

The last pot luck supper took place on November 16, 1977, the 50th anniversary of the first pot luck supper here, which took place on November 27, 1927. A reporter from the Portland Paper Company interviewed and took pictures. It was the talk of the town. The only members of the original suppers still attending were Catherine Skilling, John Skilling, and Myra Barton. Today the store is owned by Don and Shirley Boulanger, who are remodeling the first floor for an antique store and the upstairs for a sewing workshop.

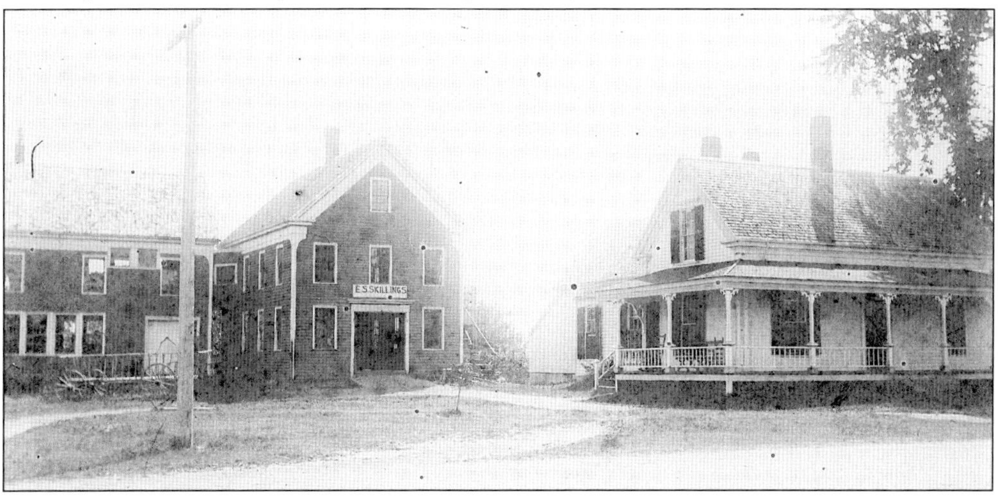

West Gray's carriage and sleigh factory is shown here in the 1800s. The building to the far left of the blacksmith shop is the factory, which was owned by Charles Allen. The connecting blacksmith shop, ran by Edwin Skilling, is where iron rims were put on carriage wheels and iron runners on sleighs. The upholstering was done by a man from Boston. The house to the right was Edwin and Ella Skilling's home; it is now occupied by Kevin and Cindy (Skilling) Trinward.

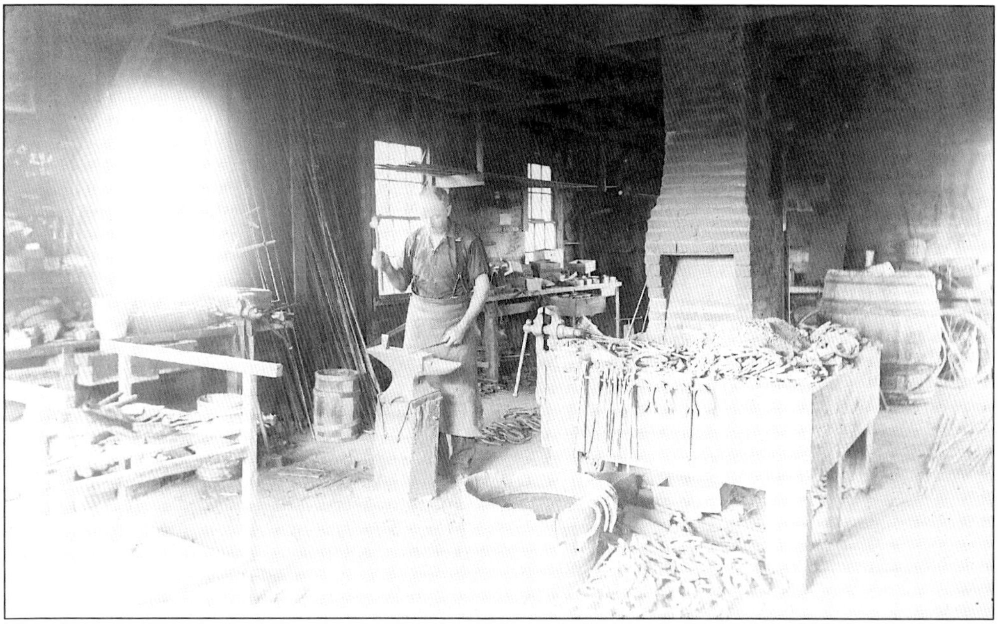

Blacksmith Edwin Skilling works in his shop at West Gray. Blacksmiths were in great demand during the 1800s and into the 1900s. They were once as plentiful as service stations are today in Gray. Blacksmiths and carriage workers were very skilled and learned their trade from the best-known factories in the area. Several of Gray's carriage and blacksmith workers invented methods of improving carriages and sleighs, and were recognized nationally.

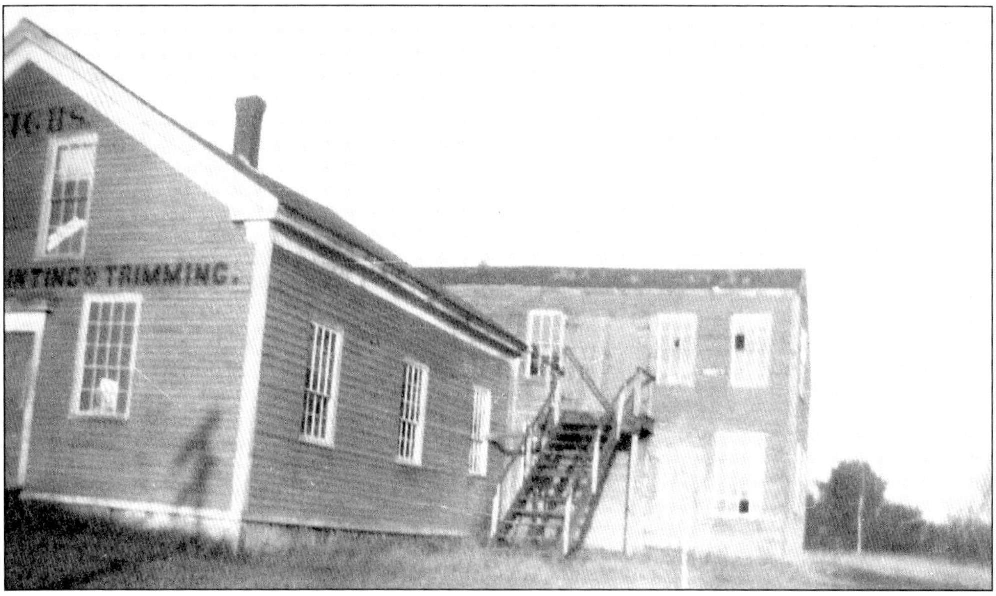

The carriage painting and striping shop was located across the road from the factory. The second floor was used for school entertainments, dances, church services, etc. The building they used to work on the carriages was eventually moved across the road and became Charles Nason's home. The blacksmith shop was moved to what is now the restaurant's parking lot and used for a garage. The carriage shop became a house. One of the carriages made in West Gray is now on display at the Willowbrook Museum in Newfield, Maine.

Two

The Bells Are Ringing

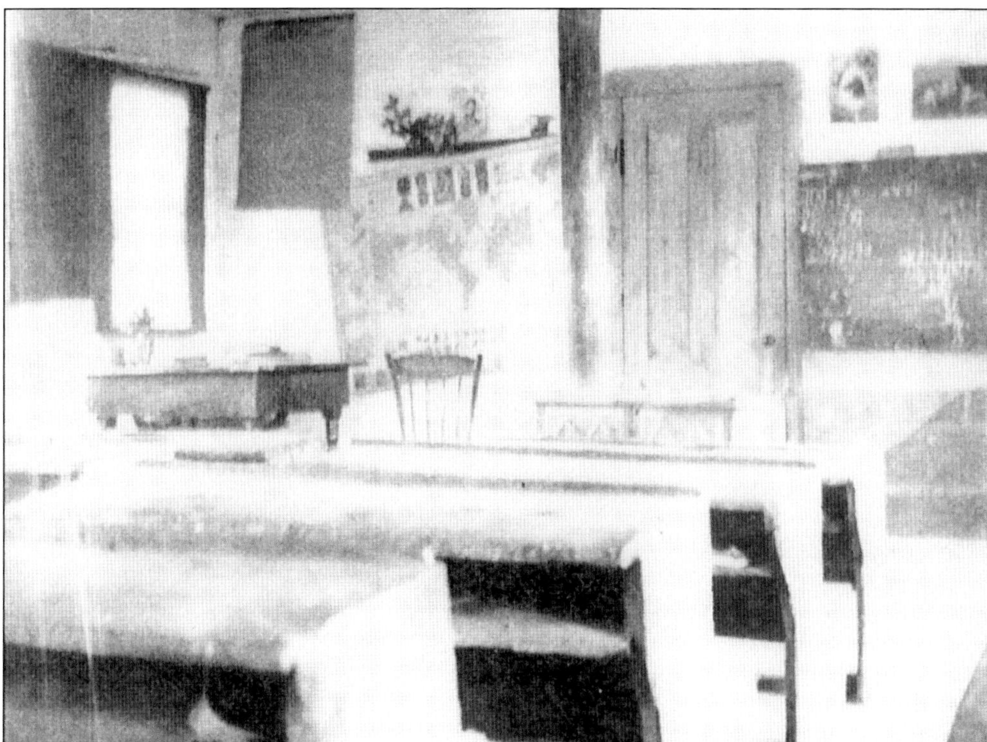

This is the interior of the District #1 schoolhouse. The first school was built in East Gray in 1793. Schoolhouses in Gray were usually built by the district and later reimbursed by the town, but before District #1 could be reimbursed for its school, the building was destroyed by fire. Another school was erected on the same spot, and it served the town for over 100 years. In 1795 Gray had four school districts; by 1878 the town had 12 districts and ten good school buildings.

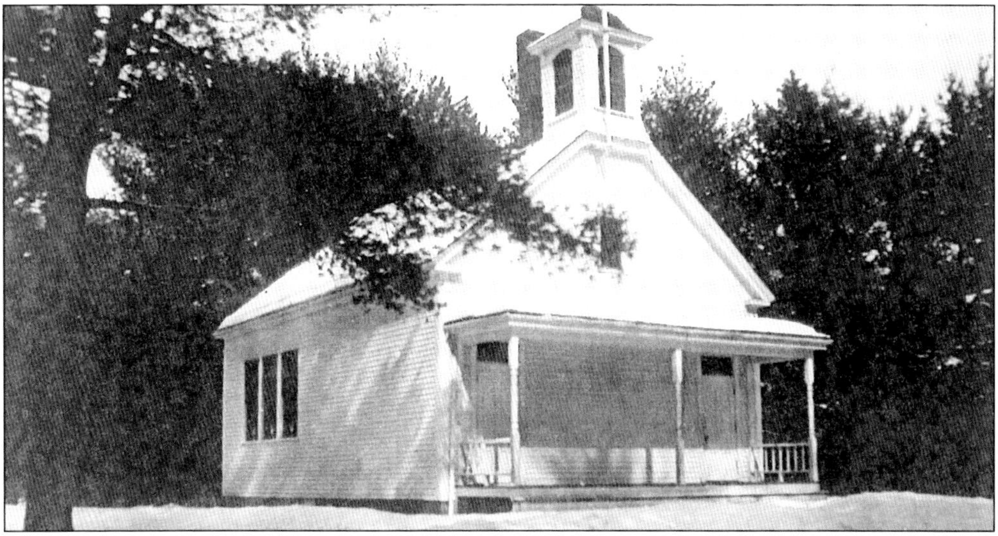

The new East Gray School, located on the corner of Mayall Road and Depot Road, was built to replace one that burned. Old records show the names of many prominent citizens who attended this school. Scholars originally had to provide their own books, but in 1889 the state legislature passed a law requiring the town to provide books for students. In 1894, the state passed a law doing away with school district system, so Gray hired W.B. Andrews as the first supervisor of schools.

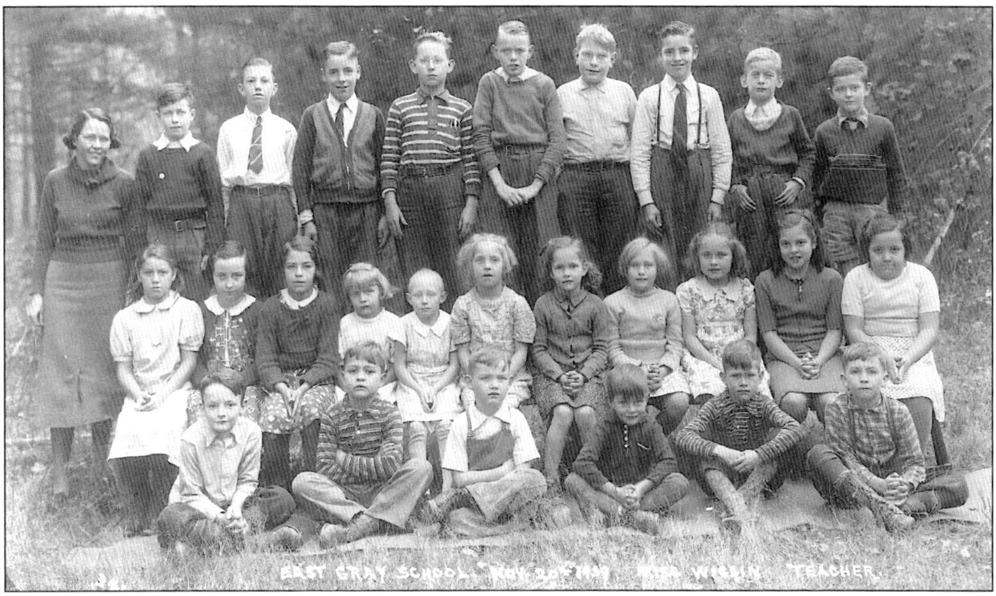

This photograph of the East Gray School was taken on November 20, 1939. At the time, the average teacher's pay was $18 per week. From left to right are as follows: (front row) Frank Partridge, Paul Jones, Gerald (Buzzy) Humphrey Jr., Lionel Jones, Richard Jones, and Lester Kimball Jr.; (middle row) Margaret Seiders, Eleanor Humphrey, Katheleen Carr, Betty Files, Vera Sawyer, Evelyn Bubier, Constance Jones, Betsy Crosby, Joanne Crosby, Nancy Crosby, and Ellen Kimball; (back row) teacher Norma Wiggin, Edward Bisco, Lloyd Wing, Frederick Carr, Gordon Kimball, George Humphrey, Charles Perry, Francis Carr, Leonard Doughty, and Malcolm MacDonald.

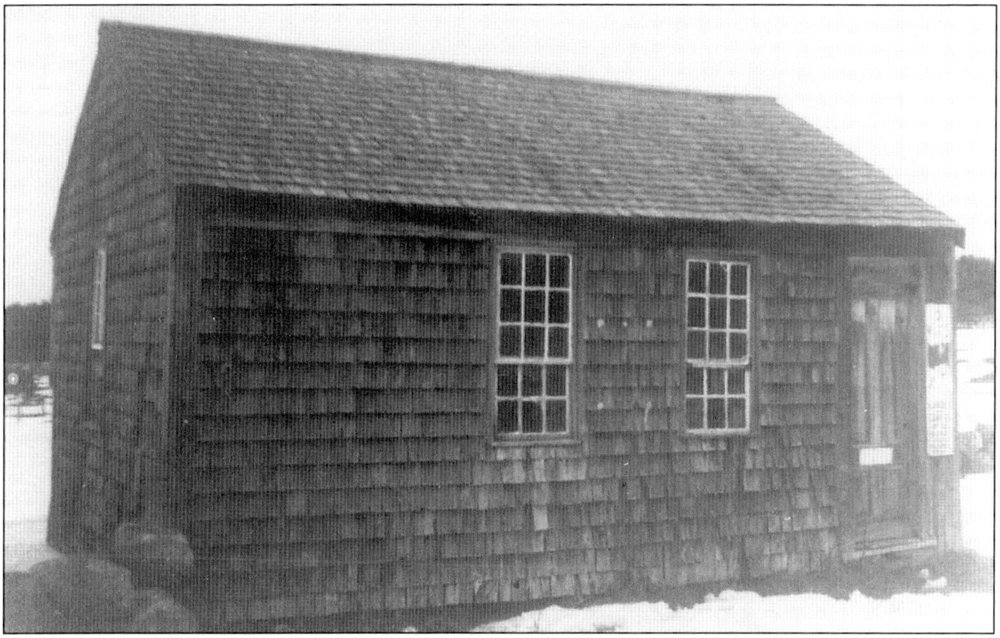

District No. 9 Schoolhouse on Long Hill was very small and primitive, serving sometimes only six or eight pupils. It was built in 1842 and was dissolved in 1894. The building and furnishings sold at an action for just $7. Two other schools were built in this area and are now residences.

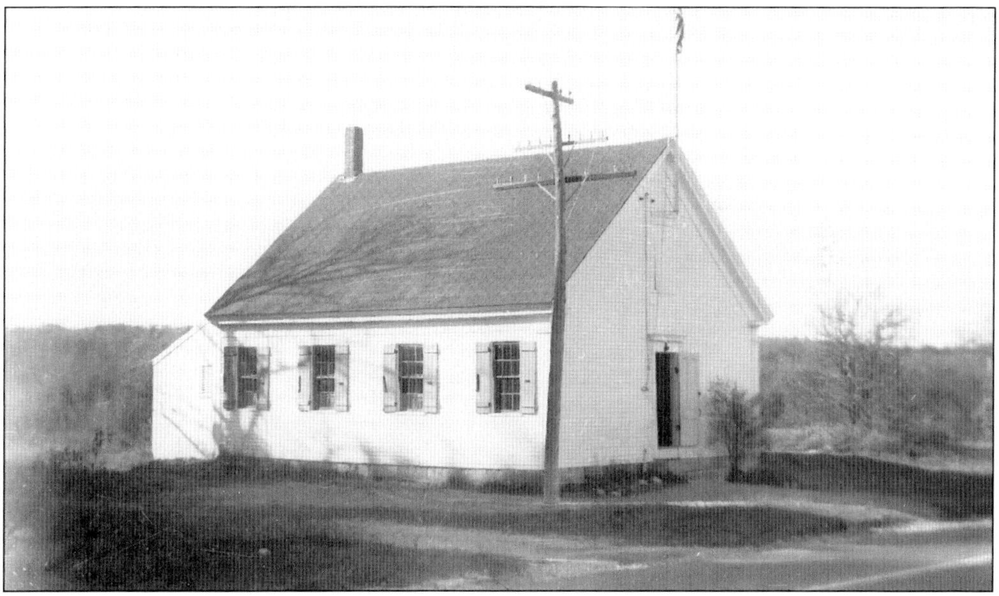

The Dry Mills one-room school, built in 1858 in District #3, became the largest ungraded school of the town in 1883. Many children received their education here. In 1959 the last class to attend this school consisted of only first and second graders. After sitting empty for many years, a group of interested people from the town made the decision in 1987 to restore the building and move it from Shaker Road to the Game Farm Road. In December of 1996 it was entered in the National Register of Historic Places. At a future date the school will be opened to the public.

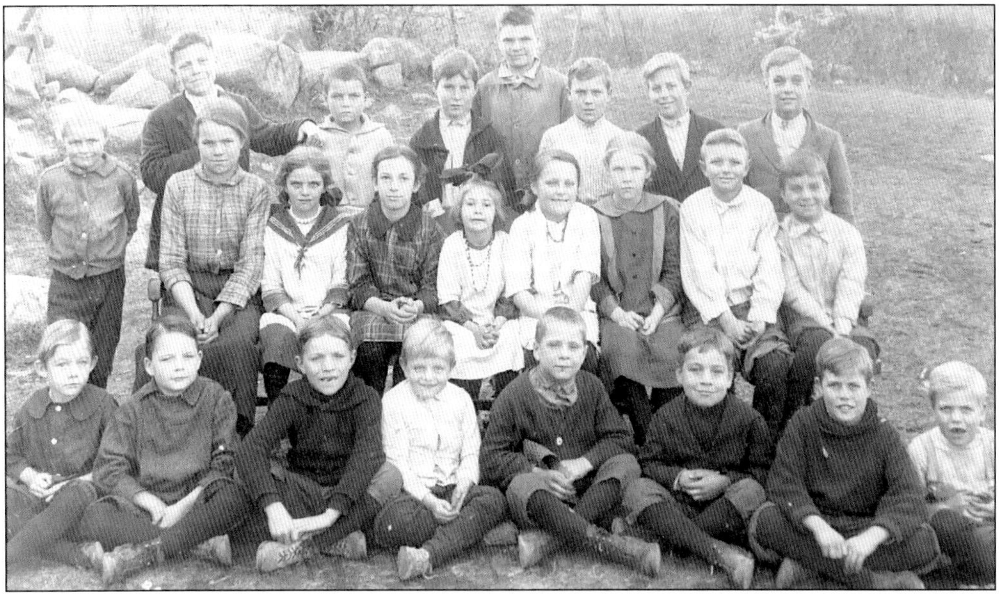

Dry Mills schoolchildren pose for a photograph in the 1910s. They are, from left to right, as follows: (front row) Merton Verrill, Howard Verrill, three unidentified students, Frank McConkey, Charles McConkey, and ? Burnell; (middle row) ? May, Grace May, Freddie Strout, Eleanor Sawyer, Edna Story, unknown, Marguerite Verrill, Cliff Strout, and Milo McConkey; (back row) Major Wing, ? May, ? Quint, unknown, Percy Quint, Clarence Quint, and Dana McConkey.

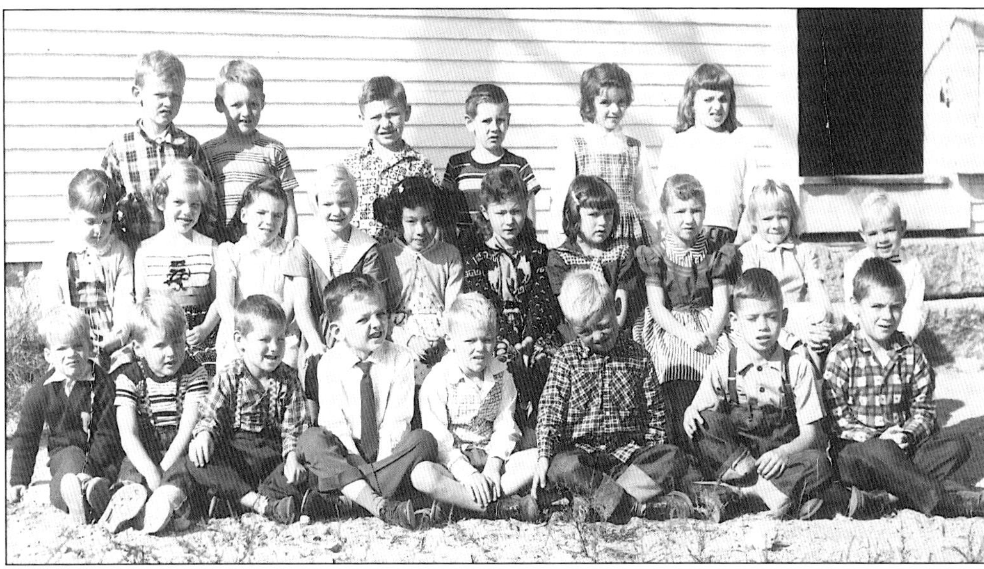

The Dry Mills School was the last of the rural schools existing in its original state. The last class to attend this school was in 1959. These students are, from left to right, as follows: (front row) Fred McCleary, Bruce Lewis, Billy Small, Kerry Walsh, Duane Ross, Mark Fogg, Michael Tardiff, and Kenneth Small; (middle row) Marilyn Walsh, Carol Robinson, Dianna Goan, Glenn McCleary, Nancy Wong, Kathleen Sayward, Carol Small, Debra Johnson, Pamela Dingwell, and Richard Dingwell; (back row) Charles Bruns, Wayne Lewis, Richard Wood, James Foster, Susan Fogg, and Elizabeth Tardiff. Their teacher was Minerva Quint.

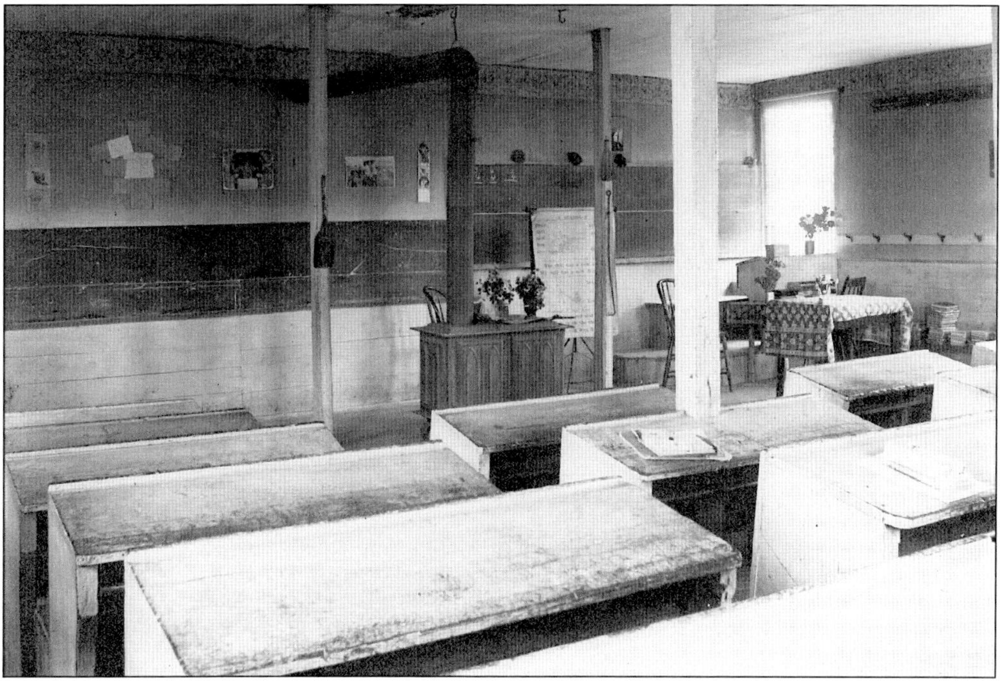

This is an interior view of the two-story, Brick School in District #5. Built in 1843, the building took the place of the wooden Center Schoolhouse. All grades were taught here, and for a while the second floor was used for students desiring more education. Having to furnish one's own transportation meant that the children usually walked to school. The teacher taught a fall, winter, and/or a spring term earning in 1893 a wage of $5 per week. The school was located on Shaker Road, opposite the present telephone company. It was torn down in 1902.

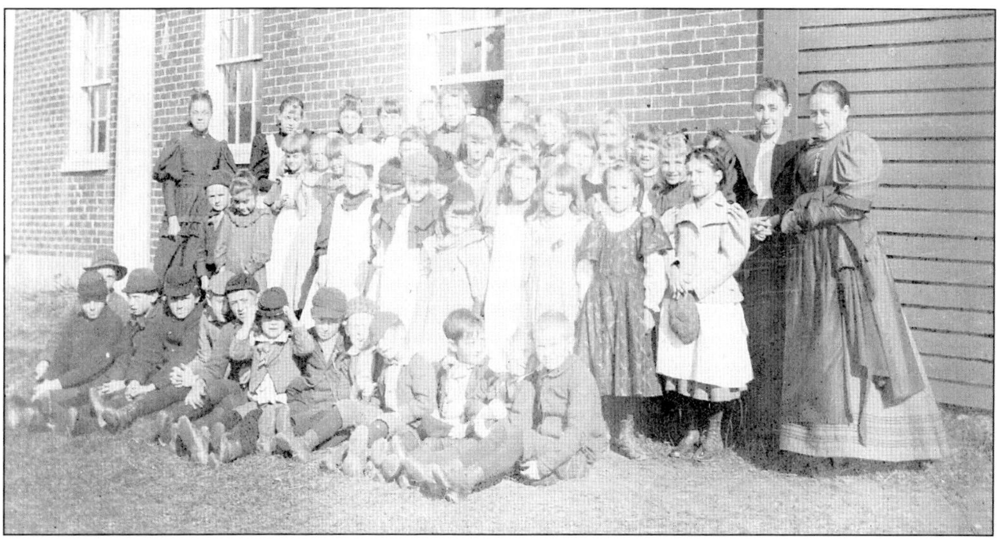

Scholars at the Old Brick School pose for a photograph, *c.* 1893. Three of the teachers were Leonora Whitney, Mabel Douglass, and Miss Abbie Sawyer. In 1893, scholars who were present every day during one or more of the terms were Julia and Harley Chipman, Bertha and Verdie Frank, Maria Haskell, Artie ?, Percy Leighton, Lewis Leighton, Ralph Morey, Cora Prince, Hattie Wormwood, Agnes Fogg, Linnie Libby, and Allie Thompson.

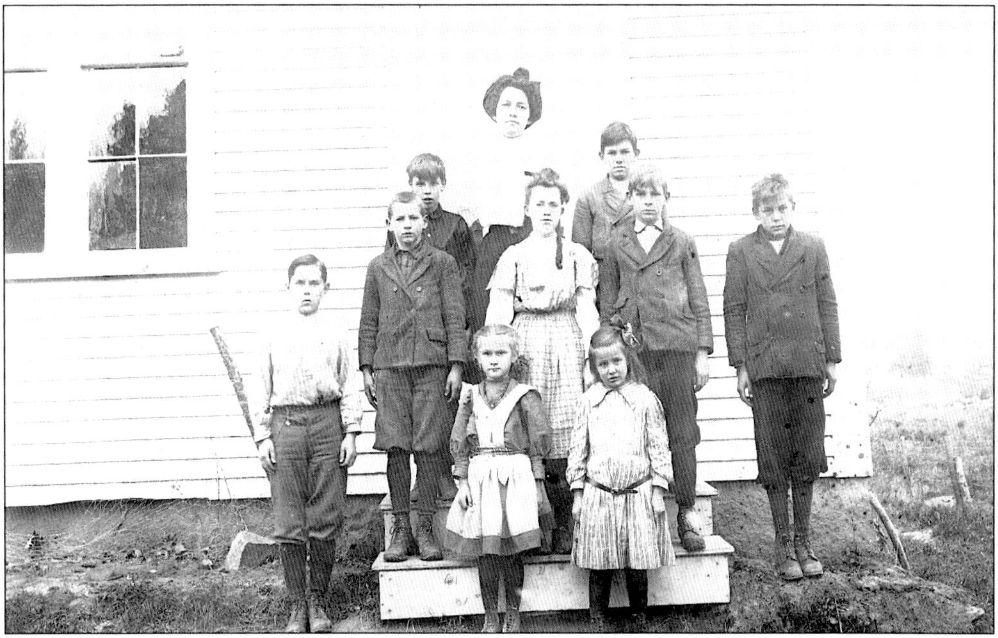

Scholars of the North Gray one-room school in District #2 pose for a photograph in 1910. Six classes are represented here with their teacher, who was paid $7.50 per week. From left to right are as follows: (front row) Mildred Yeaton and Marion Roberts; (middle row) Orin Richard, Orland Mayberry, Rachel Foster, Harold Witham, and Percy Webster; (back row) Raymond Roberts, teacher Edith Fogg, and Stanley Witham.

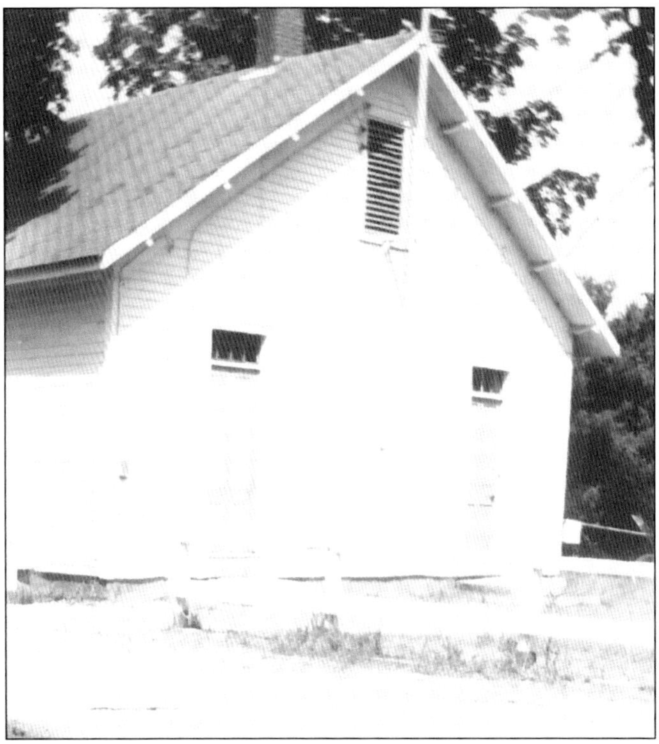

The West Gray District #9 school, later changed to #4, was located in 1849 at the corner of Cambell Shore Road and Windham Road. The building was larger than usual and was used to hold Methodist meetings, as a large majority of that sect lived in West Gray. Sometime between 1849 and 1857, against opposition, the schoolhouse was moved to the corner of Cambell Shore Road and Mountain View Road. Today the building is the Emerson's house.

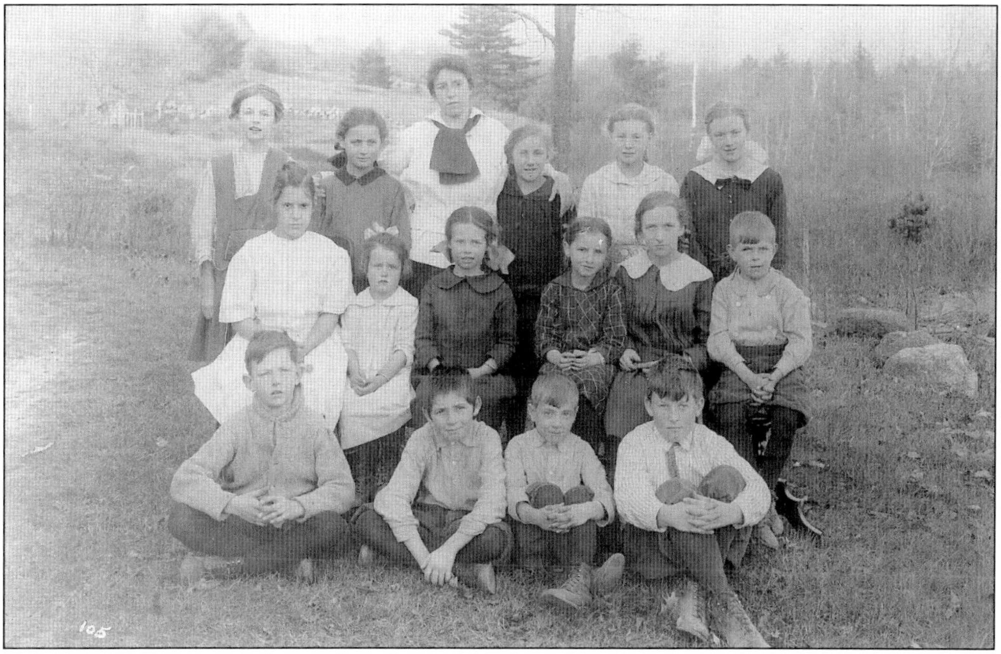

The West Gray District #4 school is shown here in 1918–19. From left to right are as follows: (front row) John Cobb, Lindsey Campbell, Carle Brackley, and Warren Libby; (middle row) Gladys Straton, ? Goodrich, ? Goodrich, Louise Campbell, Marion Pollard, and Gene Brackley; (back row) Catherine Skillings, Mary Campbell, teacher Josephine Davis, Lena Allen, Alice Skillings, and Annie Frank.

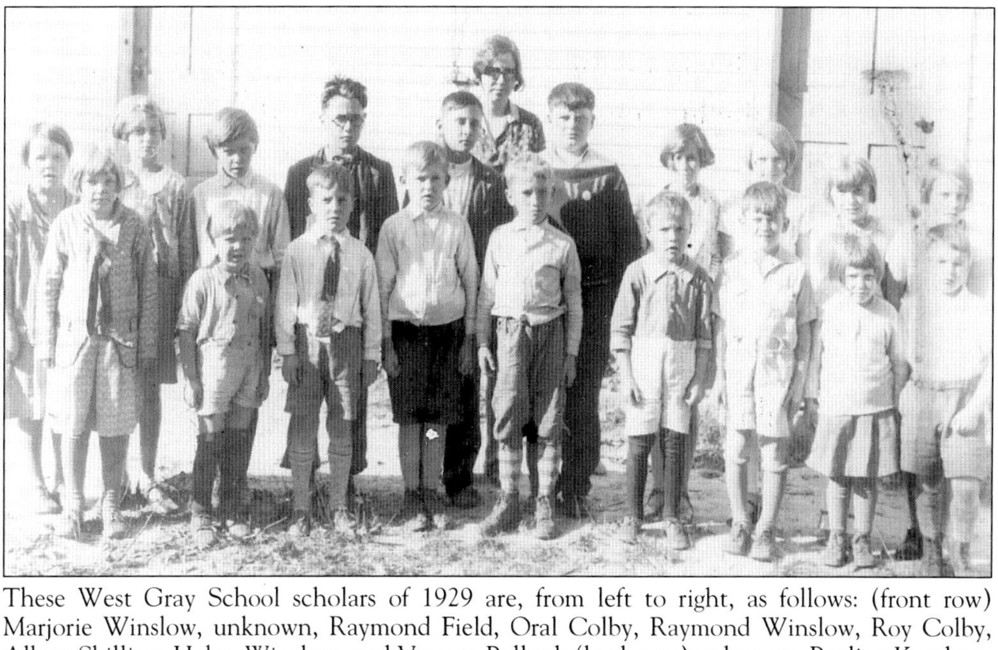

These West Gray School scholars of 1929 are, from left to right, as follows: (front row) Marjorie Winslow, unknown, Raymond Field, Oral Colby, Raymond Winslow, Roy Colby, Albert Skilling, Helen Winslow, and Vernon Pollard; (back row) unknown, Pauline Knudsen, unknown, Stanley Hall, Russell Hall, teacher Ida McDonald, Francis Knudsen, Betty Knudsen, Ruth Barton, Phyllis Winslow, and Francis Field.

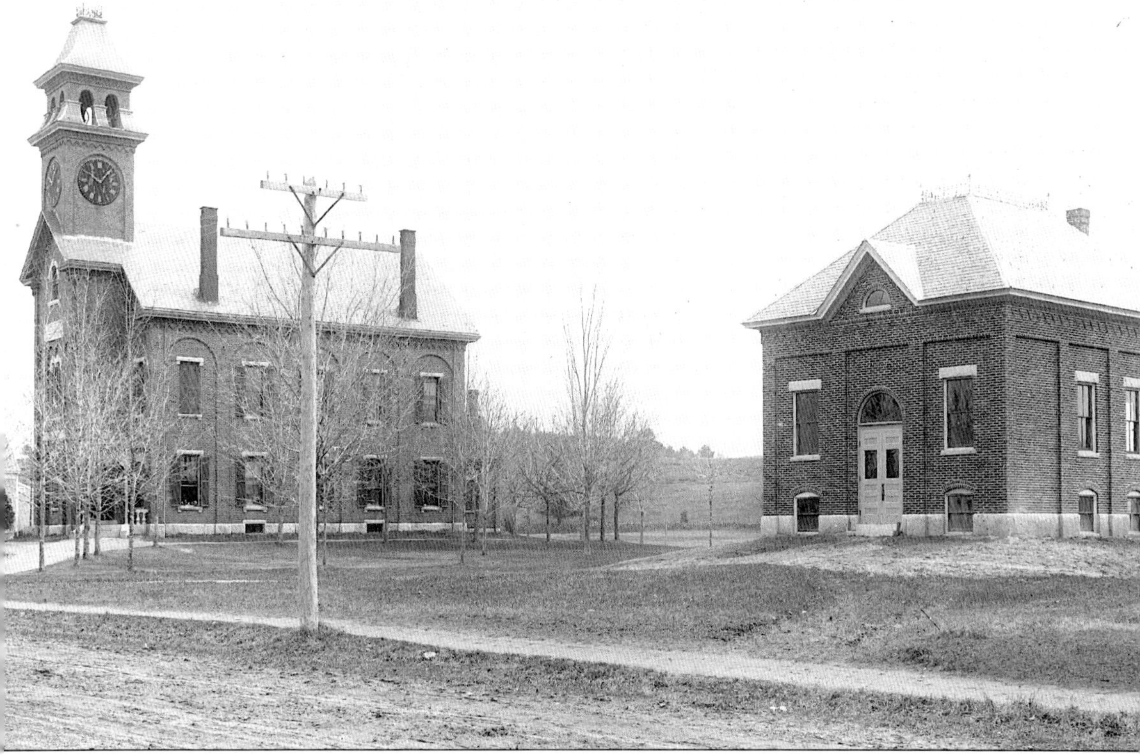

Pennell Institute was built in 1876 by Henry Goff, using the bricks from the Goff brickyard in East Gray, at the cost of $20,000, which included the clock and bell. A library was an additional $3,000 and was located on the first floor. School opened in the fall of 1886 with 122 students, and classes continued until 1962, after which there were many changes of grades. Mr. Lee B. Hunt was the first principal. The school was considered one of the finest free high schools of its kind in all of New England. Henry Pennell donated the school to Gray for the sole purpose for education.

The Science Laboratory to the right of the school was constructed in 1897 by Silas W. Foster at a cost of $1,300. The total cost was paid for by the state's appropriation of $500 and from the funds accumulated in Pennell Institute's trust fund. The *Gray News* is currently using this building. The clock in the tower has measured the days, called people to school, warned of danger, and rung in celebration. After years of use, it needed a major repair job, which was done in 1997. Pennell Alumni with the help of the townspeople raised the $50,000 to repair the "town clock," allowing it to ring once again on the hour and the half hour. Pennell Institute is on the National Register of Historic Places.

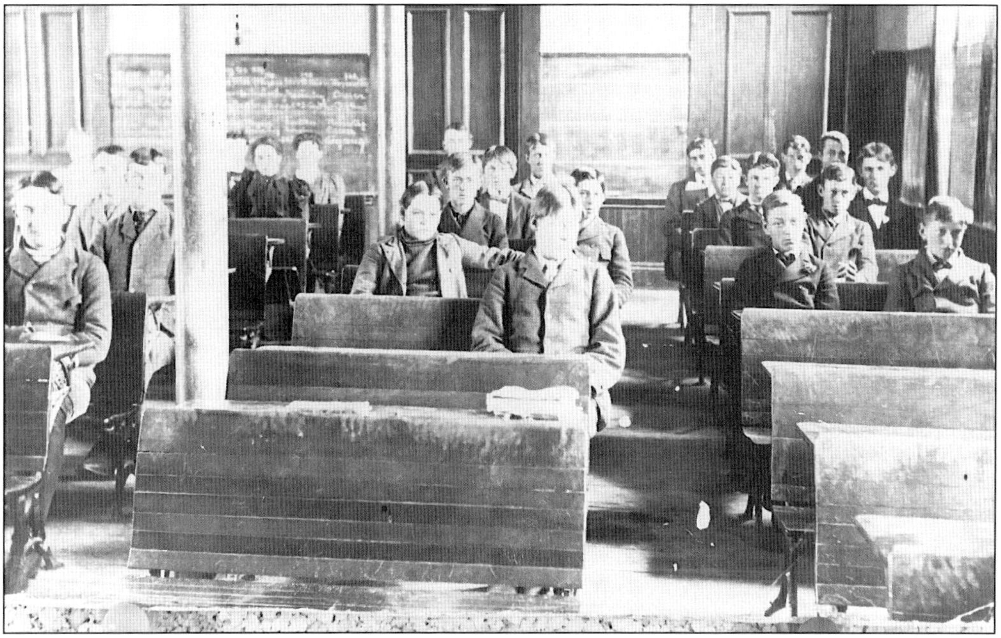

The first classes at Pennell Institute began in 1886; at that time, there was no grading in the common schools. Boys and girls sat separately. Nearby towns with no high schools sent students to attend. In 1889 the first class to receive their diplomas from Pennell were Annie Bean, Arthur Bennet, Grace Dow, Kate Leslie, Kate Libby, and Mabel Libby. Three went to college and three became successful teachers. This photograph was taken *c.* 1903.

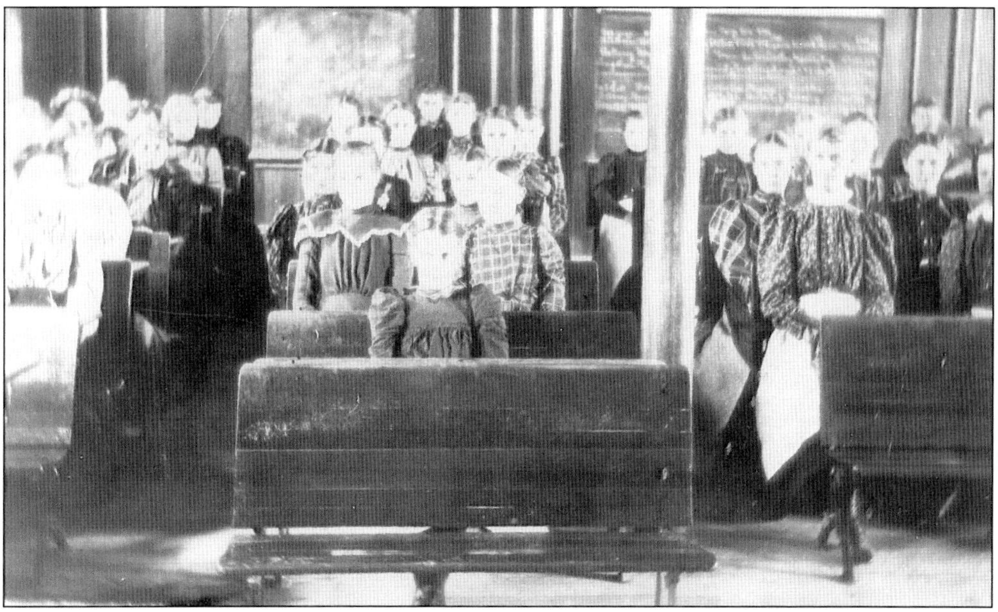

The two girls in the front row on the right side are the Bohnsen twins, Jennie and Minnie. This photograph was also taken *c.* 1903.

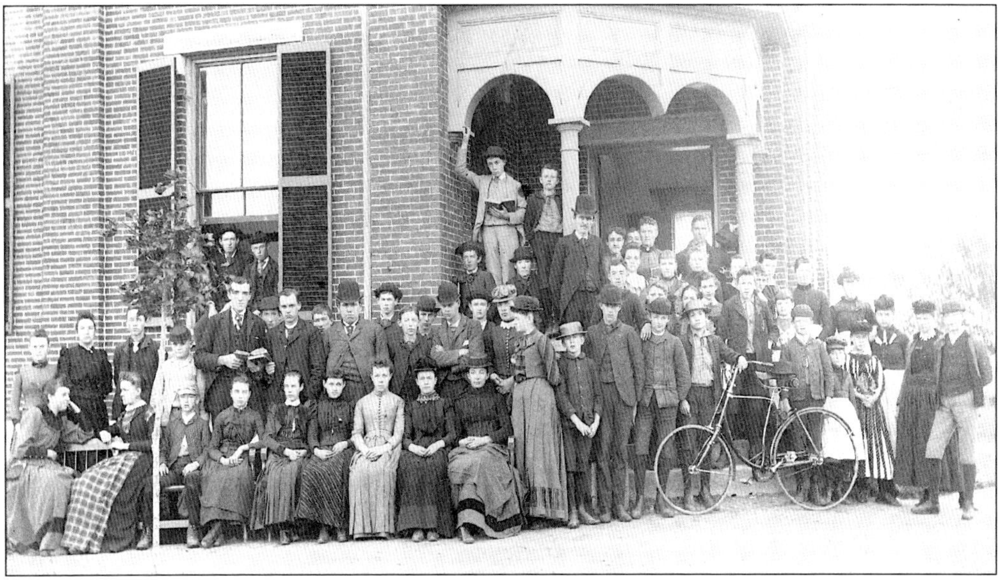

Students at Pennell Institute are shown here at the turn of the century. Many of them boarded at nearby homes because they were from out of town. They either walked to school or rode bicycles, horses, or horse-drawn wagons. Horses had to be left at the stables, which were close by.

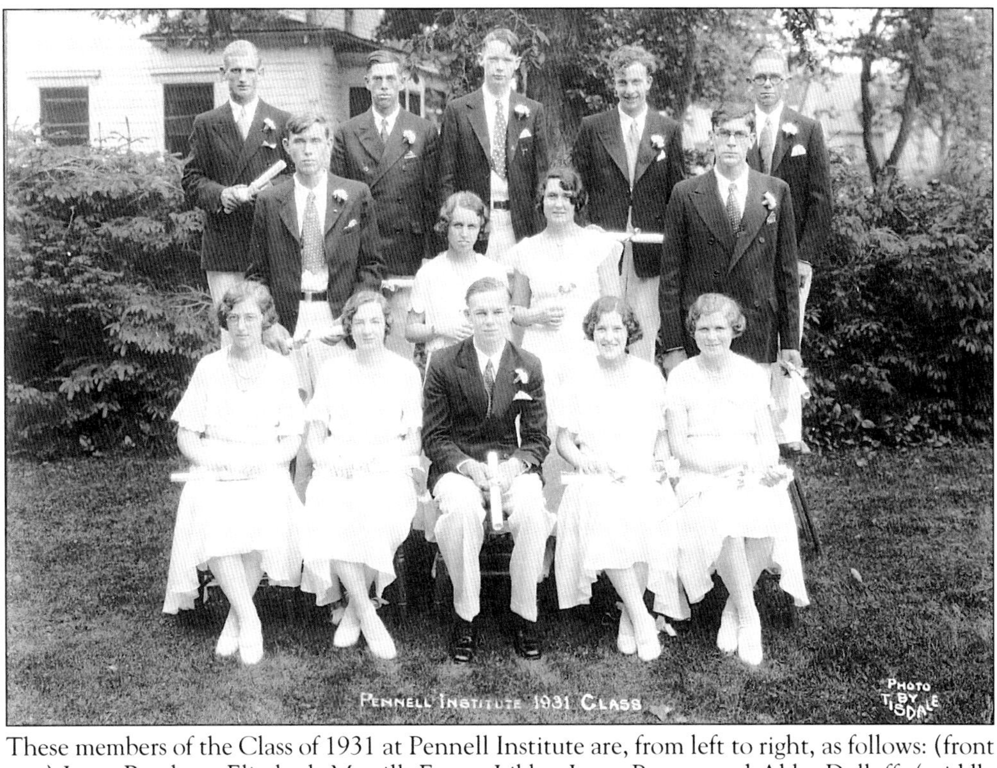

These members of the Class of 1931 at Pennell Institute are, from left to right, as follows: (front row) Loan Brackett, Elizabeth Merrill, Ernest Libby, Irene Potter, and Abby Dolloff; (middle row) Raymond Simpson, Frances Manchester, Alice Coffin, and Arnold Tripp; (back row) John Hancock, Leroy Sawyer, Erwin (Pat) Barton, Allen Tripp, and Norman Dolloff.

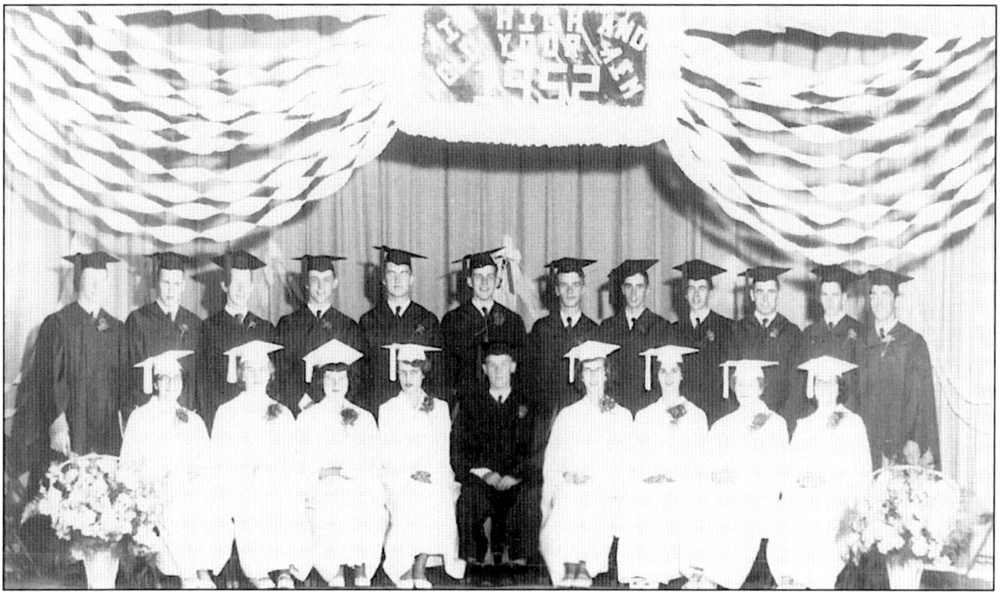

The Class of 1952 at Pennell Institute was composed of the following students, from left to right: (front row) Elizabeth Ferri, Nancy Webb, Barbara Pollard, Carol Nason, Lawrence Libby, Charlene Tripp, Judith Libby, Joanne Bunnell, and Anne Ferri; (back row) Robert Skilling, Roger White, Frederick Merserve, Clinton Barter, Jay Rand, Charles Qualey, Ralph Lashua, Eugene Leach, Warren Whitney, Ralph Taylor, Wilbert Whitney, and Malcoln Brown.

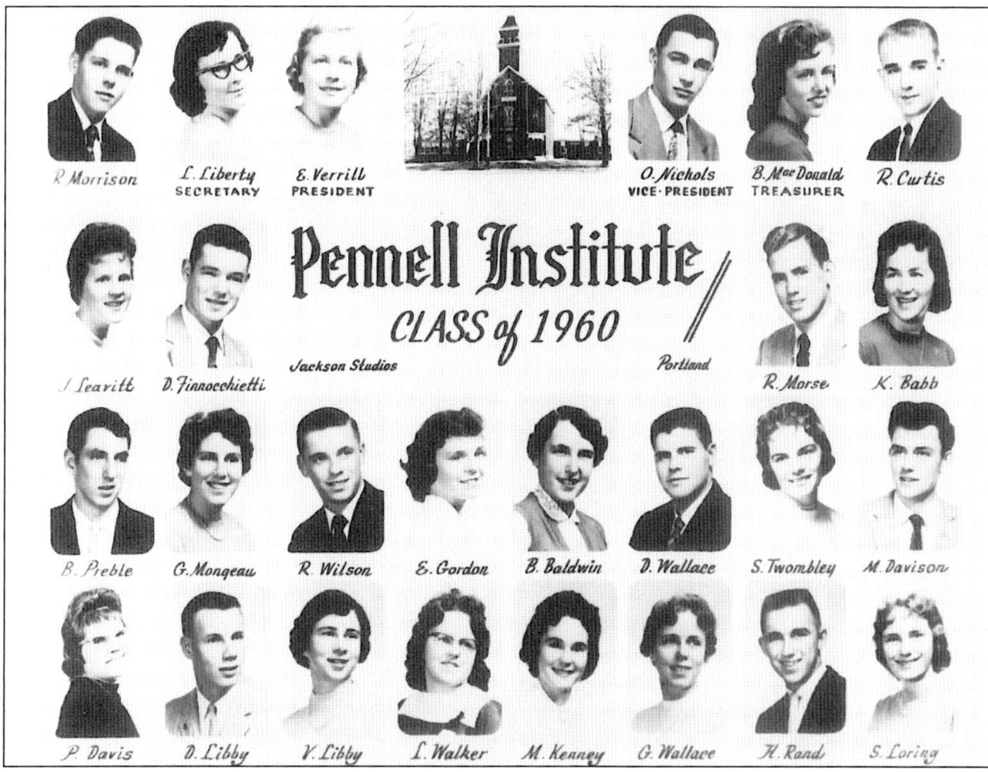

The Class of 1960 posed individually for a class photograph.

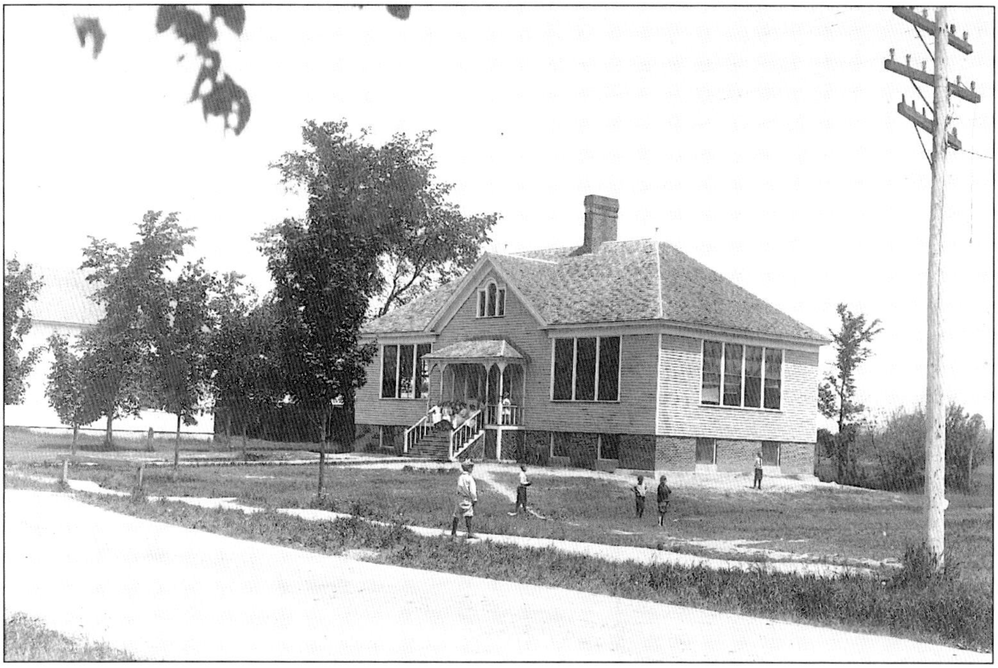

The Primary School, also known as the Grammar School, was built in 1902 to replace the Old Brick School. Six grades originally attended this two-room school, but after 1948 only primary grades attended school here. Presently, the building houses the offices of School Administrative District #15, which includes the towns of Gray and New Gloucester.

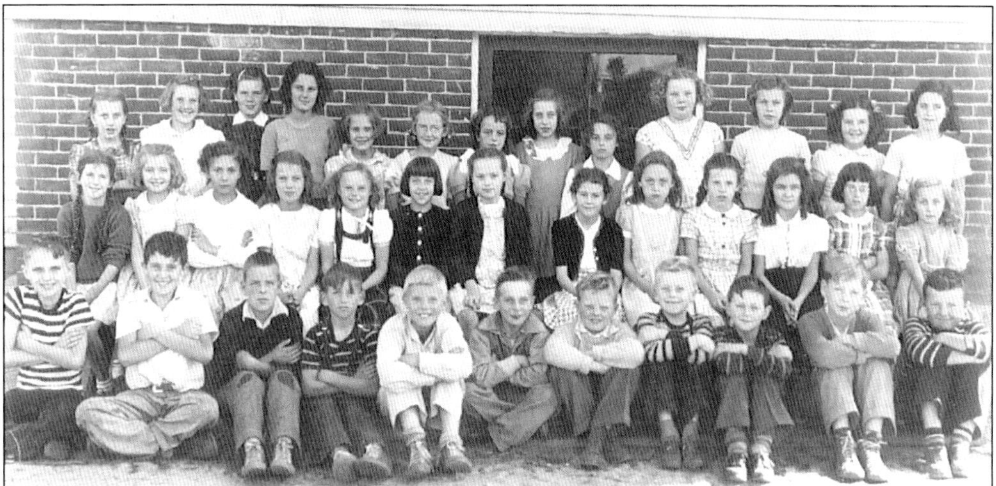

This 1948 photograph taken at the Gray Primary School shows the following students, from left to right: (front row) Marvin Kenney, Allen Tripp, Everett Berry, Lyle Hunt, Harold Swinington, Billy Griffin, Donald Jergensen, Lee Mains, Bobby Adler, Donnie Bibber, and Jack Gibbs; (middle row) Yvonne Skilling, Dawn Bryington, Lucy Ayer, Lorraine Hunt, Jean Sawyer, Carolyn Cray, Margaret Davis, Sandra Brown, Eileen Thomas, Nancy Hamilton, Elaine Quint, Sally Cray, and Nancy Carll; (back row) Patty Libby, Agnes ?, Eileen Copp, Eva Tardiff, Wilhelminia Latham, Katherine Lashua, Sandra Ordway, Mary Finocchietti, Patsy Carr, Barbara Foster, Patsy Liberty, Barbara Caswell, and Louise Hunt.

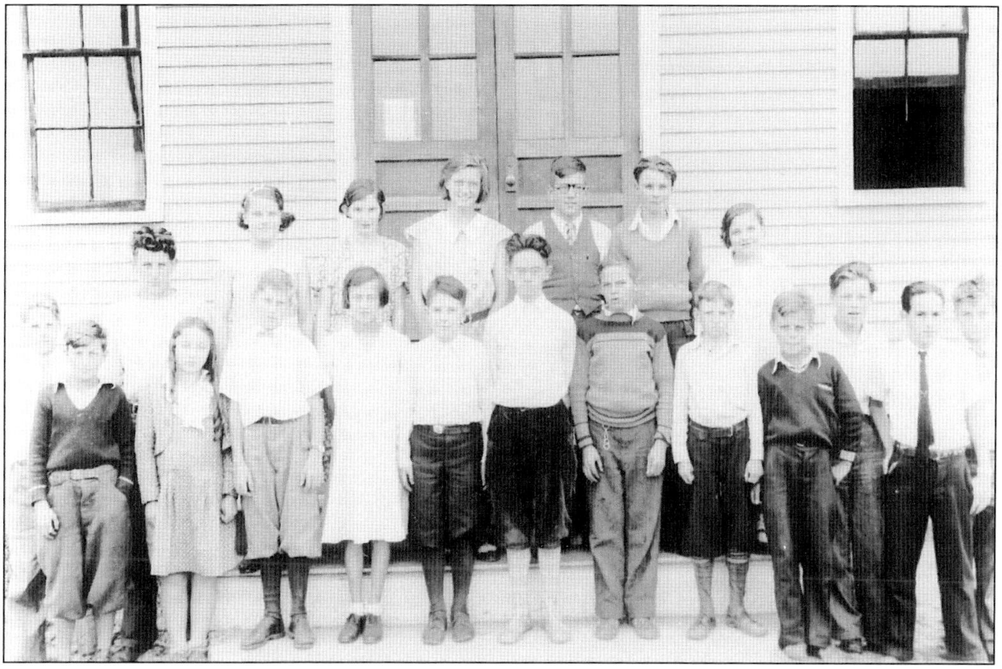

Hancock School was located on Skilling Road, which turns off of Greenleaf Street. It was built in 1920 as a junior high school. These members of the Class of 1933 are, from left to right, as follows: (front row) Walter Hinds, Miriam Bisbee, William Taylor, Arvilla Humphrey, Sidney Leavitt, William Duplisea, Clayton Davis, Jimmy Colley, Everett Doughty, George Small, Clyde Cobb, and Harold Nason; (back row) Joe Sawyer, Urban Roberts, Mildred Hayes, Esther Ellinwood, Nancy Carter, Willis Hancock, Irvin Hill, and Grace Thompson.

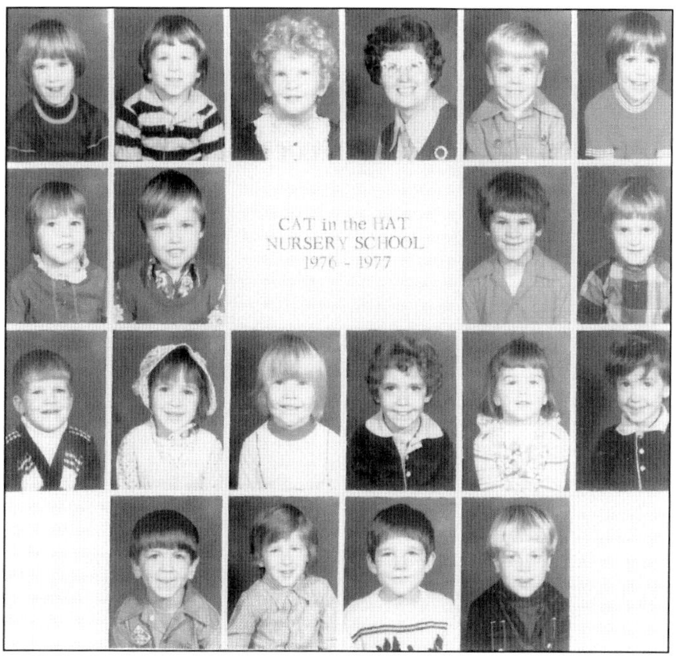

The first co-op nursery, The Cat in the Hat, was founded in 1976 by Fran Hutchings and Yvonne Merrill. From left to right are as follows: (front row) Scott Moynihan, Shawn Butler, Danny Wink, and Matt Joy; (second row) Kenneth Knapp, Holly Libby, Russell Grant, Andy Hutchings, Carrie Stevens, and Jemery Hutchings; (third row) Bethany Coffill, Jason Tupper, Dana Wallace, and Kristin Ehnstorm; (back row) Jennifer Jannarone, Jerermy Gorden, Jennifer Bullock, teacher Arlene Lundy, Steven Emmons, and Jennifer Kenney.

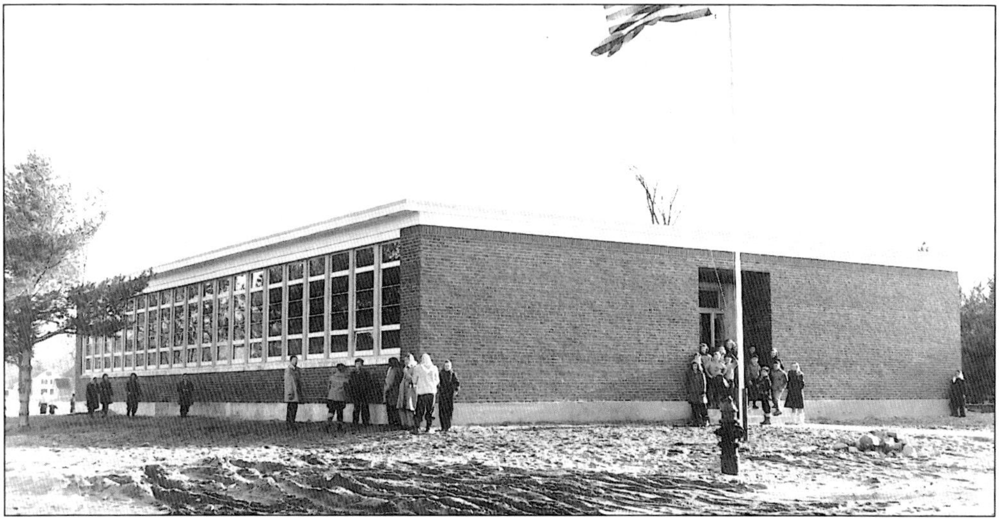

The four-room elementary Russell School located on Grange Street was built in 1948 by John T. Doughty at the cost of $40,000. The cinder block, brick-faced building measures 85 by 58 feet. The third, fourth, fifth, and sixth grades each had a large classroom surrounded by an attractive and well-lighted building. There was plenty of space for expansion and a playground. Since 1948 there have been three additions to the school. The building was named for James W. Russell, a Gray native who died in World War II.

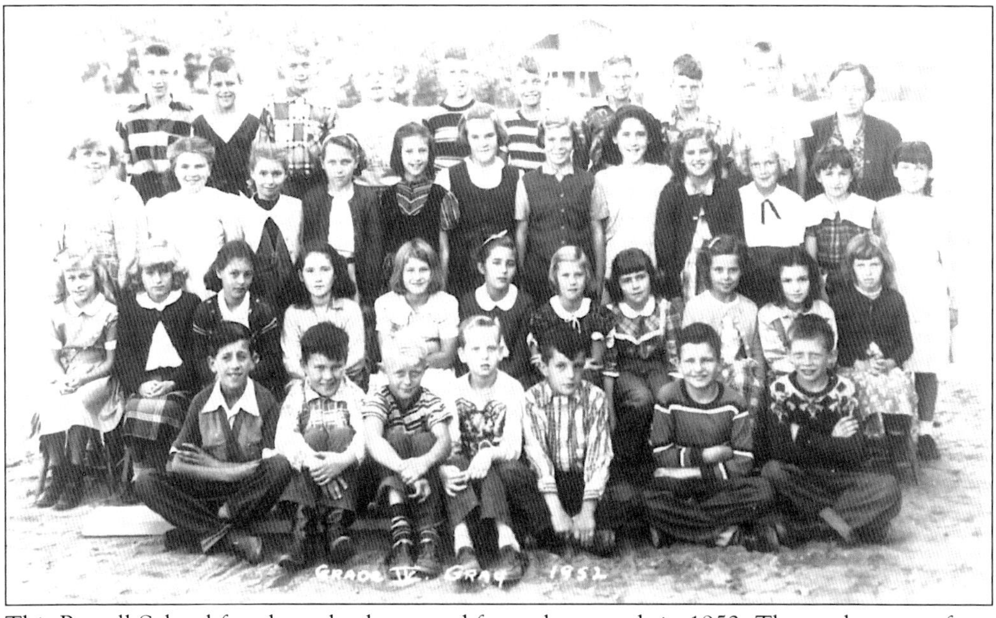

This Russell School fourth grade class posed for a photograph in 1952. The students are, from left to right, as follows: (front row) Dennis Durgin, John Henry, and John Palmiter; (second row) Judy Steeves, Jackie Scribner, Donna Stevens, Nancy West, Ruth Smith, Livia Ustic, Beverly Smith, Karen Wallace, Patricia Morrison, Jean Bryant, and Janet Johnson; (third row) Judith Burnell, Helen Swinington, Sheila Boynton, Sally Kimball, Dorine Kelly, Dianna Nichols, Elizabeth Libby, Jackie West, Rebecca Cole, Kathy Dolloff, Gail Neal, and Rosalie Baker; (back row) Stanley Liberty, Richard Rand, Paul Ross, Ronald Doughty, Paul Dougthy, Forrest Grant, Donald Whitney, David Leavitt, Paul Pittis, and Mrs. Doughty, the teacher.

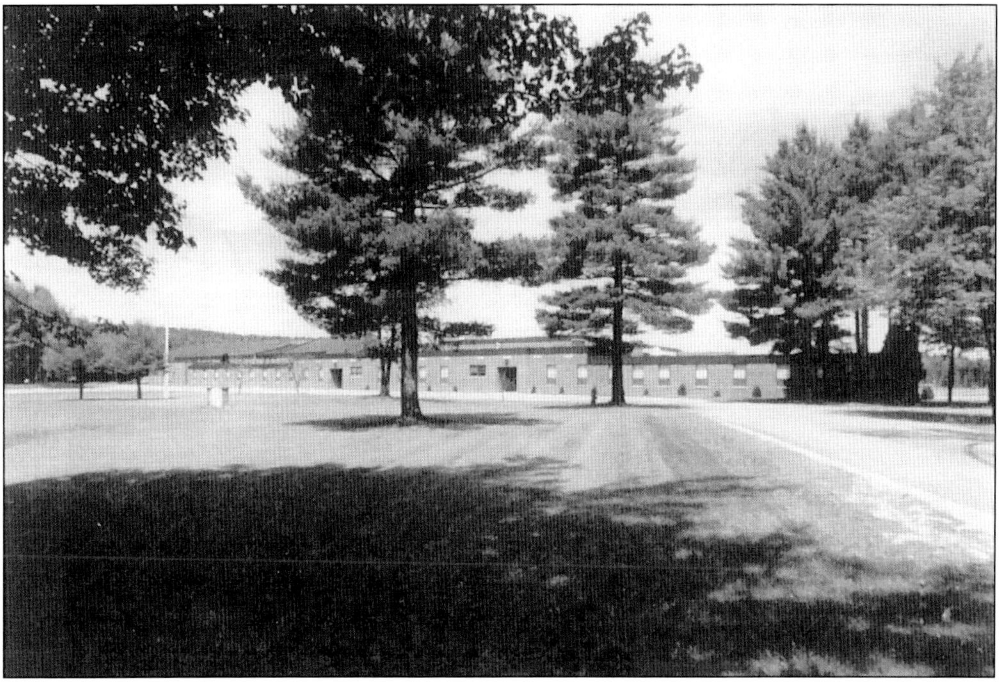

The Administration District #15, which includes the towns of Gray and New Gloucester, was formed in 1960. In 1962 the Gray-New Gloucester High School was built on Libby Hill Road. The building was enlarged in 1976–77 to accommodate both junior and senior high school classes. Nearly 750 pupils attended this new and ultramodern facility in 1977. Gray has always held a high standing in educational matters. The school received the Presidential Excellence in Education Award for the years 1984–85.

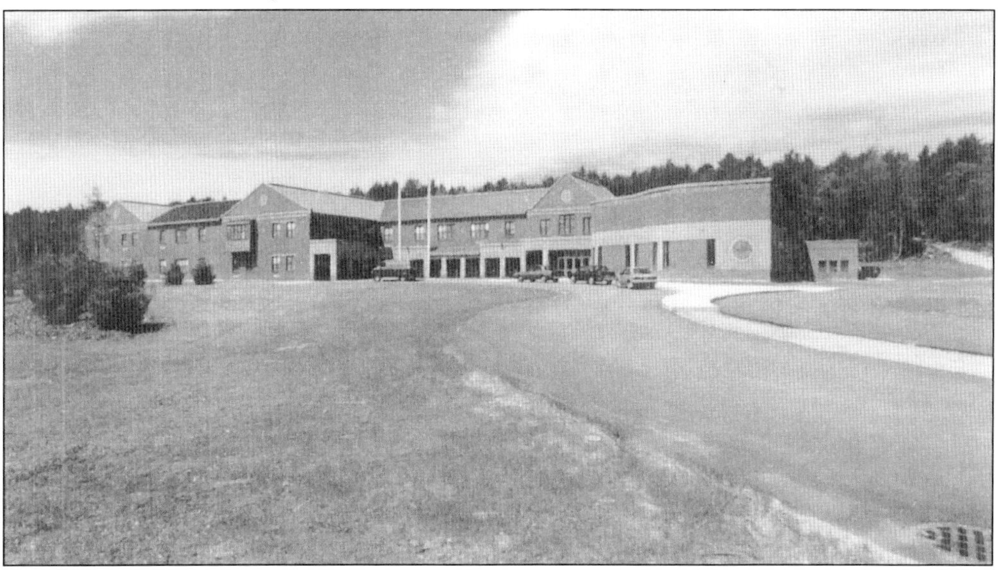

The Gray-New Gloucester Middle School was built in 1989 to accommodate grades five through eight. This unique school is located on Libby Hill Road, just up the road from the GNG High School. In 1984–85, the GNG Junior High School received a national award for excellence.

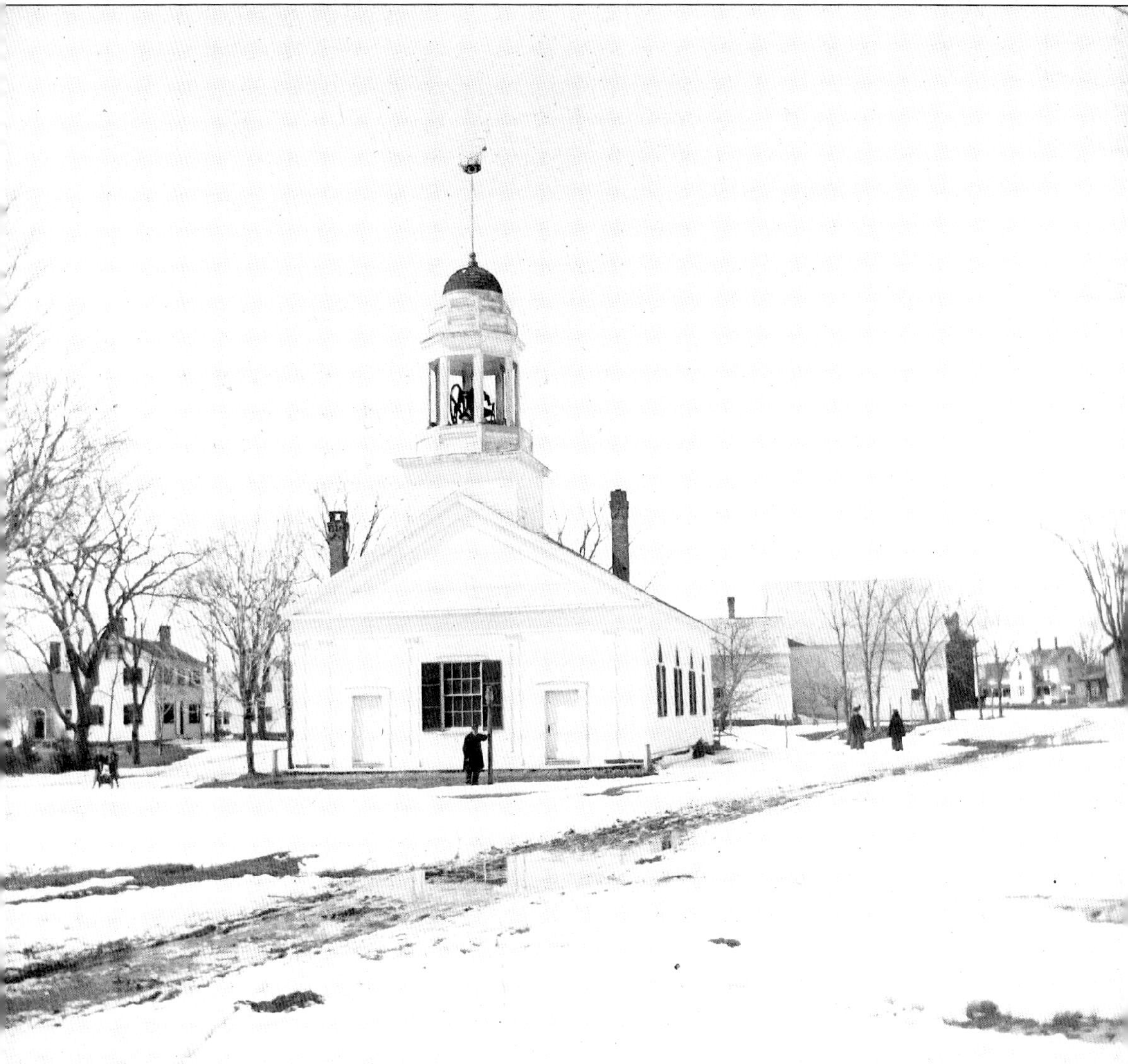

The First Parish, a Congregational denomination, was organized in 1774 in a small church located where the main entrance to the cemetery is now. The first minister was Rev. Samuel Nash, a Brown University graduate. In 1783 he was replaced by Rev. Samuel Perley, a Harvard graduate, who revived the religious society in a Presbyterian form. After 1803, the Congregational Society was reorganized and has continuously existed for over 195 years.

In 1828, the parish church building had to be removed to make way for the present Portland-Lewiston Road. The congregation built a Colonial-style church (shown above) at the intersection of Brown and Greenleaf Streets. Early in the year 1900, the old church structure was torn down; a new building was completed by the end of 1900, at a cost of about $7,000.

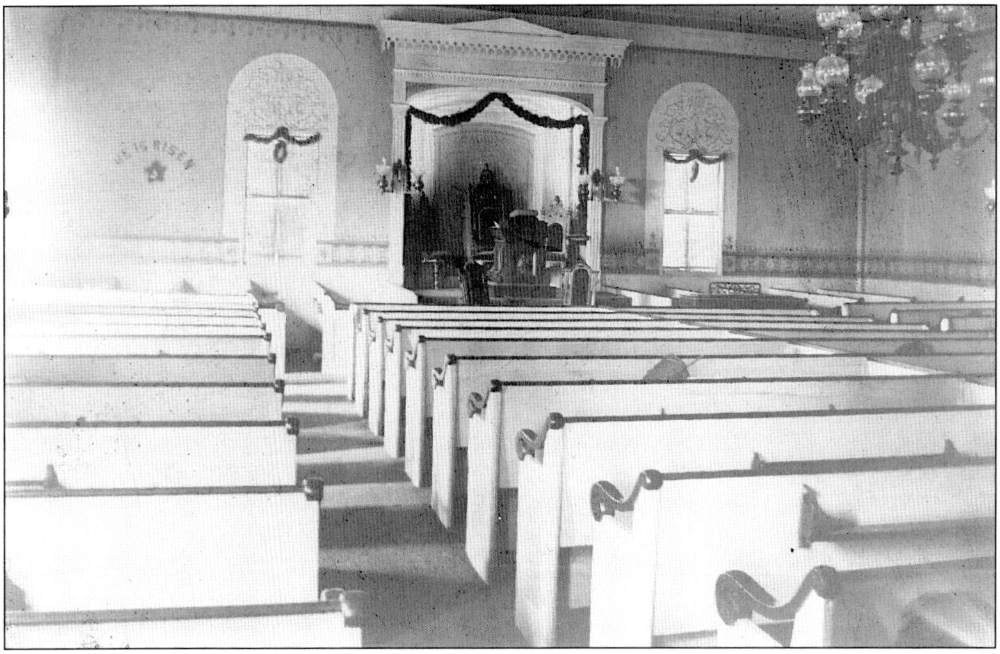

This interior view of the Congregational church was taken on the last Sunday of its existence in 1900. The area was very wet, causing the foundation of the church to deteriorate beyond repair.

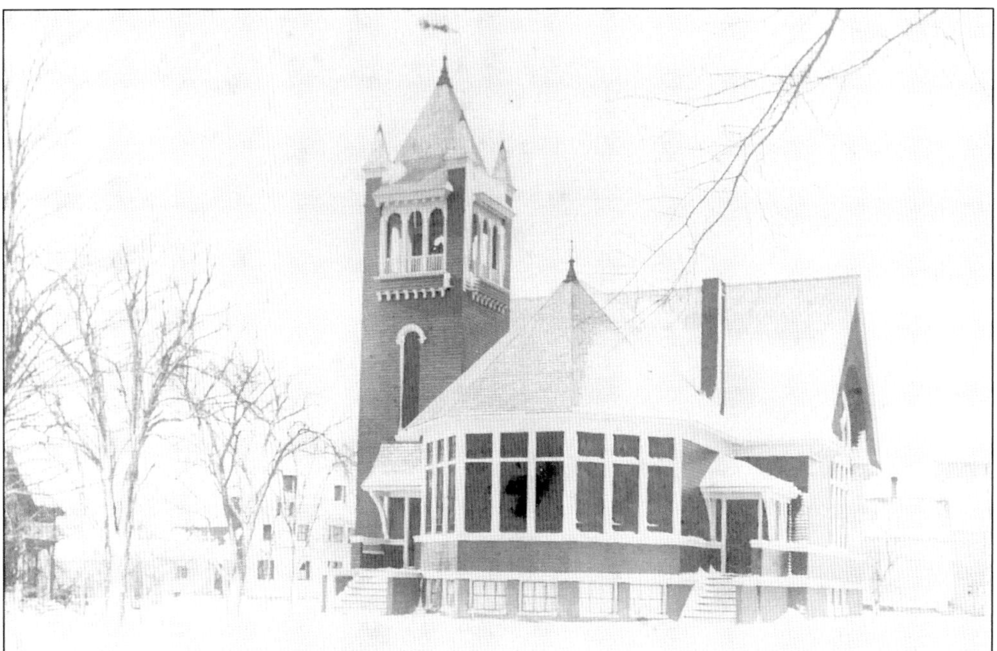

The present Congregational church was dedicated on January 2, 1901, the first Sunday of the 20th century. Herbert L. McCann served the church from 1899 to 1909. Today the church is known as the First Congregational Church of Gray.

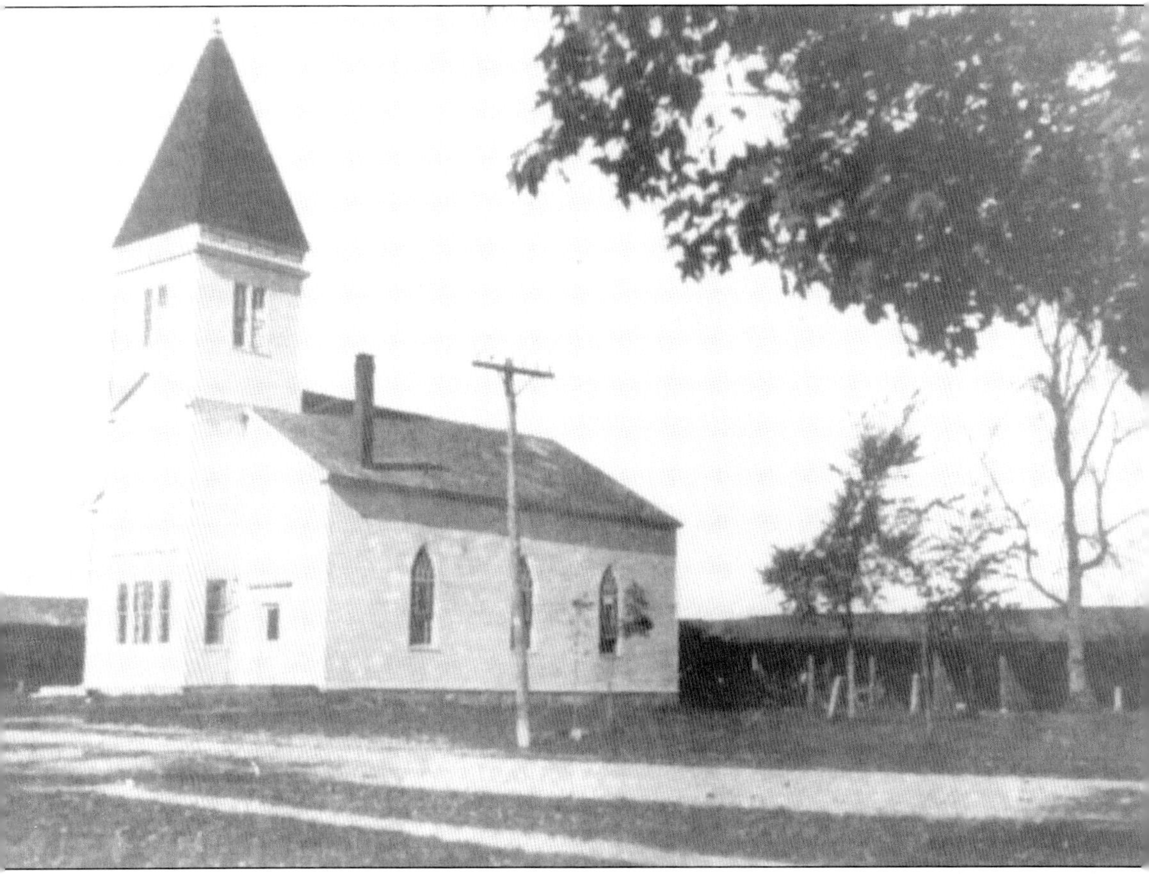

The Baptist Society in Gray was founded by Nathan Merrill, who came here in the 1760s and built his home on what is now known as the Mayall Road in East Gray. In 1782 the Gray and New Gloucester General Provision Anti-Pedo Baptist Church was organized.

In 1830, at the cost of $1,500, the Universalist Society constructed the building on Shaker Road, next to the old fairgrounds, that became known as the Free Baptist Church of Gray (it also served as the Union Meeting House). In 1856 the building was sold at public auction for $300 and turned over to the Baptist members, who used it until it was sold in 1983. Originally the church had a much taller steeple, but in 1905 this was removed. Over the years other remodeling has somewhat changed both the exterior and interior of the building. In 1983 the Free Baptist Church building was purchased and it has served as an antique shop ever since. Notice the carriage and horse sheds at the back of the church.

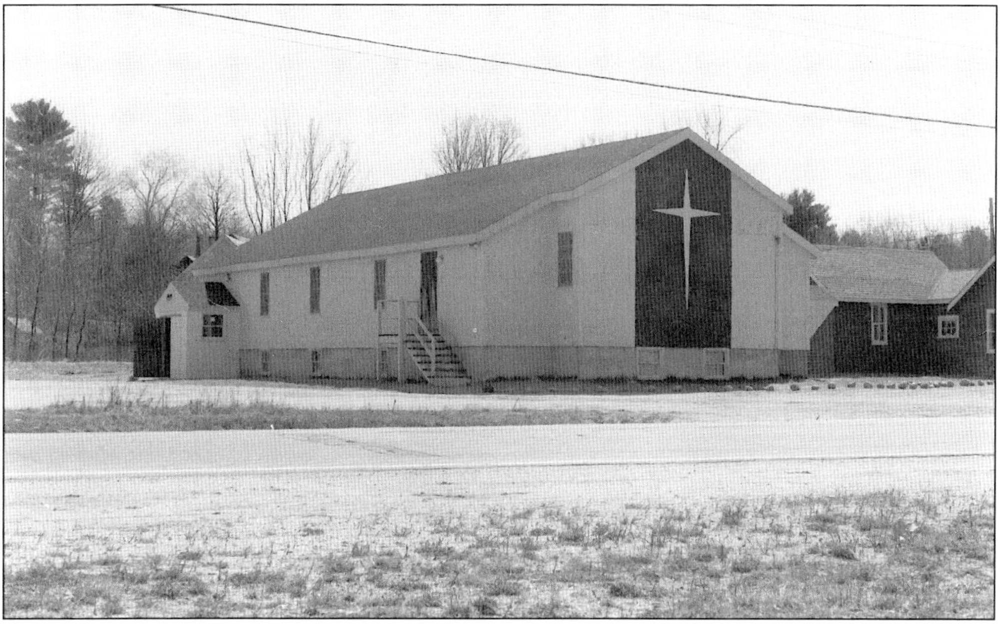

The Trinity Assembly of God held its first service in February of 1956 at the home of Mr. and Mrs. Percy Mason on the Town Farm Road. Rev. Edward Granholm conducted the service. From 1958 to 1960 meetings were held in various locations. In 1973, the present church was built north of Gray Corner on the east side of the Lewiston Road. It was dedicated on Palm Sunday, April 17, 1974.

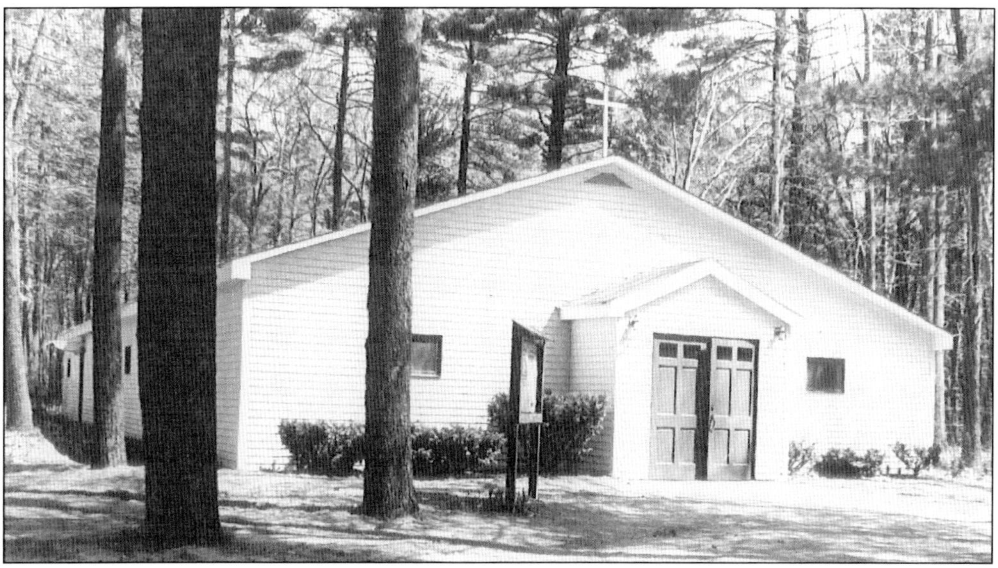

In 1959, through the efforts of Father James Knox, summer residents, and the Cathedral Parish of Portland, St. Gregory's Church was built at St Gregory's Boy's Camp on Crystal Lake. It was winterized in 1964, and the first Mass was held that year at midnight on Christmas Eve. In 1967, St. Gregory the Great's Parish was formed and Father Knox was appointed pastor. Shortly thereafter, a priest's residence and parish hall was built. The boy's camp discontinued in 1974, and the parish acquired the property in 1977. It still serves Gray and surrounding towns as a parish today.

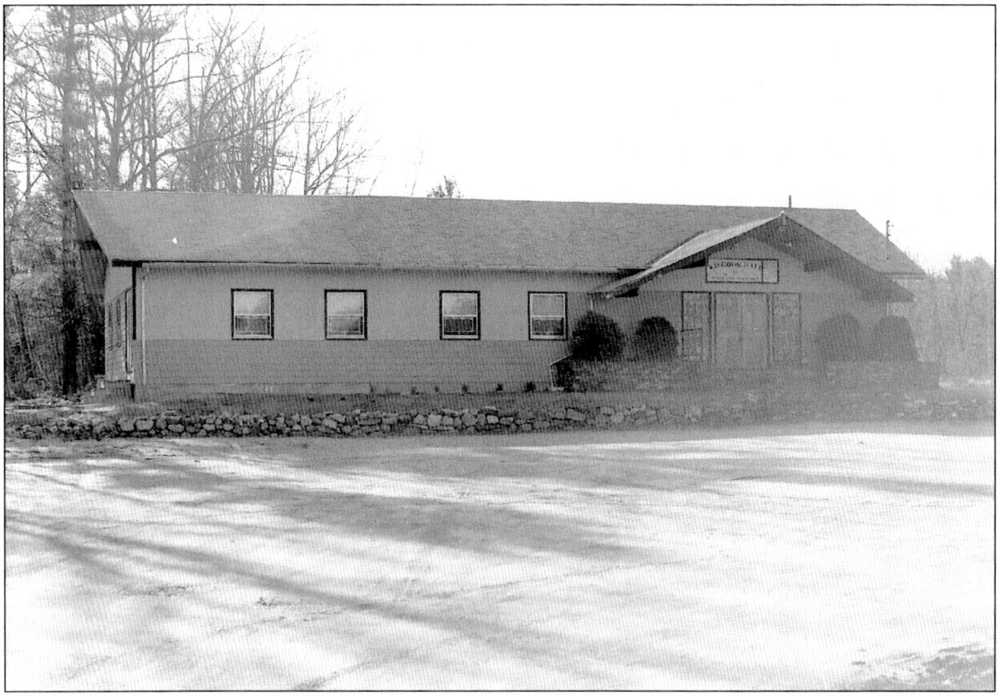

In 1961 a congregation of Jehovah's Witnesses was formed in Gray. They originally met in the building now occupied by Mark Stimson Associates. The Kingdom Hall of Jehovah's Witnesses in South Gray is located on Route 100. It was built in 1967, dedicated in 1968, and is still in use today.

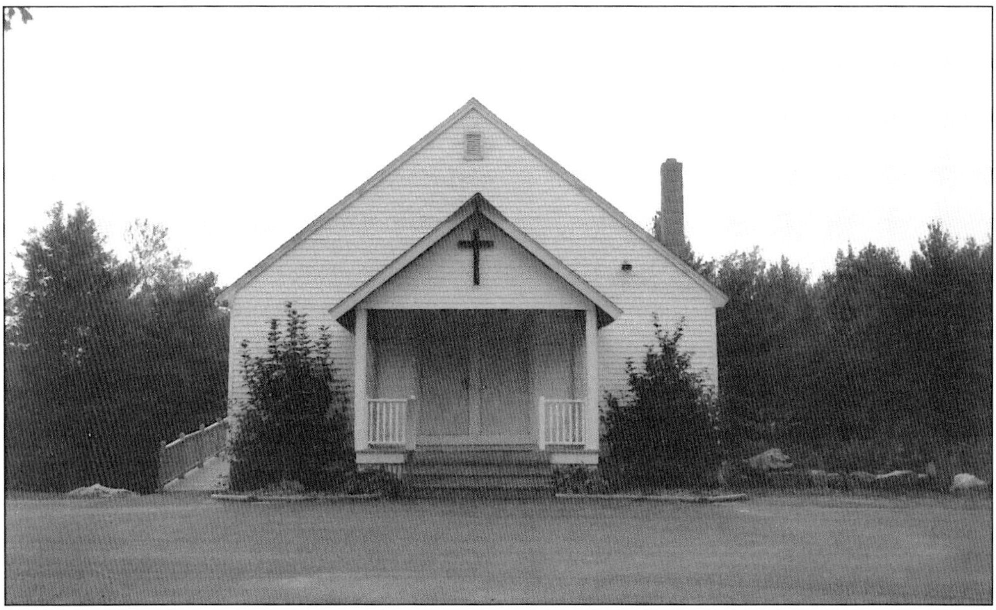

The Bible Believing Baptist Church was organized on October 1, 1978. The groundbreaking day for the new church, which was located on the Old Portland Road, was November 1, 1980. It was dedicated in May of 1981 with Rev. Beal as pastor. Rev. Darwin Vail became pastor in 1981. In June of 1986, a new auditorium was dedicated.

Three

Home Sweet Homes

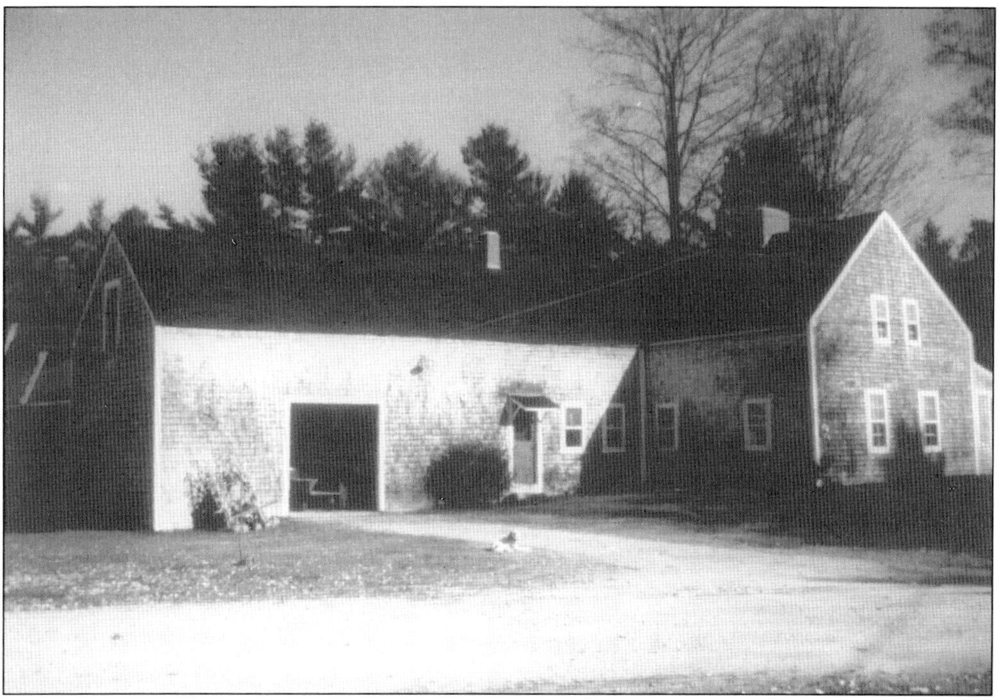

The first framed house in the area was built in 1766 by Rev. Nathan Merrill, who lived alone; it was built to suit his own personal taste, and included many large rooms. He was ordained under the apple tree near the front doorway. Later, the house was owned by George Doughty. It is now the McKeen's home.

Gray has many charming old homes. The following have been chosen because of their date of construction, historic interest, and/or architectural styles.

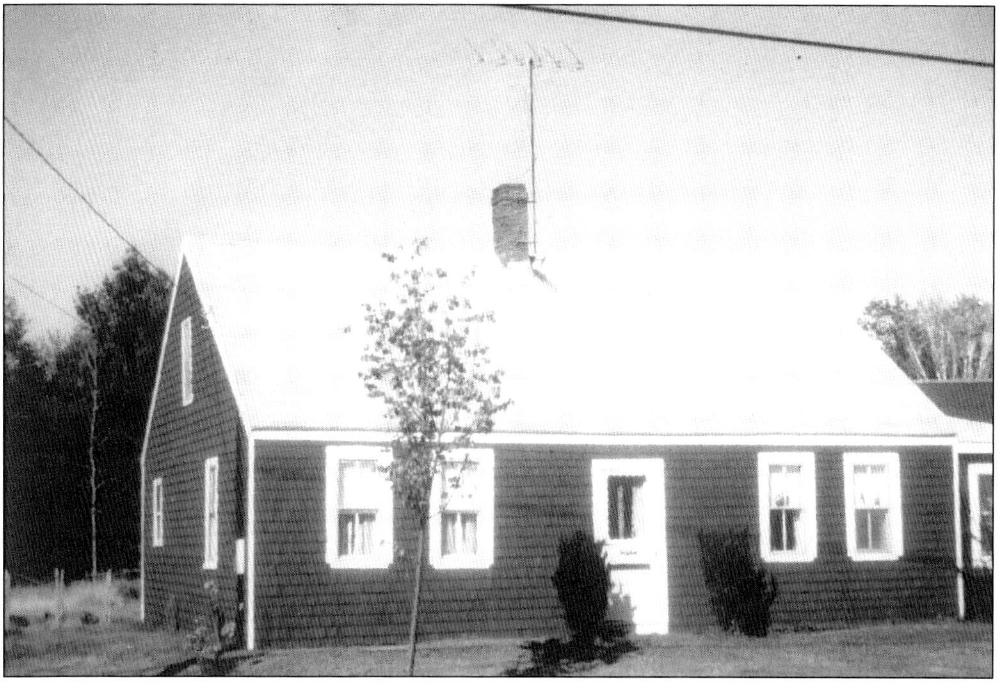

This Cape-style house (now painted red) was built in the 1770s and is located on Route 115 heading toward North Yarmouth.

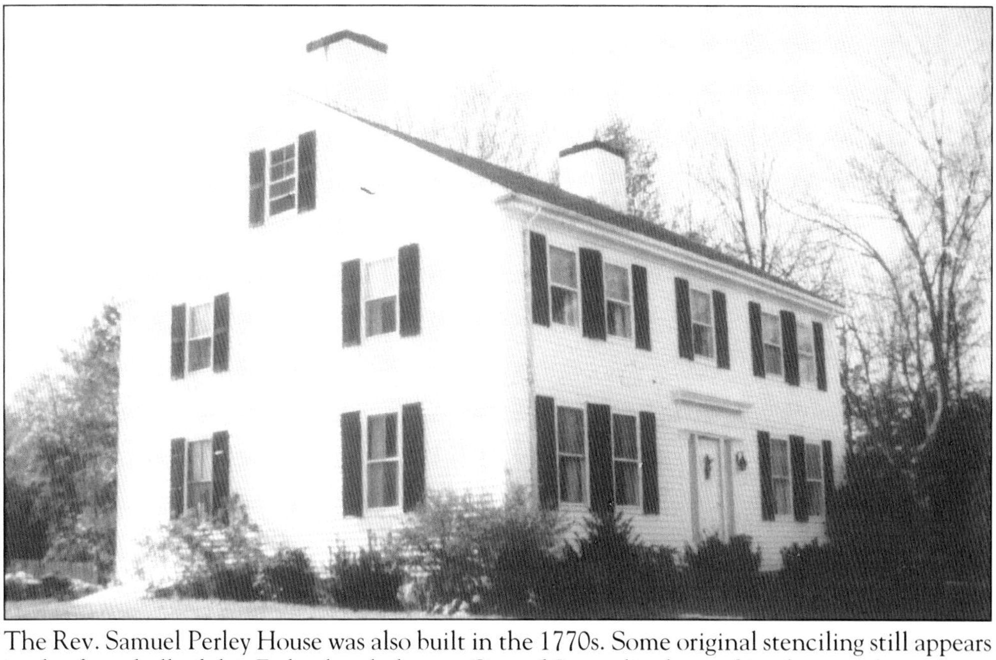

The Rev. Samuel Perley House was also built in the 1770s. Some original stenciling still appears in the front hall of this Federal-style home. One of Samuel's closest friends was John Adams, who later became the second President of the United States. Samuel was born in 1742 in Massachusetts, and came to Gray in 1784 to pastor Gray's first church. He remained the pastor until 1791. For the remainder of his life he practiced medicine and law, and is considered the town's first physician.

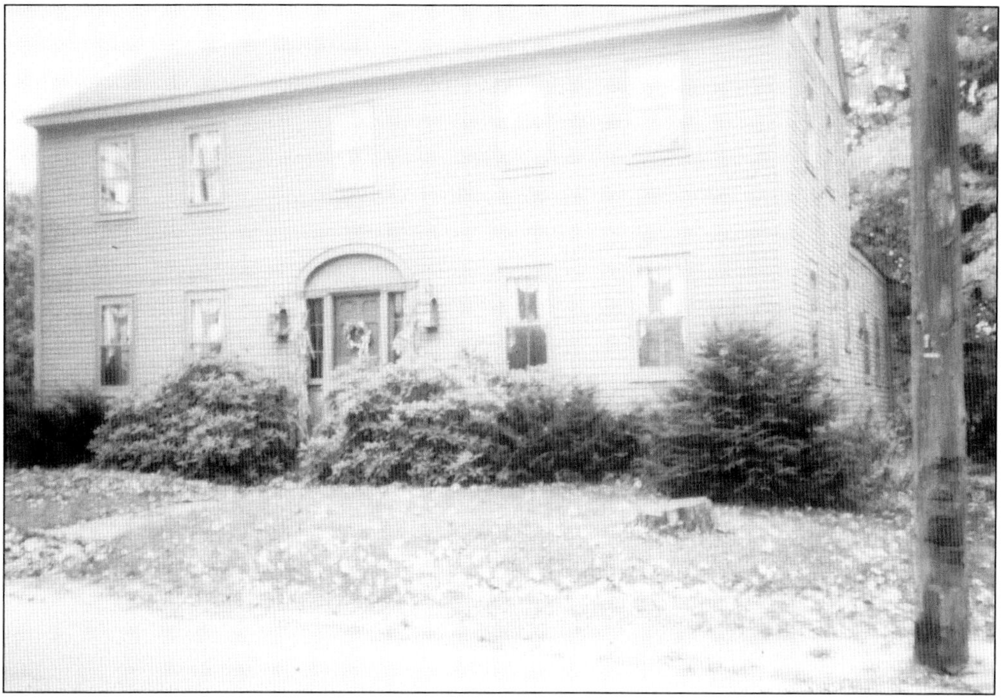

The original Baptist parsonage, built in 1840s, is where Daniel Green lived. He was active in financial affairs, owned land on the eastern side of Main Street, and operated a store. The parsonage, located on the south side of Greenleaf Street, is currently a residence.

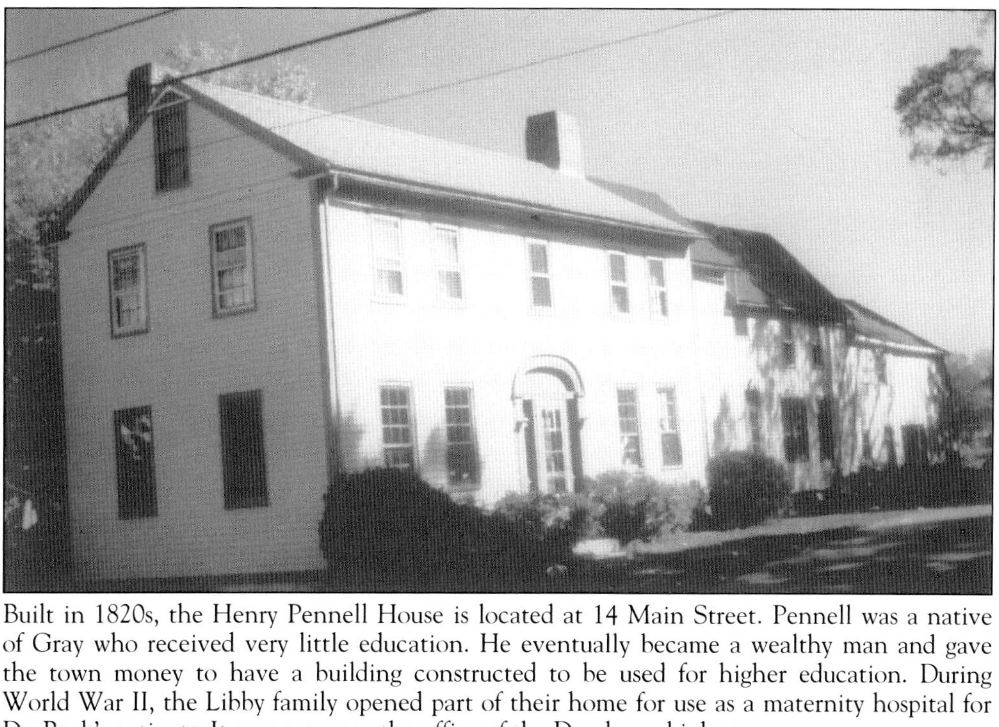

Built in 1820s, the Henry Pennell House is located at 14 Main Street. Pennell was a native of Gray who received very little education. He eventually became a wealthy man and gave the town money to have a building constructed to be used for higher education. During World War II, the Libby family opened part of their home for use as a maternity hospital for Dr. Beck's patients. It now serves as the office of the Dombrowski doctors.

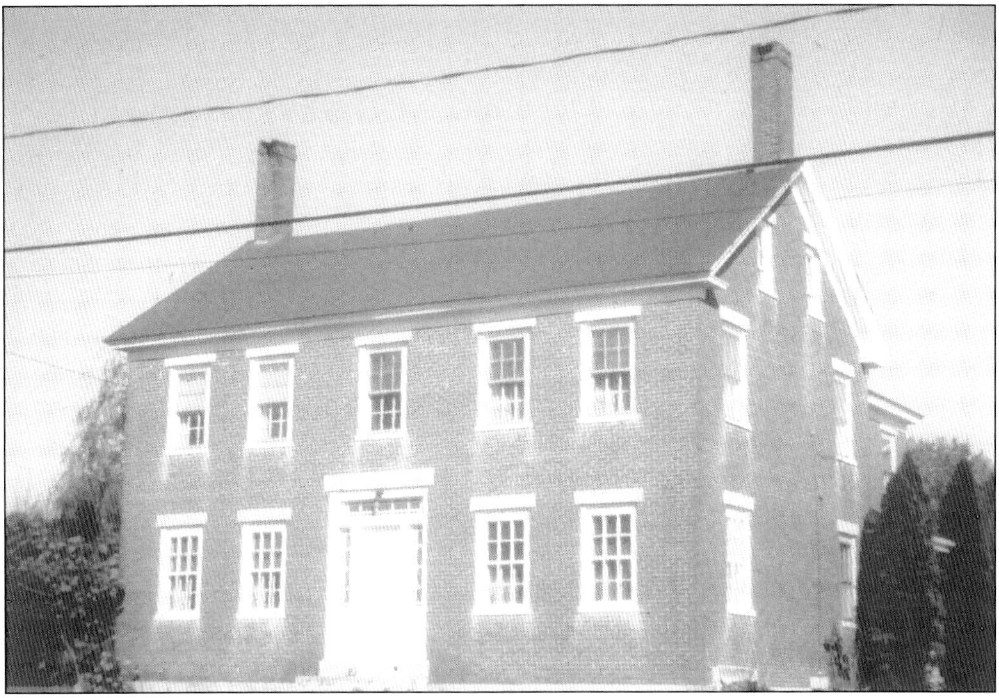

The old alms brick house, built in 1830s by Theophilus Stimson, has been known as the John W. Frank farm, the Town Farm, and Hansen's farm. The rear of the property is currently occupied by a ladder company.

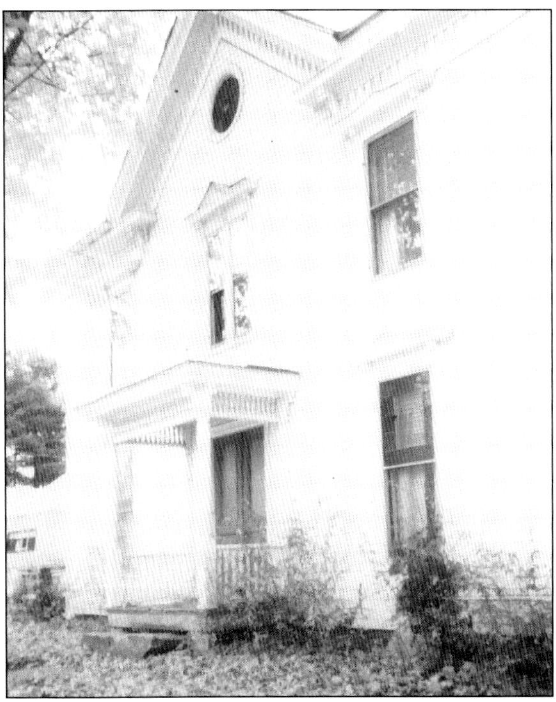

This ornately trimmed, two-story, wooden clapboard house is located on Route 100 just south of Gray Corner. It is typical of many farmhouses in Maine.

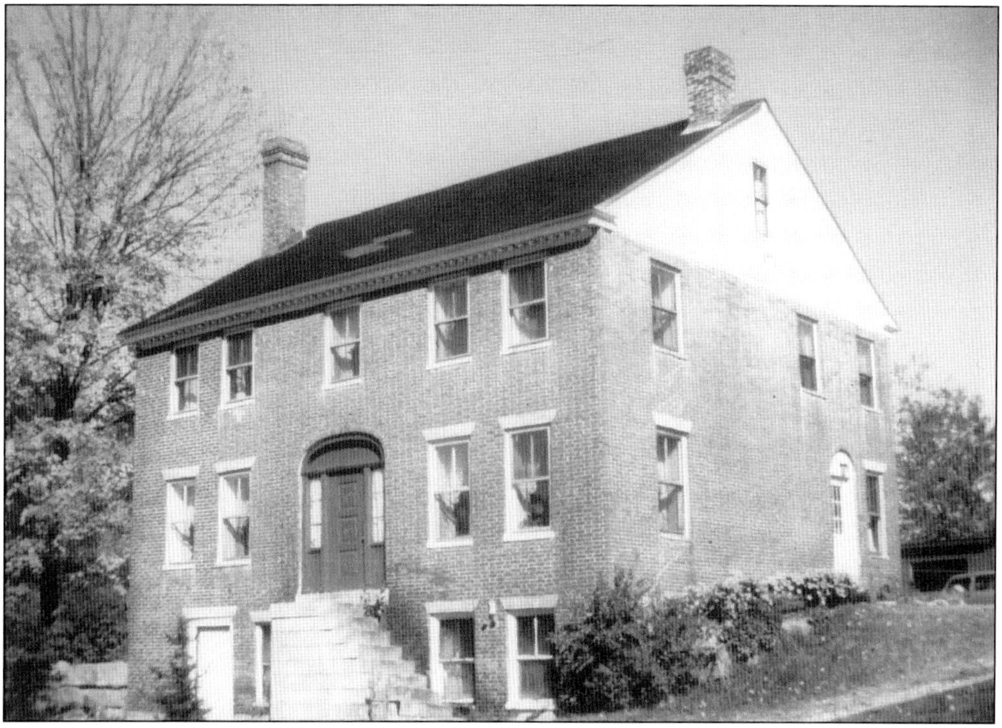

This brick Federal-style early tavern was built between 1810 and 1820. It is located on the east side of Route 100 in South Gray, and is now a private residence.

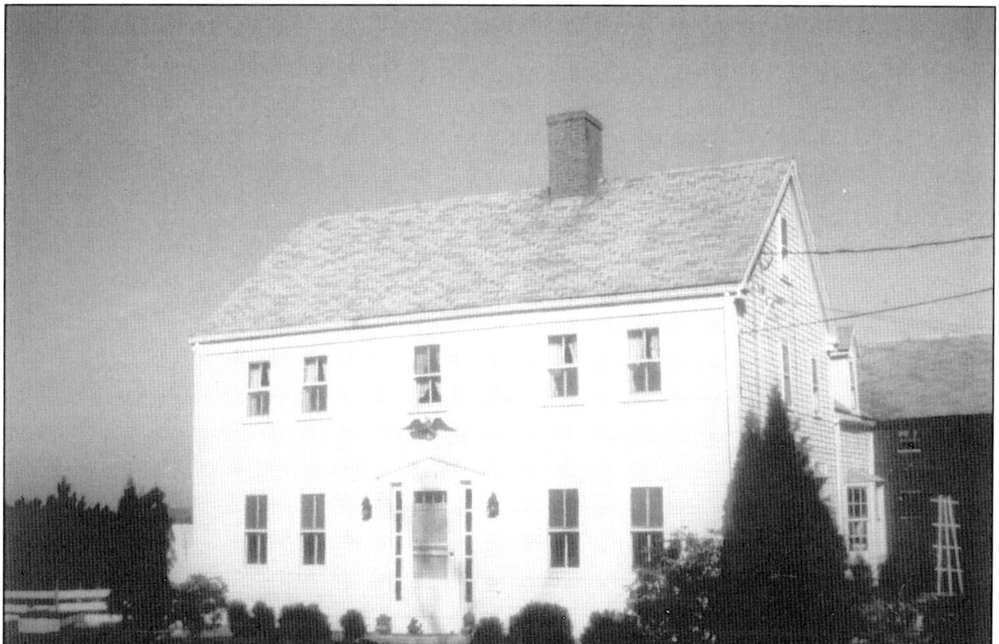

Nathaniel Youngs lived in this farmhouse in East Gray, which was built in 1776 on the east side of North Yarmouth Road. George Washington's secretary once lived here. Today, the house is owned by Jim Gillies, who has been restoring the buildings to their original style.

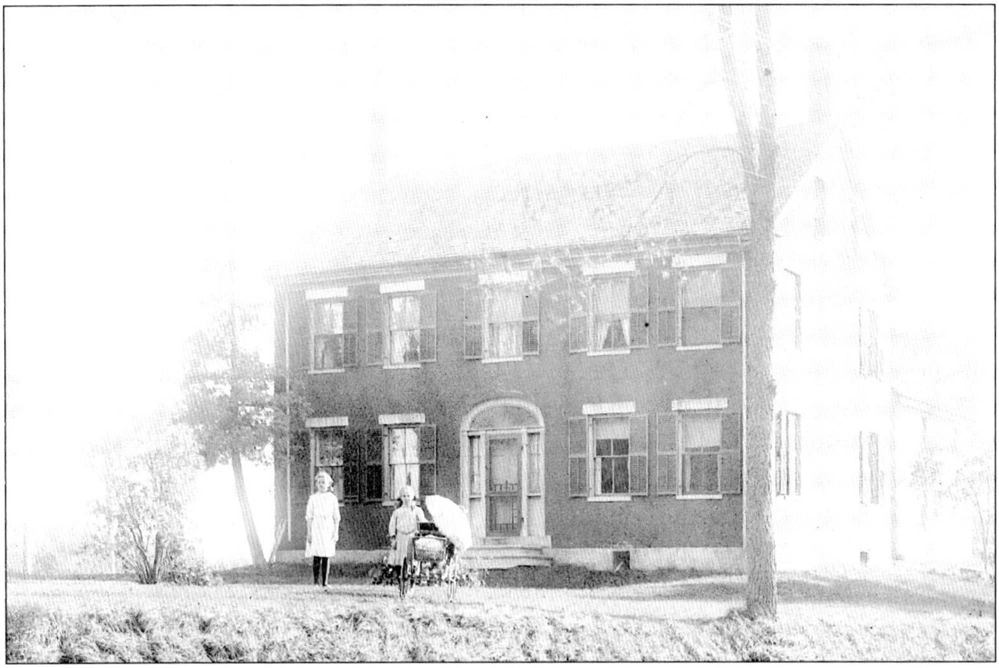

This picture shows the front view of the Federal-style brick building known as the Snow House. It was built in 1830s by the Mayall family and is located at Gray Center on the corner of Route 202 and the Old Portland Road. The front looks the same as it did in the Colonial days.

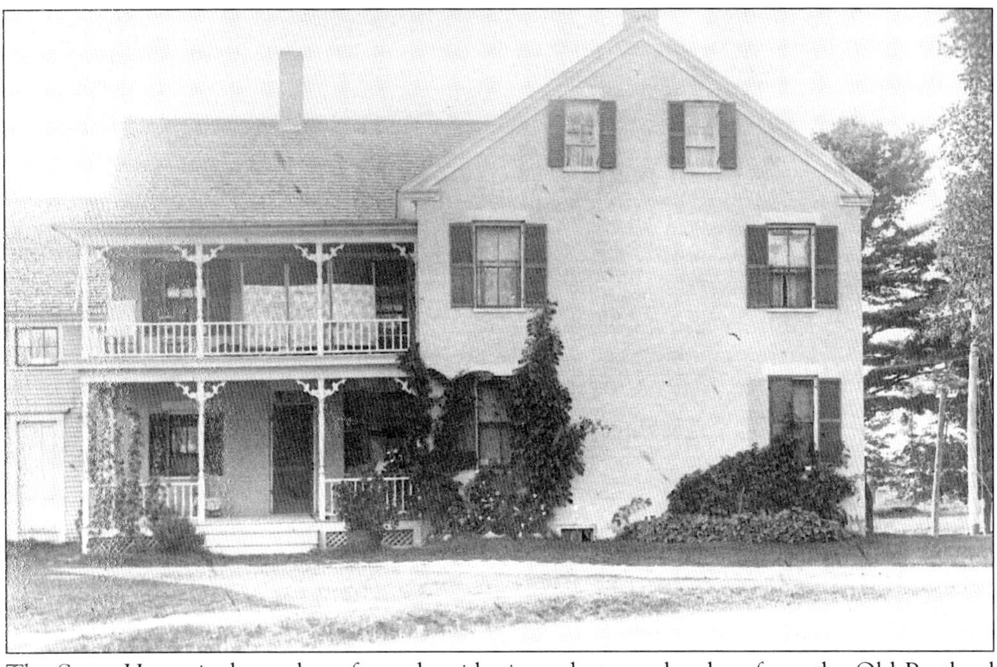

The Snow House is shown here from the side, in a photograph taken from the Old Portland Road. Notice the Victorian gingerbread design added to the Federal-style house. The porches have since been remodeled.

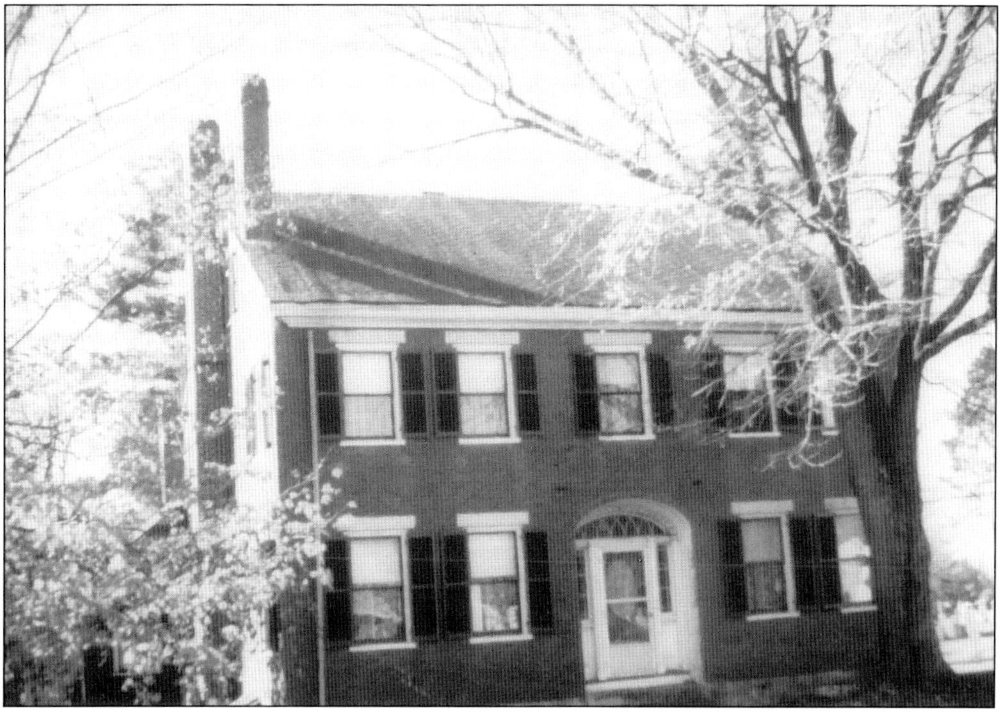

The Federal-style Morrill House was built in 1830s in the center of town. It's on the National Register of Historic Places and is currently the home of Evelyn Morrill Durgin.

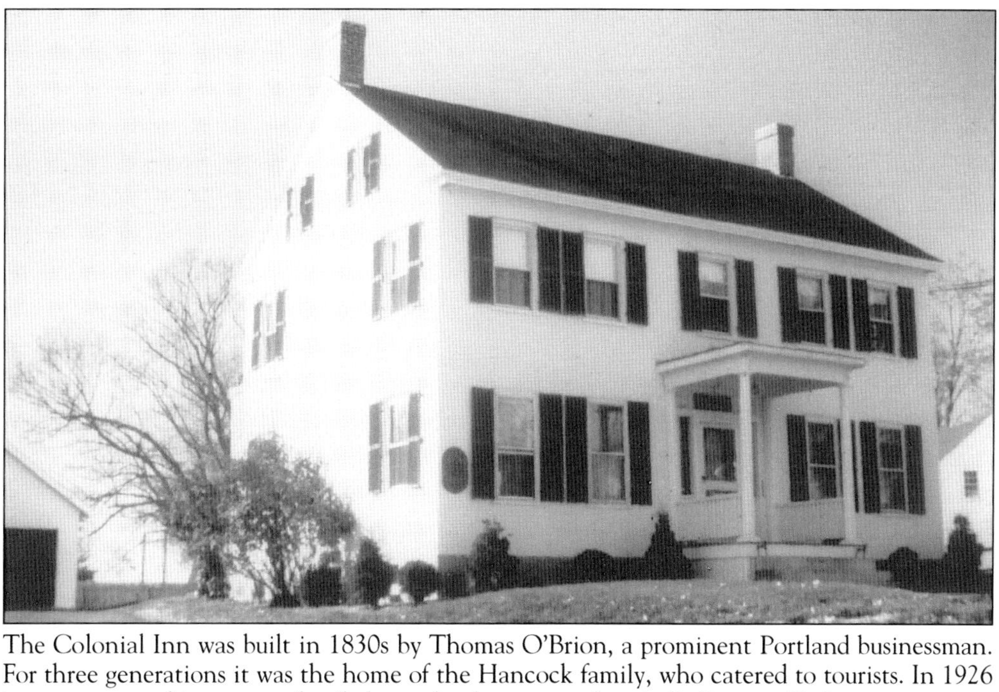

The Colonial Inn was built in 1830s by Thomas O'Brion, a prominent Portland businessman. For three generations it was the home of the Hancock family, who catered to tourists. In 1926 it was converted into a two-family house by then-owner Jennie B. Sawyer. Today it remains an apartment house.

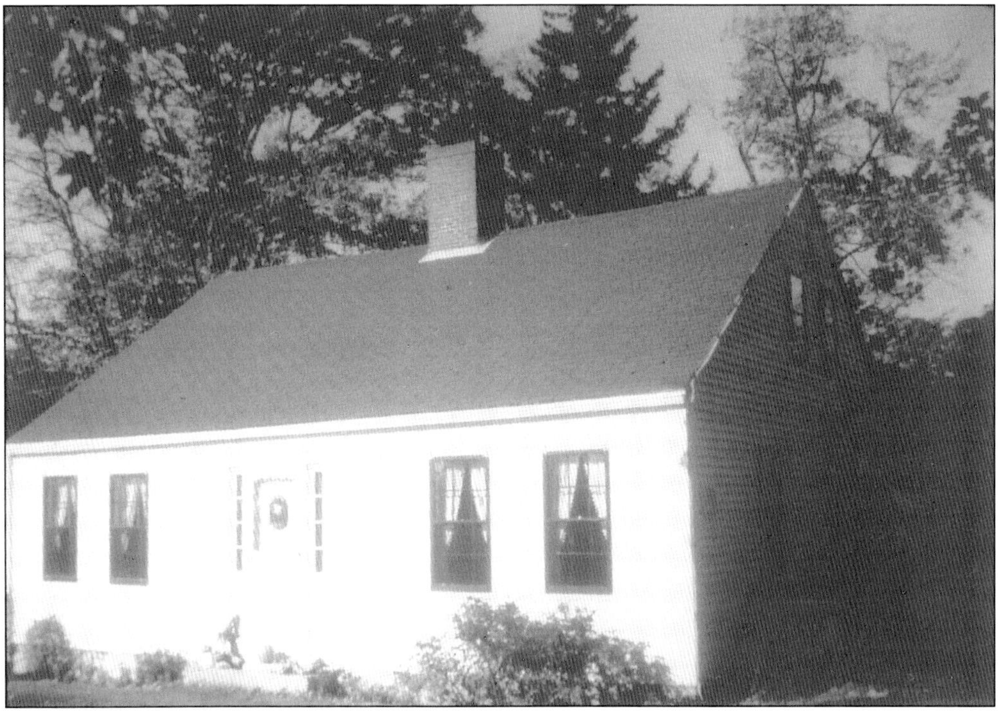

The Cape Cod-style Fogg House was built in 1789 and is located across from Cole Farms Restaurant on the west side of Route 202.

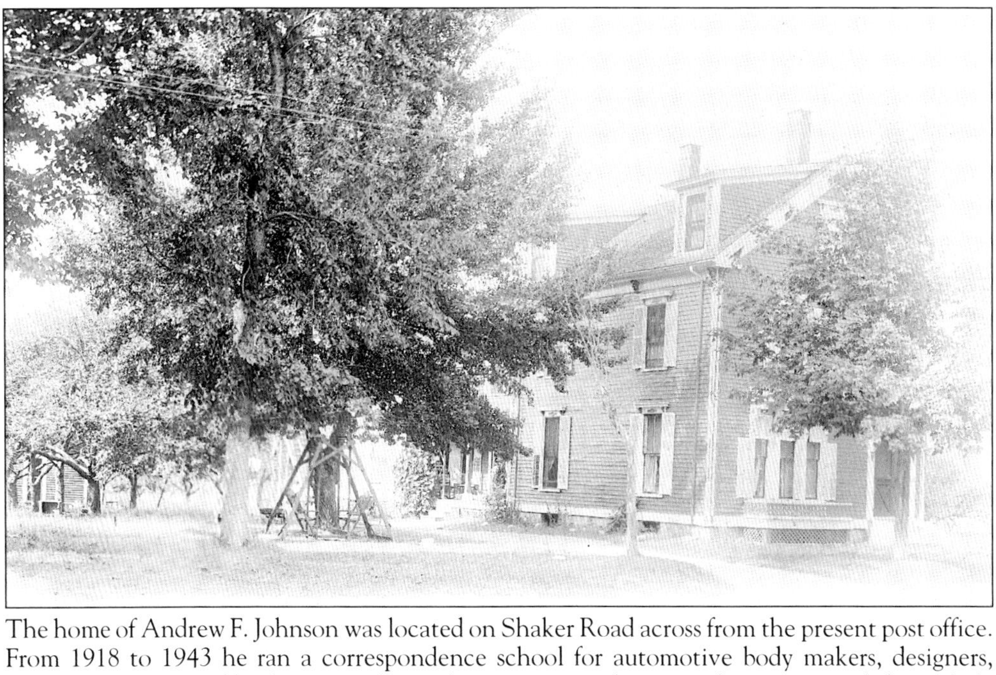

The home of Andrew F. Johnson was located on Shaker Road across from the present post office. From 1918 to 1943 he ran a correspondence school for automotive body makers, designers, and draftsmen out of his home, and was the major contributor to the origins and the orderly development of automobile body design. After coming back to Gray, he took a great interest in town affairs and was one of the trustees of Pennell Institute.

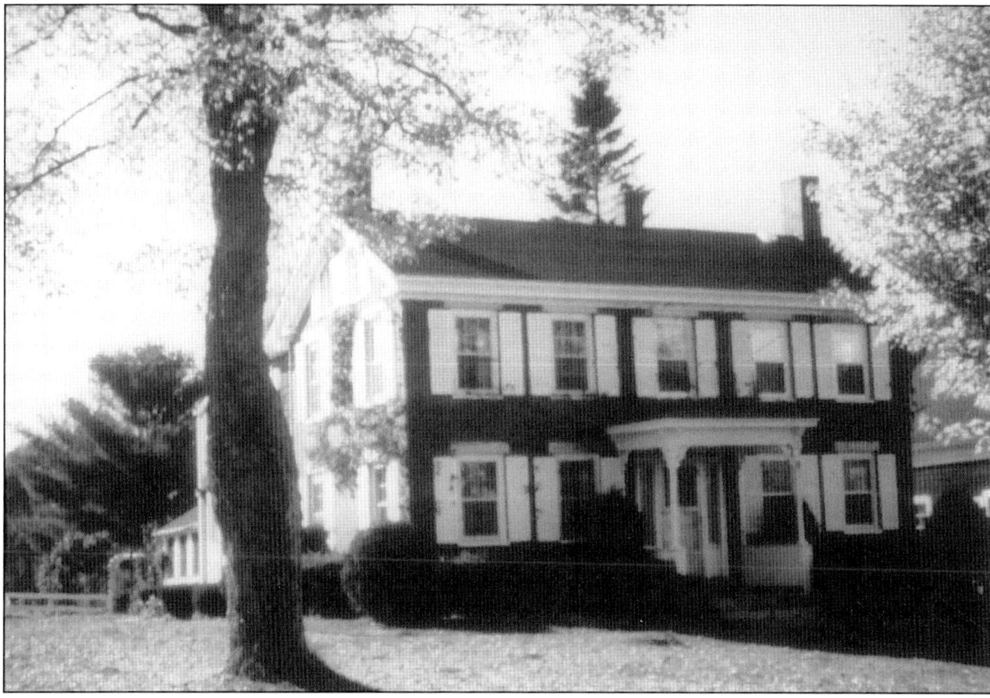

Hiram Hunt's house is an early Greek Revival building erected in the 1830s on Hunt's Hill Road.

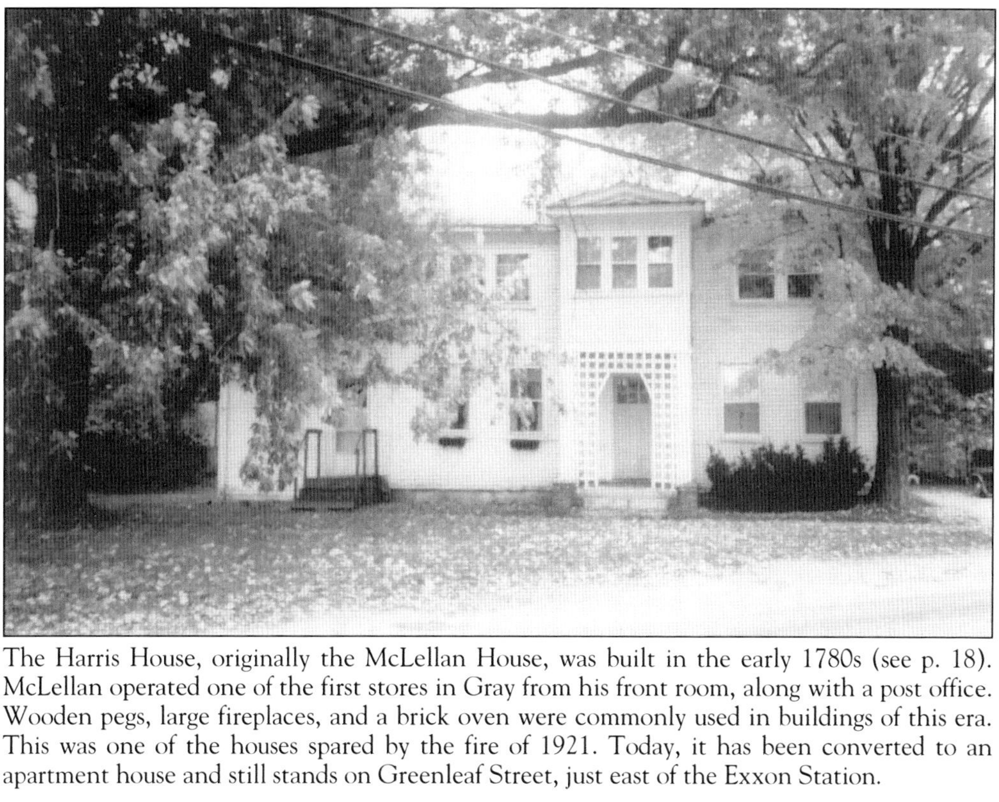

The Harris House, originally the McLellan House, was built in the early 1780s (see p. 18). McLellan operated one of the first stores in Gray from his front room, along with a post office. Wooden pegs, large fireplaces, and a brick oven were commonly used in buildings of this era. This was one of the houses spared by the fire of 1921. Today, it has been converted to an apartment house and still stands on Greenleaf Street, just east of the Exxon Station.

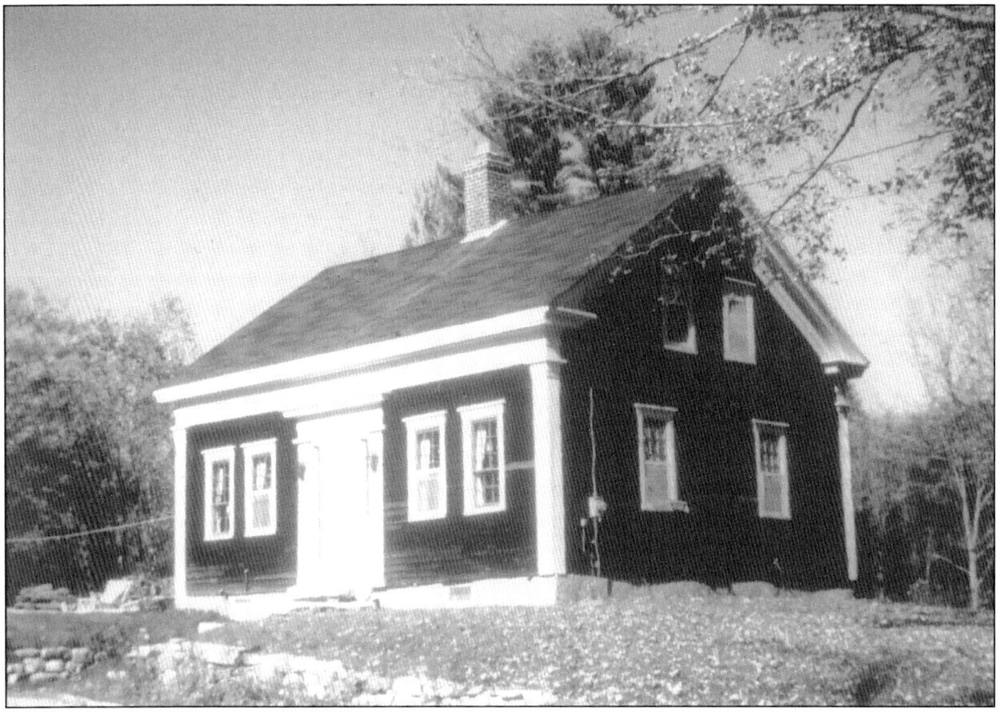

This Greek Revival structure is located on Dutton Hill and was built in 1840s.

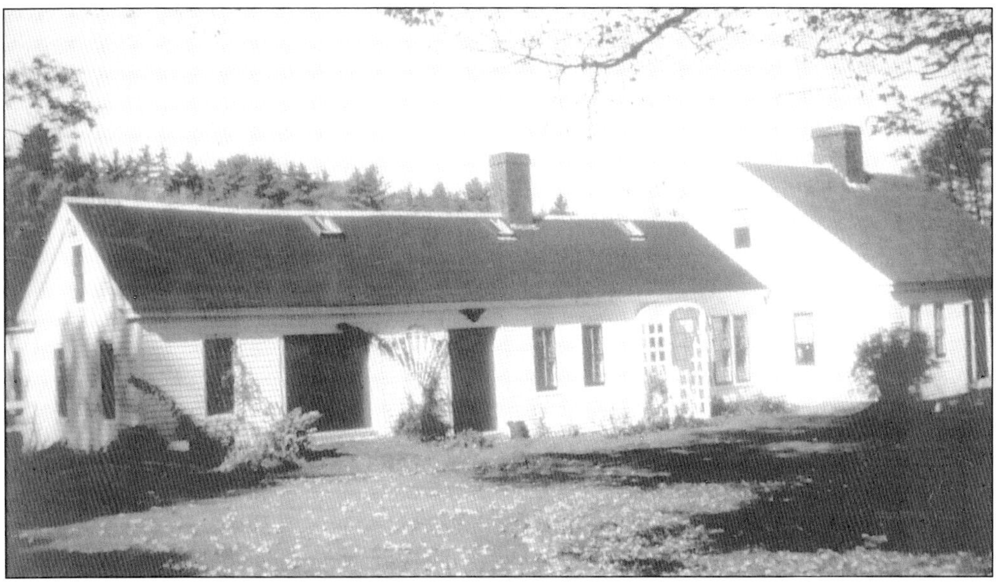

The Freeman Homestead was built in 1779. This West Gray home is a rural Cape that has been built onto over the years by the Freeman family. George Freeman was an engineering expert for the construction of the foundations for many of the San Francisco Bay bridges. Today, his son George lives here.

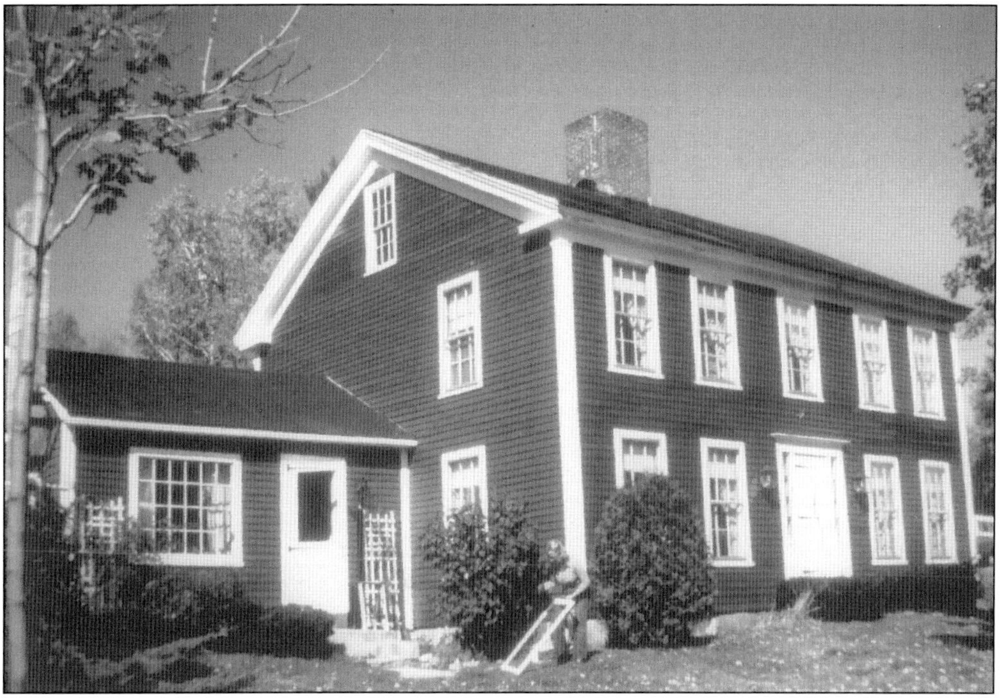

The Libby House in West Gray was built in 1790. Note the large central chimney. The house has had many owners over recent years.

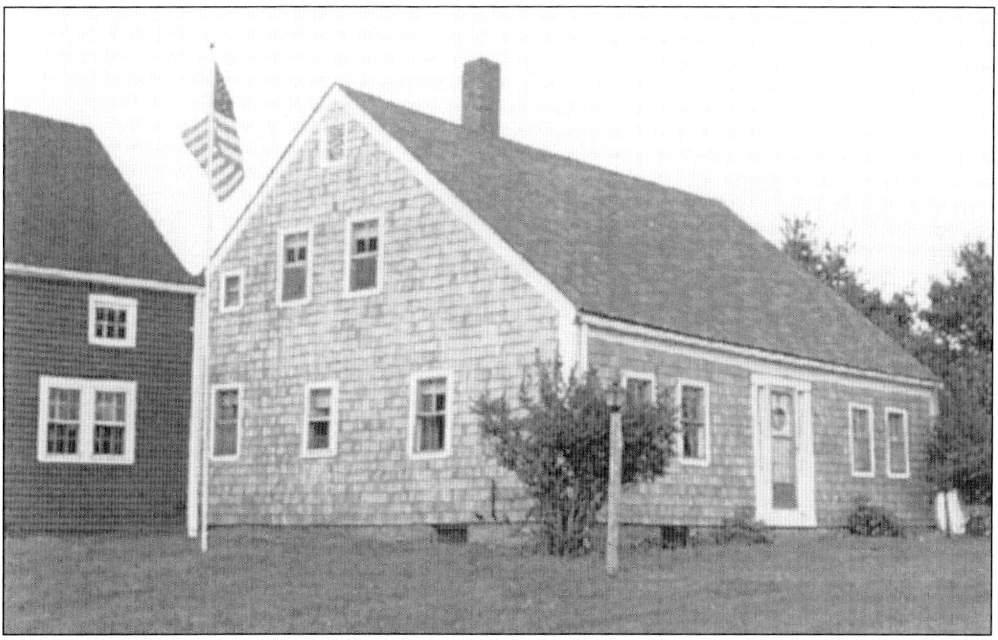

The Week's Homestead was built on Lot #34 in 1762, before the present North Yarmouth Road had been built. When the North Yarmouth Road was built, the barn had to be moved back 14 feet. The house was built by Benjamin Weeks, who tilled the soil, nurtured apple trees, had three children, and minded his own business, as people reported. Other owners were Oscar Weeks, Frank Hill, and Perley Sawyer. It is now owned by the Stansfield family.

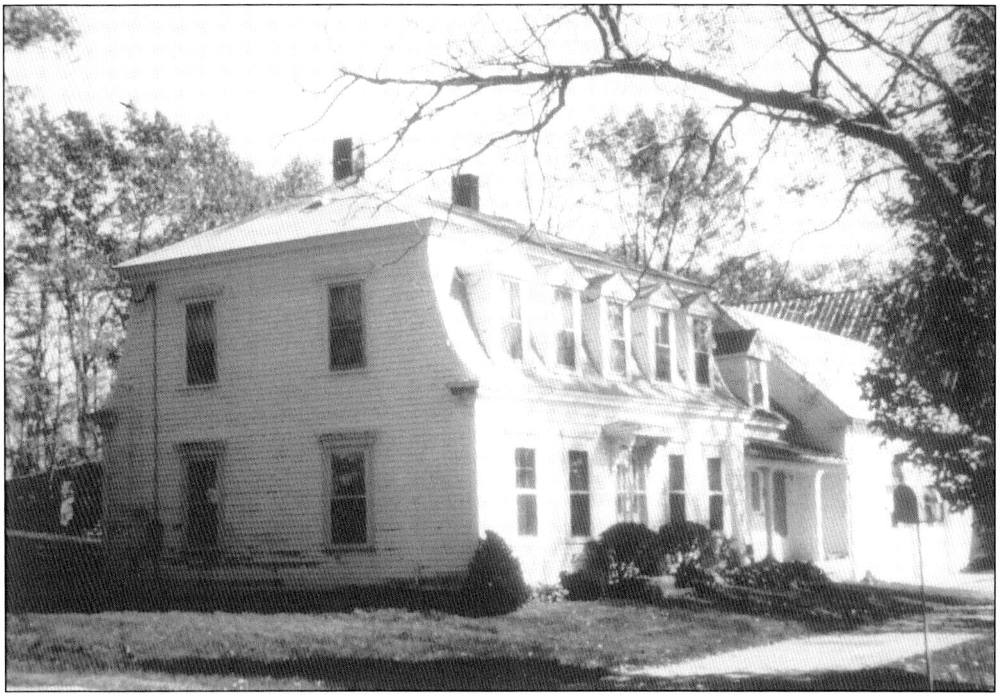

Almost on the town line of Windham, this Mansard-style home of the 1870s is now owned by the Werner family.

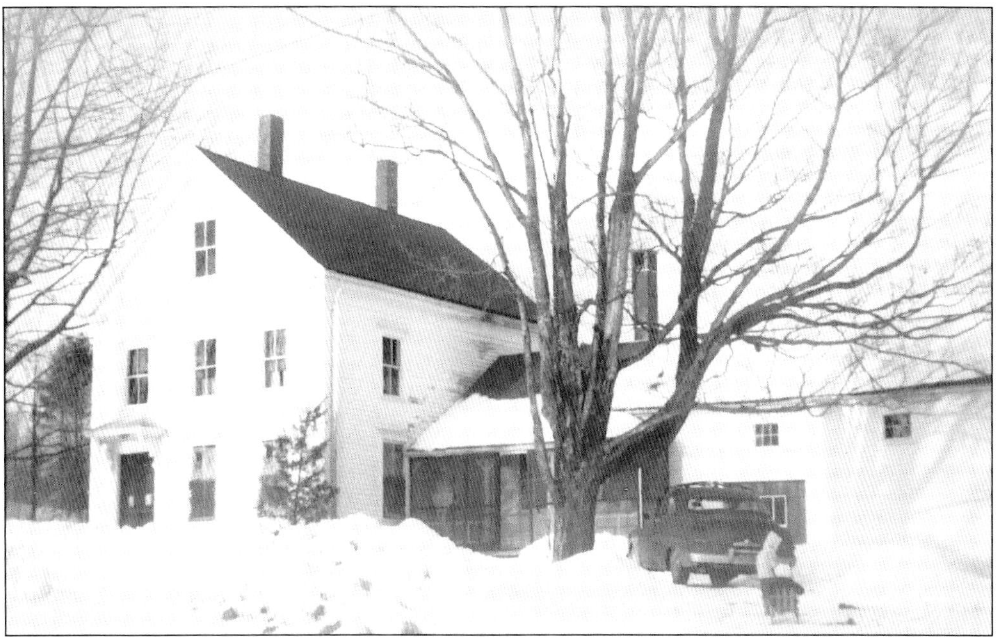

This house on the Cambell Shore Road was built by the Shaw family, probably Calvin Shaw, in the early 1830s. It stayed in the Shaw family until 1897. After that no one lived in the house on a regular basis until Hubert and Carole Cobb bought it in 1960. It had no electricity or plumbing at the time of the purchase. They have updated the house considerably and live there today. The children shown in the picture are Helen Cobb and Hubert Cobb Jr.

Four

Railroad Ties

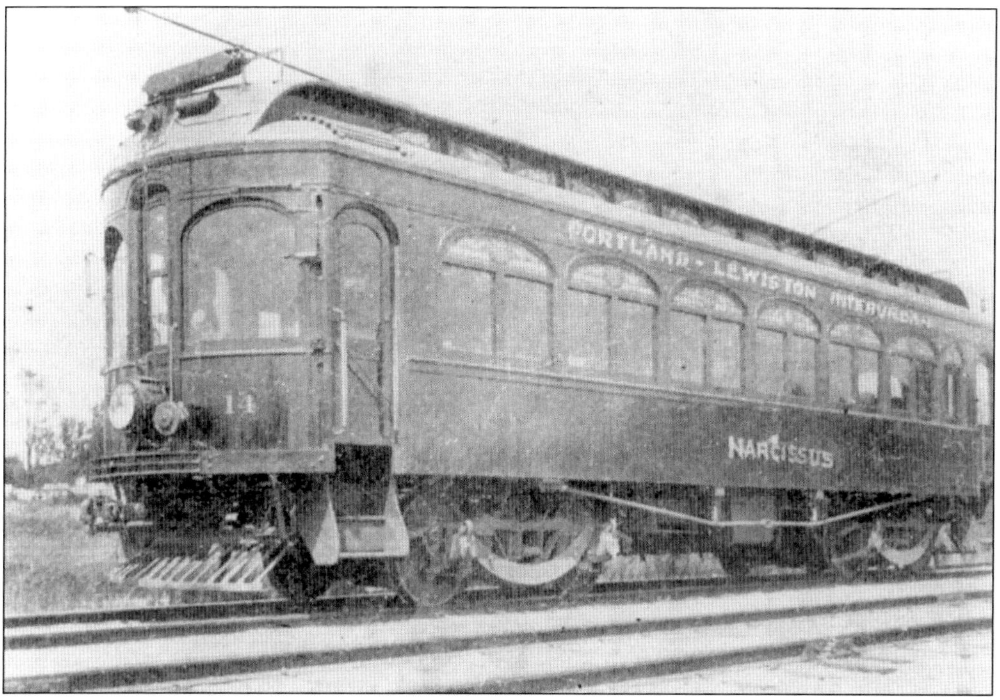

The Portland-Lewiston Interurban Railroad served the Gray area with high-speed electric cars featuring mahogany interiors, bronze metal work, heavy plate-glass windows, and skylights of leaded art glass. Fifty-two people could be seated on the reversible green plush seats or the leather seats of the smoking compartment. Most of the cars were named for flowers. "Narcissus" was the name of car No. 14, which was built by the Laconia Car Company in 1912. Narcissus was the first passenger car to run the entire new line.

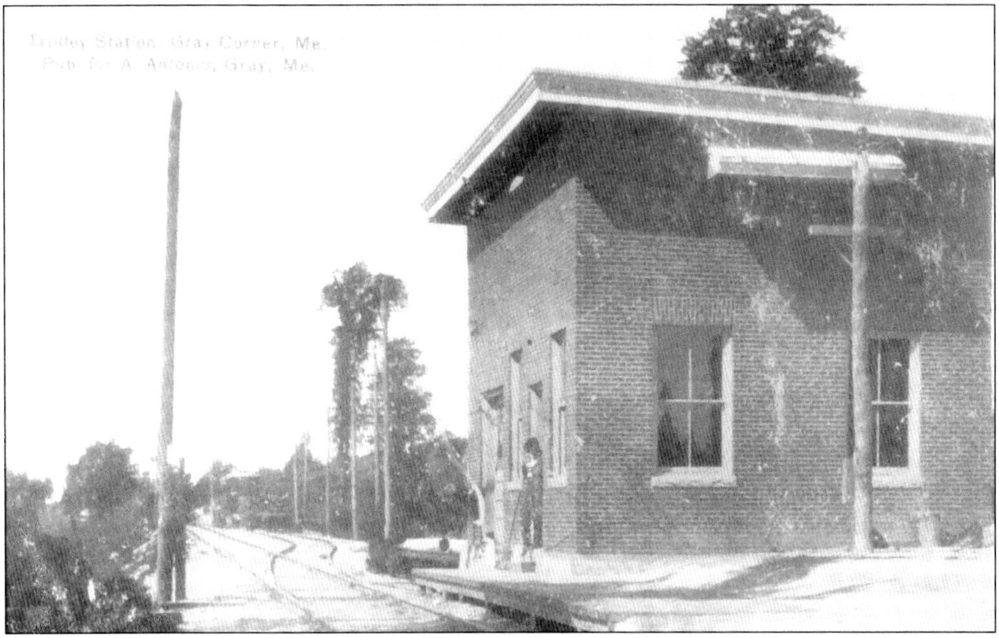

The Portland-Lewiston Interurban Railroad's sub-station at Gray opened in 1914. The sturdy brick sub-station was located at the foot of Week's Hill on the north side of the Yarmouth Road. The building, which also doubled as a passenger waiting room, housed 300 KW rotary convertors and three 100-KW step-down transformers. Another building, known as the car shed, was used for storing the work cars and locomotives. The final run of the Portland-Lewiston Interurban Railroad took place on June 29, 1933.

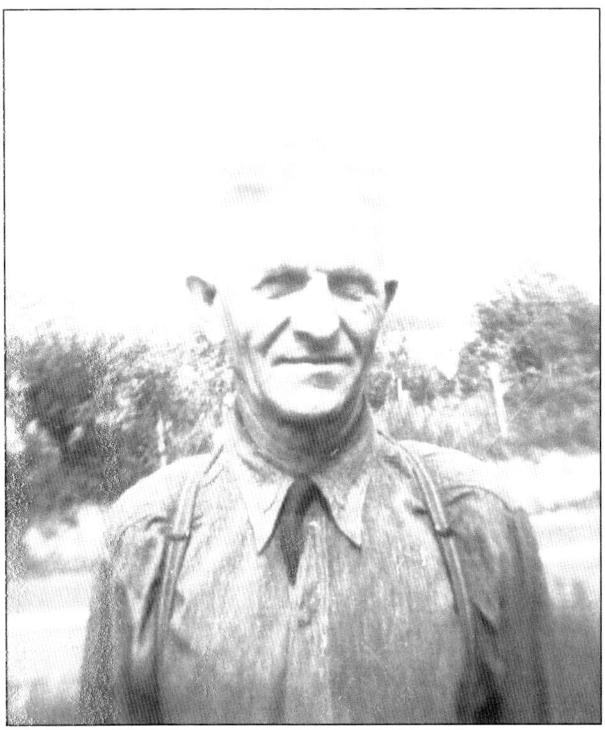

This is a 1938 picture taken of Mark Marcus Muzzy, a day agent/operator at Gray's sub-station, frequently referred to as the "mayor" of Gray. Gray's sub-station served as a gathering place for those who had little else to do besides sit and chat. Muzzy was a prominent man in the town, and when he was on duty he had many visitors. He worked the entire length of time that the Interurban was in operation.

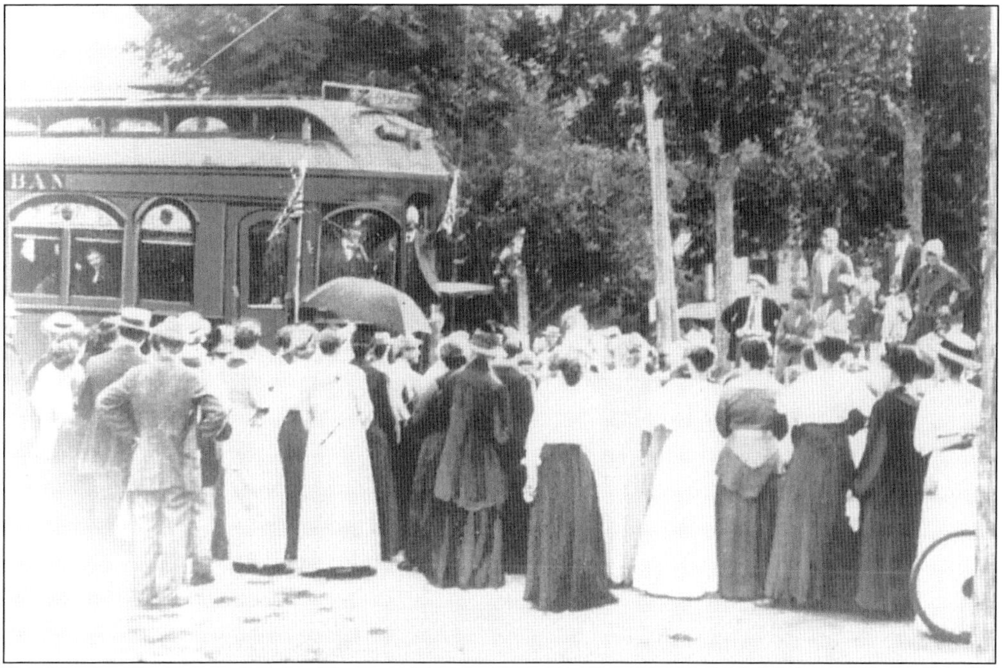

On August 18, 1914, the Portland-Lewiston Interurban Railroad had its most distinguished passenger: ex-president Theodore Roosevelt. "Teddy" is shown on the train at the rear door addressing a gathering at Gray's sub-station. He was given a ride in the parlor car *Merrymeeting*.

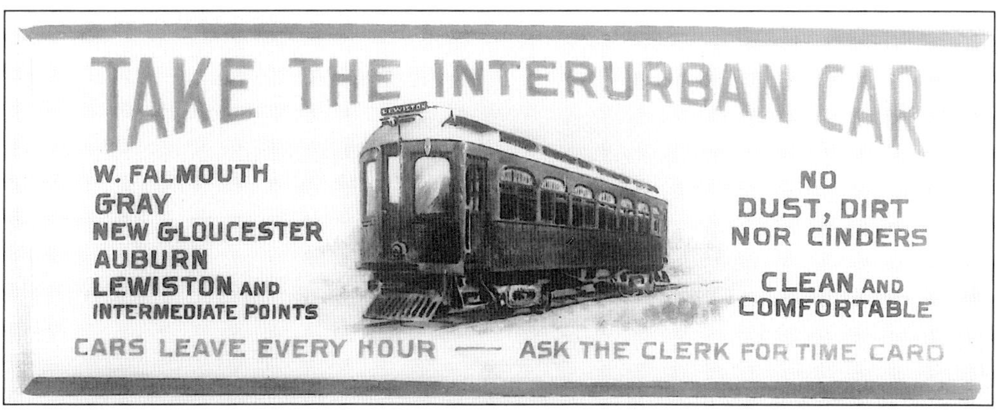

Porcelain tile plaques were used to advertise the Interurban service. Only one such plaque is known to exist today. The lettering and reproduction of cars pictured were shown in color.

PORTLAND-LEWISTON

INTERURBAN

RAILROAD

TIME TABLE

GEO. S. WILLIAMS, General Manager   P. E. WEYMOUTH, Superintendent

For the first ten years, the Portland-Lewiston Interurban Line was a consistent money-maker. Sixteen round trips were made daily in each direction. Their busiest days were in 1920, Maine's centennial year.

FAST FREIGHT SERVICE

TWO TRAINS

DAILY

BETWEEN MAINE'S TWO

LARGEST CITIES

Portland Office
20 PORTLAND STREET
Tel. 1147

Lewiston Office
116 MIDDLE STREET
Tel. 866, 867

Freight and express service commenced in 1915 with two daily round trips. They always ran as extras, and a brisk commercial business developed for Gray.

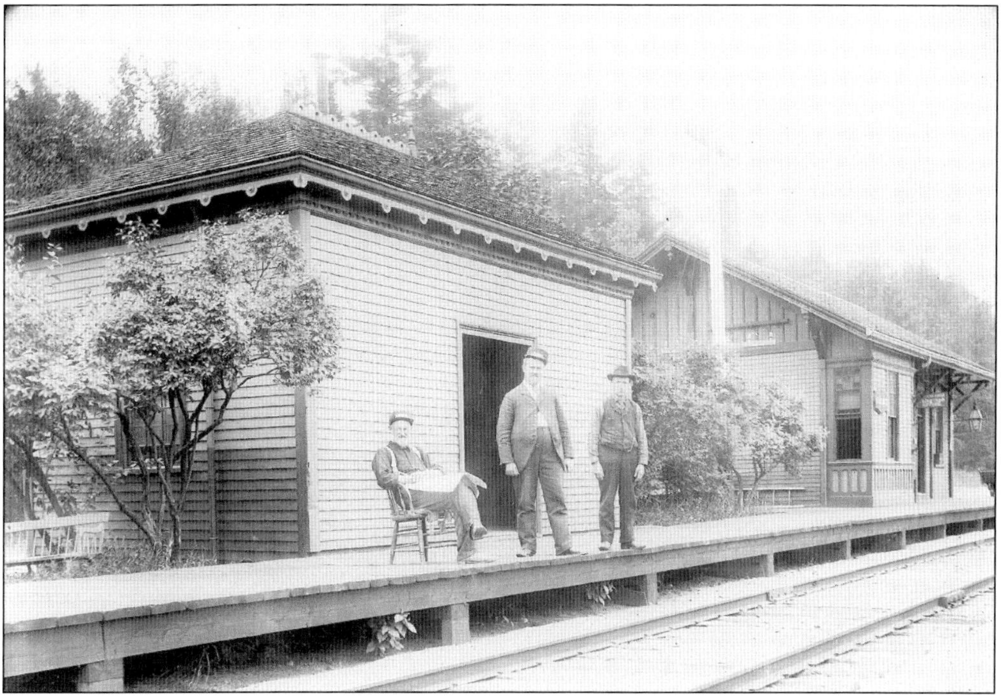

The Maine Central Railroad station in East Gray, known as Gray Depot, opened in the 1870s. It played a vital role in the success of farming and lumbering, making this one of the busiest sections in town from 1879 to 1933, when Maine Central Railroad closed. The station received grain in carload lots to supply the farmers. Coal came in by the carload and was then hauled by horses to the village. During the summer of 1907, 96 carloads of hay were shipped out of Gray Station to the Boston market. Milk was another commodity that was sent by rail. The services of the MCR were in great demand.

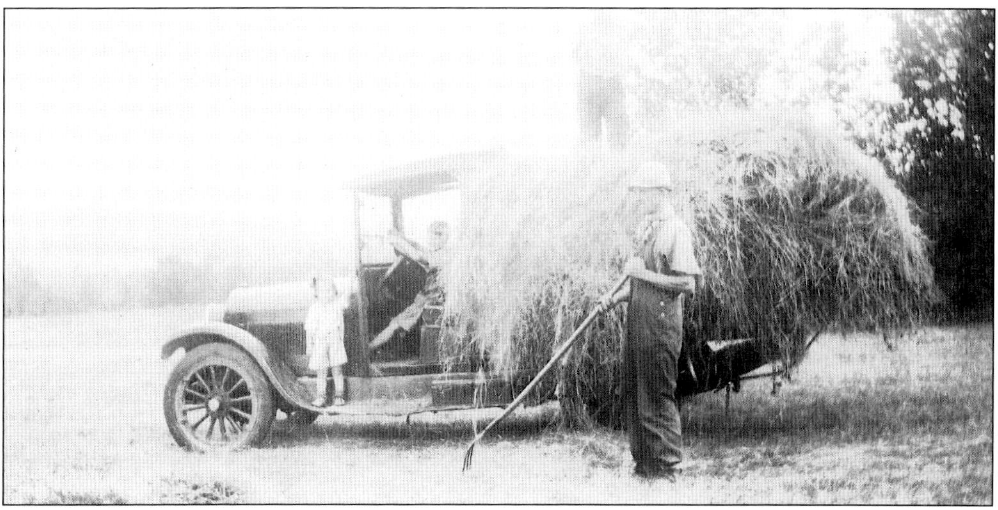

Summertime saw a lot of haying, c. 1940. Any hay that was not needed by local farmers was pressed into bales and put onto the trains for sale to the Boston market. Members of the Muzzy family are shown here working in their fields. They are, from left to right, Carole, Mark M. Jr., Carlton, and Mr. Mark M. Muzzy.

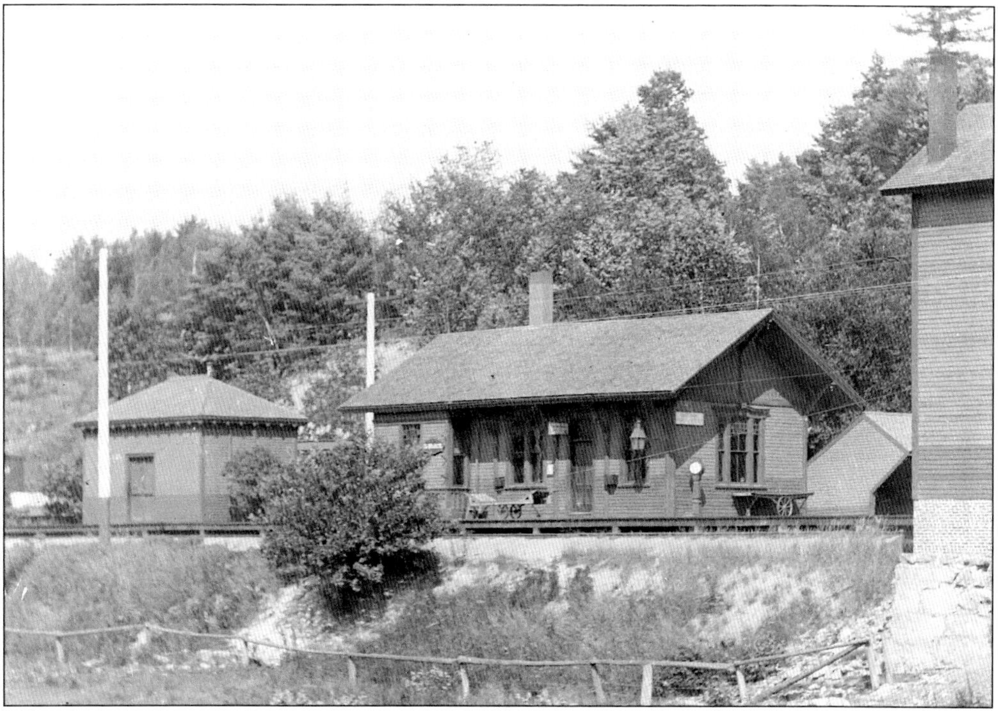

Maine Central Railroad provided many years of telegraph, passenger, and mail services to Gray Depot. The mail was taken from the train by the postmaster and distributed to various parts of Gray by stagecoach. There were many station masters over the years, including C.J. Perley, E.N. Roundy, R.S Andrews, W.B. Holt, E.L. Patten, E.S. Wood, W.W. White, E.S. Colbath, and G. Humphrey. Frank Witham, a mail carrier for 24 years, met the final passenger and mail train on April 27, 1957.

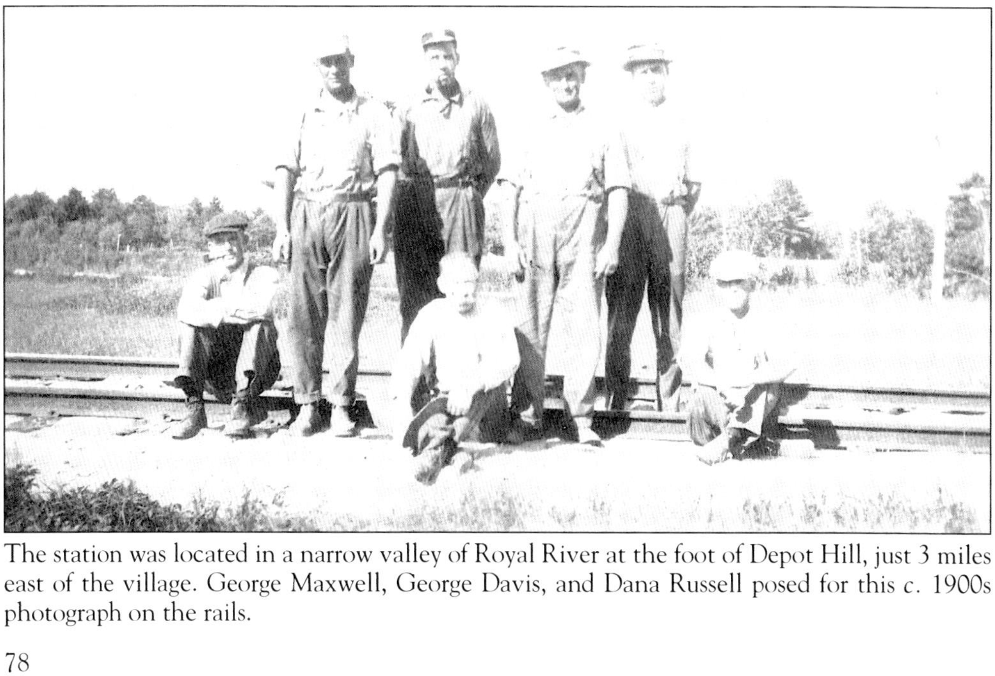

The station was located in a narrow valley of Royal River at the foot of Depot Hill, just 3 miles east of the village. George Maxwell, George Davis, and Dana Russell posed for this *c.* 1900s photograph on the rails.

Five

Spinning Yarns

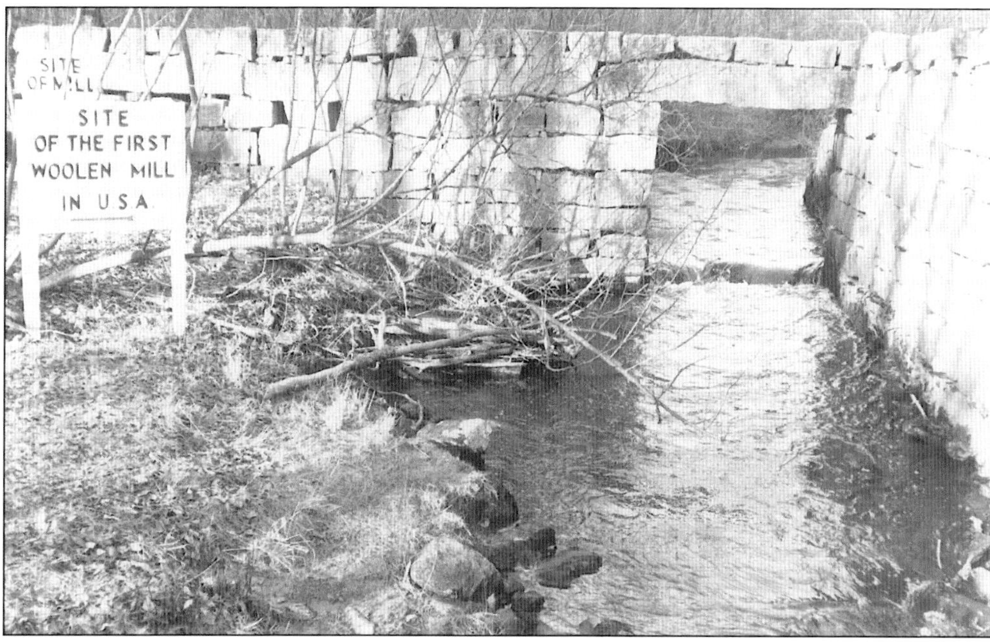

On this site in North Gray, Samuel Mayall established the first water-powered woolen mill in the U.S. Samuel converted an existing wooden gristmill with machinery he had smuggled from his native England. With his technical experience and talent, Samuel was processing wool here by 1791. Nearby farms supplied the wool; Collyer's Brook provided water power and a route down the Royal River to the coast. In 1806 Samuel advertised new, faster machinery and added a dyeing operation to the carding, spinning, weaving, and fulling processes. The Mayall Mill flourished, and the "upper mill" was built in 1816. Samuel trained his children in the mill business, so after his death in 1831, daughters Mary and Phanela took over and contracted to have the brick "lower mill" built in 1834. The mills were then leased to a series of managers including Tyng Wilson, who ran it for many years. Blankets for Union soldiers in the Civil War came from Mayall Mills. This photograph was taken in 1950.

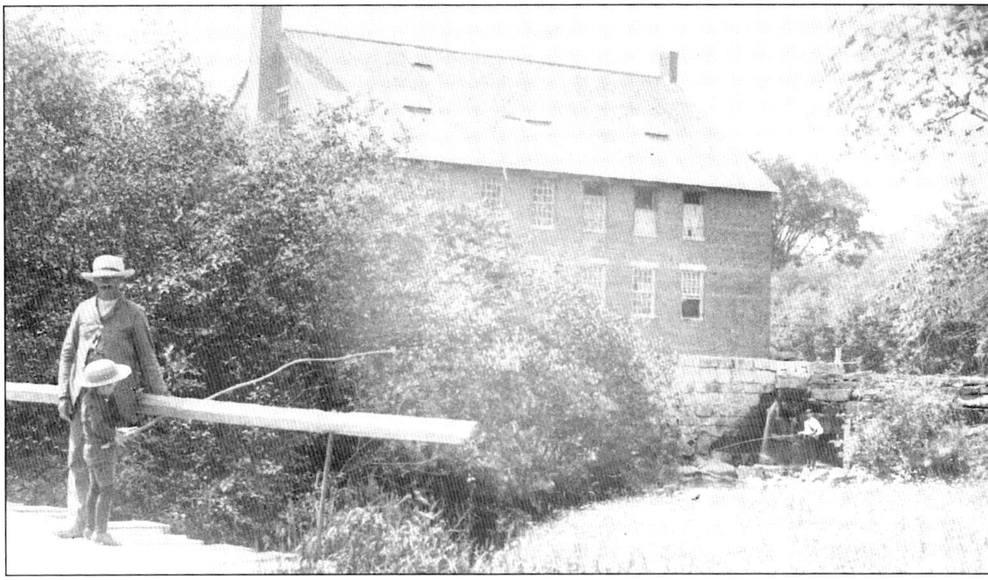

This 1885 photo by Elbridge Cobb at Mayall Mills shows Adam Purvis with Cobb's son and Eugene W. Sawyer. The mills at that time were owned by William Beatty, who had purchased them from the Mayalls in 1879, when the original wooden mill was still standing. Beatty had managed the mill since 1871, advertising "ladies cloths and woolen goods, custom carding and cloth dressing . . . [and] . . . machinery repair." By 1886 the Mayall Mills had been renamed The Falmouth Woolen Mills, and Beatty's billheads carried the message, "manufacturer of repellents, cloakings, satinets." In 1886 the upper mill burned and cloth-making here ceased for a few years.

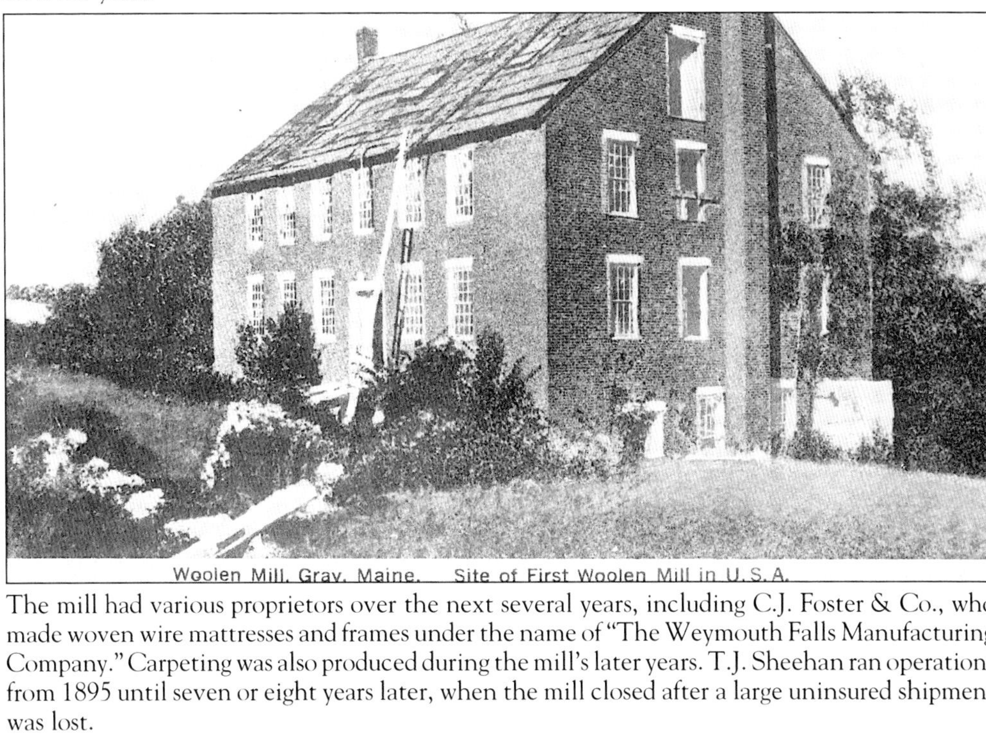

The mill had various proprietors over the next several years, including C.J. Foster & Co., who made woven wire mattresses and frames under the name of "The Weymouth Falls Manufacturing Company." Carpeting was also produced during the mill's later years. T.J. Sheehan ran operations from 1895 until seven or eight years later, when the mill closed after a large uninsured shipment was lost.

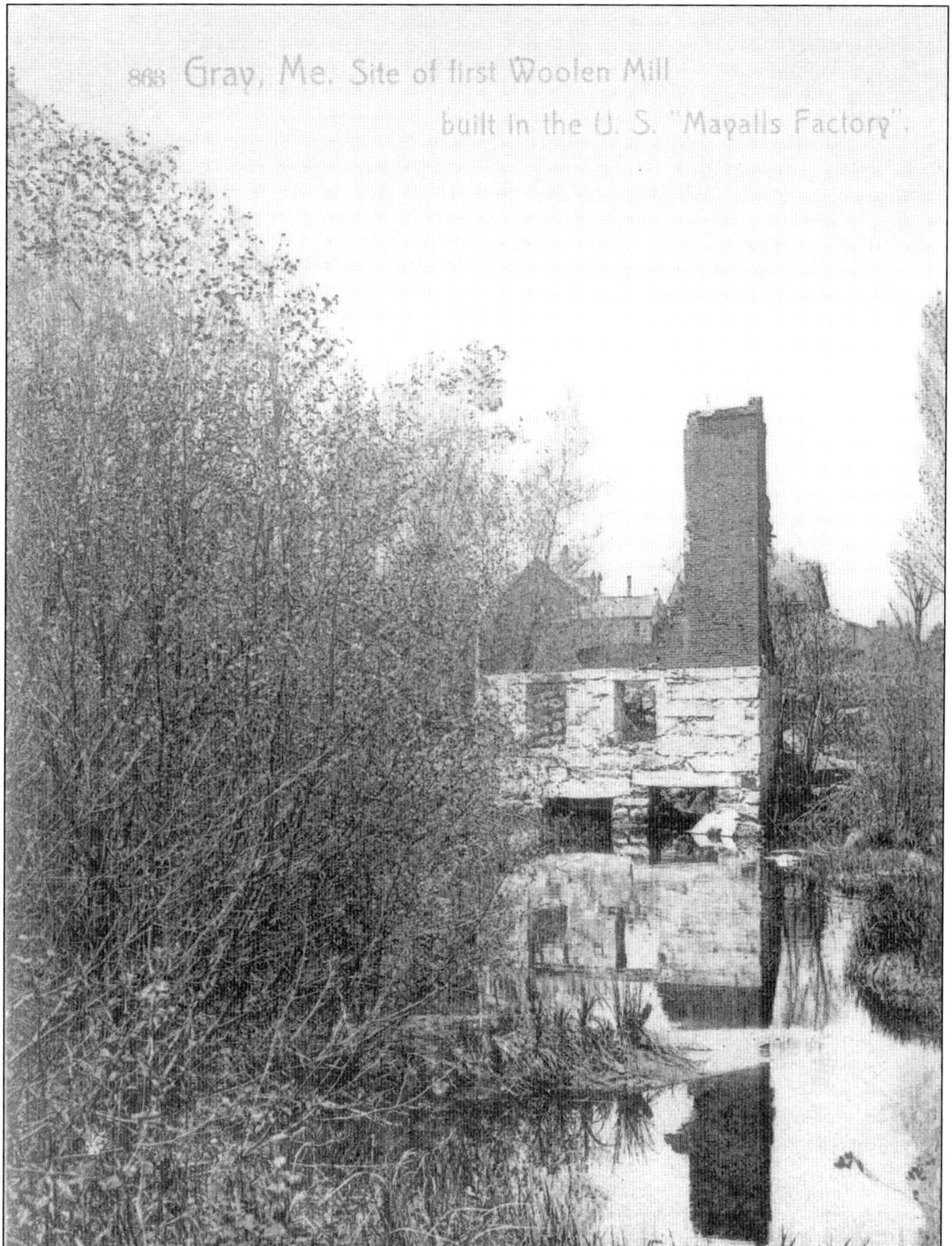

Crumbling brick ruins and a thick stone wall beside Collyer's Brook are all that is left of the Mayall Mills, well over two centuries after Samuel Mayall started his first mill. The original wooden building was still standing in 1879 but no trace of it remains. Bricks from the other buildings were used in the construction of Pineland State Hospital in Pownal. One building that has survived from the days of the Mayall Mills is a large three-story house, located on the north side of Mayall Road and a short distance to the west of the mill site, which once served as a boardinghouse for 19th-century mill workers.

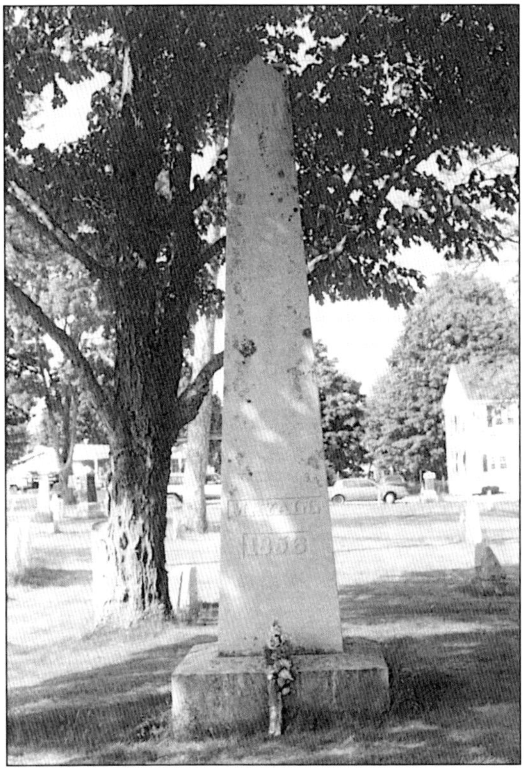

This monument marks the Mayall family plot in the Gray Village Cemetery. Samuel Shaw Mayall was born in England in 1761. He has been called "The Father of the American Wool Industry," and also served as a selectman of Gray. Samuel and his wife, Anna Hicks, had three daughters and five sons. He died in 1831 and was laid to rest on the Mayall property. Later, his remains were interred here.

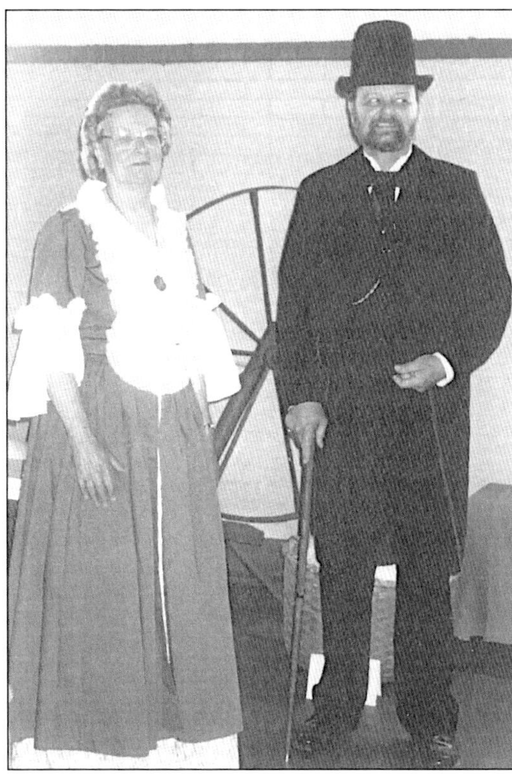

Samuel Mayall Day was sponsored by the Gray Historical Society in the summer of 1997. Mill founder Samuel Mayall and his daughter Phanela were portrayed by Howard Black and Margaret Sawyer. Highlighting the day were Samuel's reminiscences of a life of perseverance, achievement, and danger. This glimpse into the 1790s through the 1830s revealed the difficulties Samuel faced in defying strict English laws meant to prevent American competition with their textile industry.

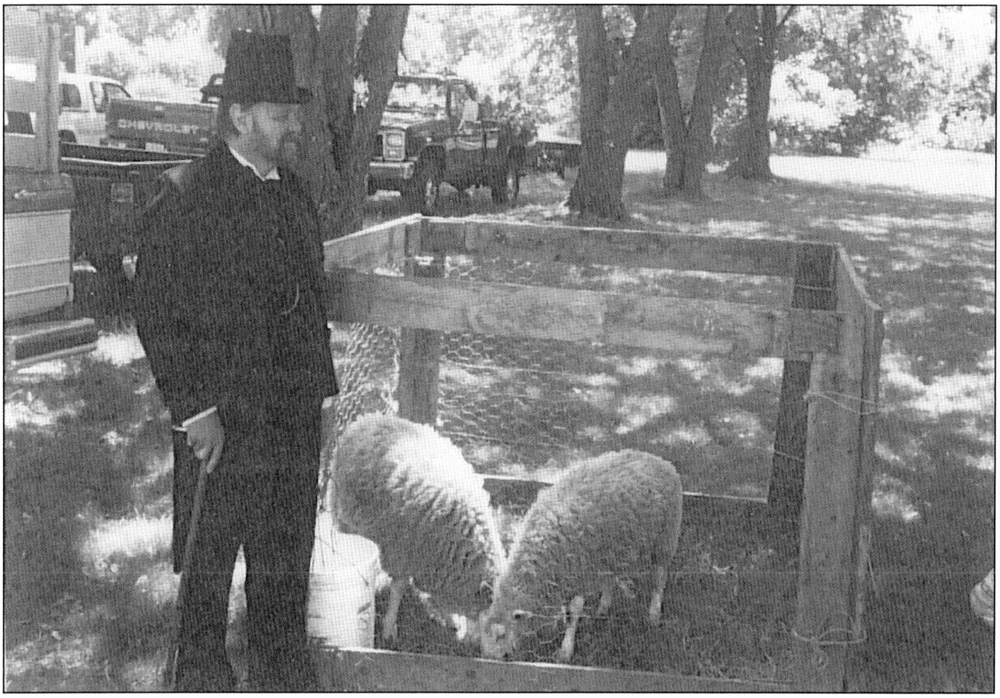

"Samuel Mayall" watched sheep from area farms graze at the celebration, a reminder of their essential part in the birth of the mechanized woolen industry in Gray.

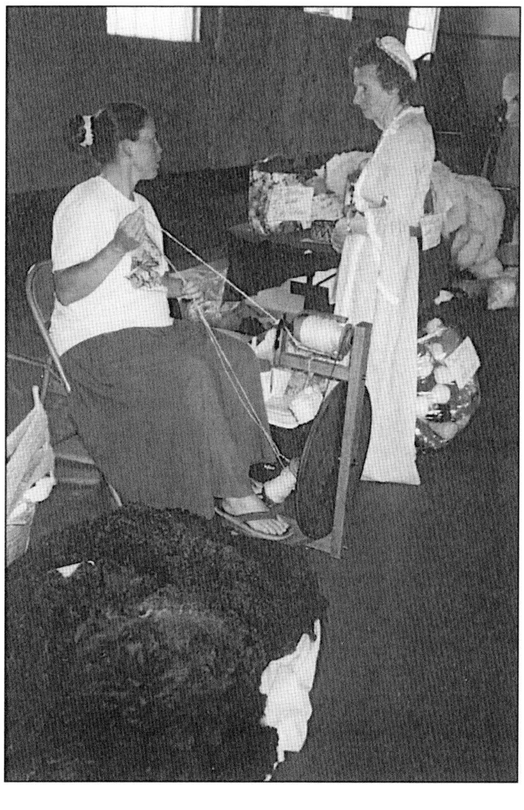

Despite the mechanization of the textile industry, earlier methods survived. Laurie Hughes, shown here with Mae Beck of the Gray Historical Society, was among the spinners and weavers demonstrating their craft on Samuel Mayall Day.

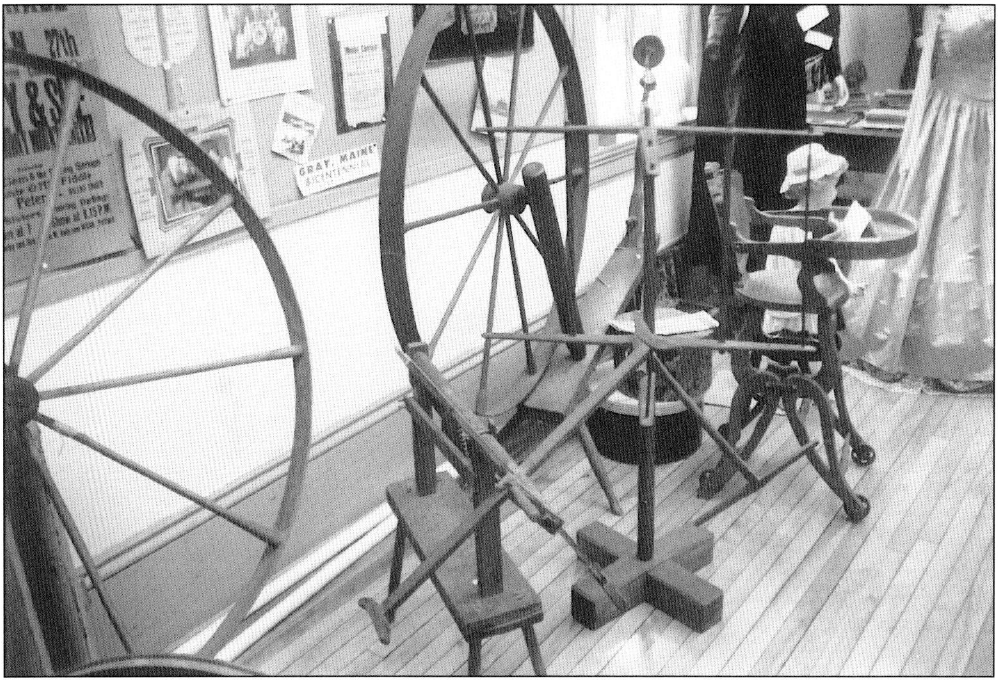

Spinning wheels from the Gray Historical Society Museum were part of the exhibit showing devices used in individual homes in the 1800s.

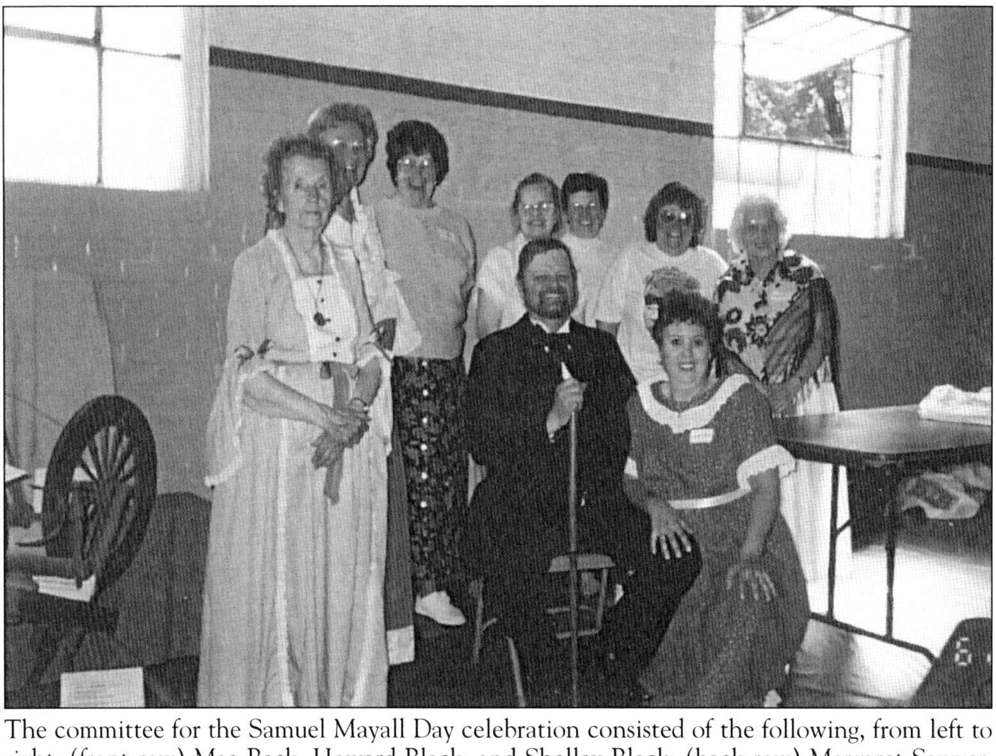

The committee for the Samuel Mayall Day celebration consisted of the following, from left to right: (front row) Mae Beck, Howard Black, and Shelley Black; (back row) Margaret Sawyer, Louise Knapp, Jean Szendrei, Judy Steeves, Karen Taylor, and Helen Davis.

Six

All in a Day's Work

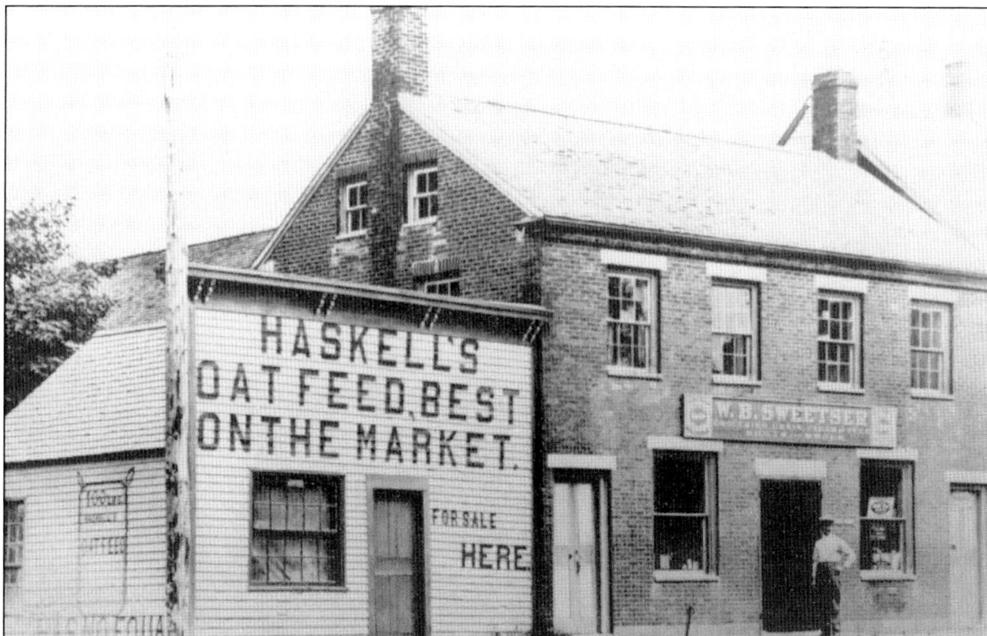

Here we see the Grain Store and the W.B. Sweetser General Store at about the turn of the century. The dirt sidewalk in front of the Grain Store became a great spot to play marbles in the springtime. The rest of the stores had brick sidewalks. The Grain Store building has housed many businesses, from a shoe repair shop to a fish market. At one time, the W.B. Sweetser General Store included the post office, and the second floor had an apartment and a barber shop. This store also had many proprietors.

Gray has often been called the "Crossroad of Maine," and many businesses here have centered around meeting the needs of the traveling public. The center at one time had four taverns (which today would be hotels). The paving of highways brought additional growth to Gray in many forms, including gasoline stations and restaurants.

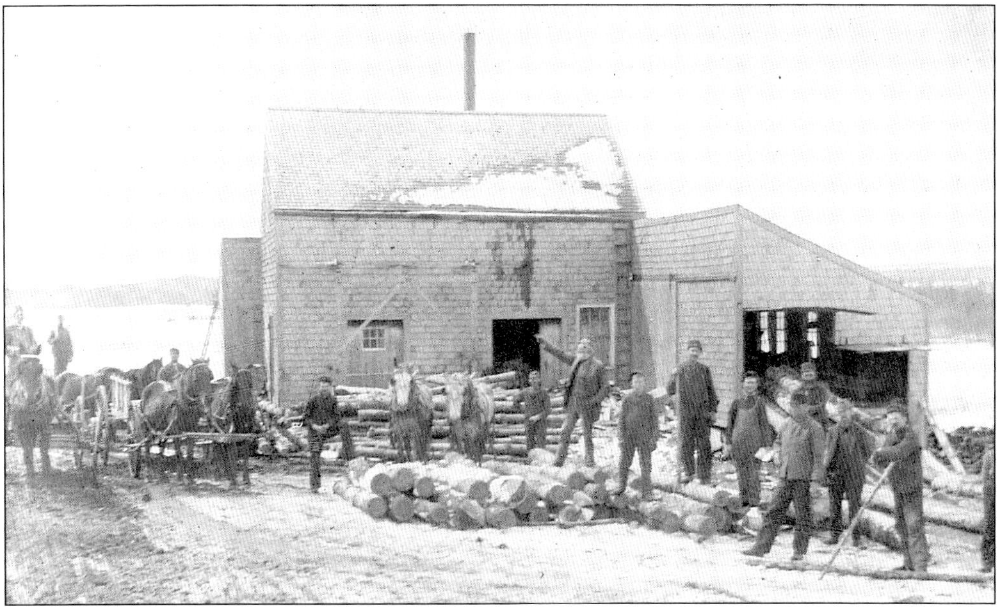

Northwest of Dry Mills, another large mill thrived for decades at Douglassville, also called Suckerville. Lumbering was the town's first industry, and it remained very productive for over one hundred years. By 1760 water power was created by building dams, allowing many different industries to be located in the same area, including gristmills, stave mills, and cooper shops. By the 1800s streams began to be used to power boilers and engines. In the 1900s gasoline engines came into use.

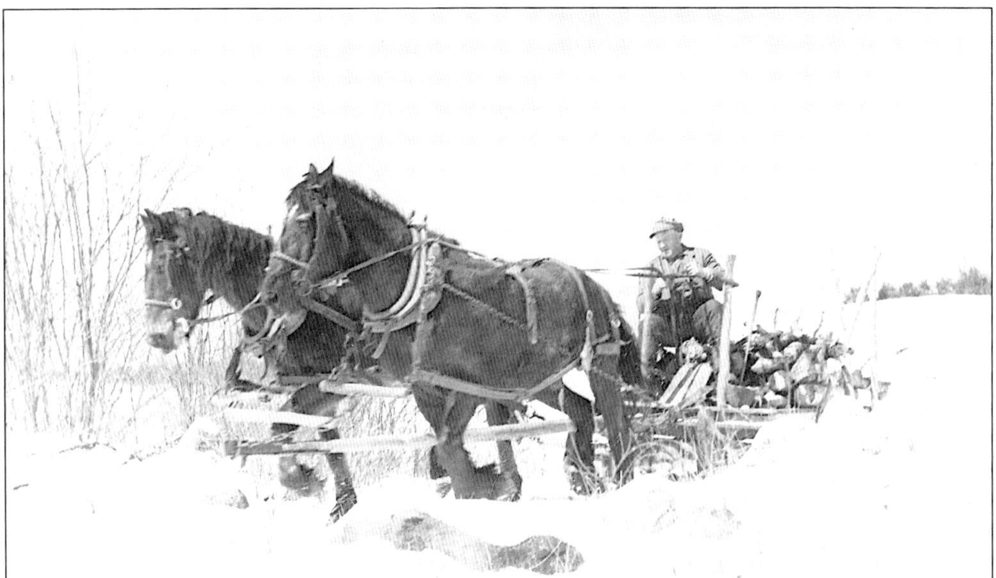

A pair of work horses named Ned and Ted were owned by Albert Cobb. Albert lived on Cambell Shore Road in West Gray.

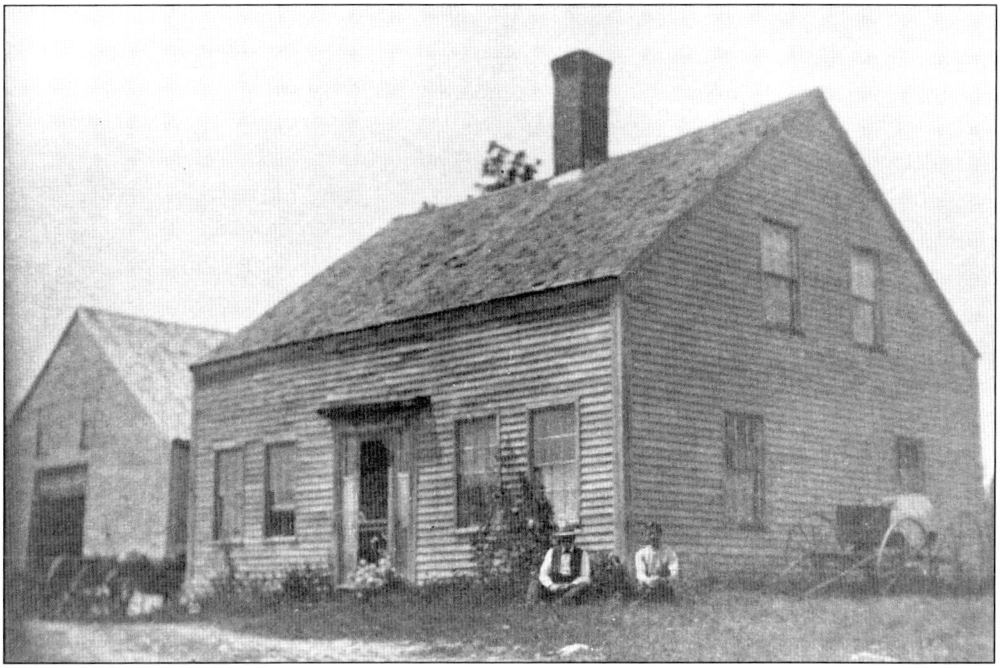

Mr. Goff's home was located off Shaker Road, on Libby Hill Road. Mel and Willis Goff are sitting in front of the house. In 1907, Will was moving his portable sawmill between lumber areas with his ten-horse team. Portable mills became very popular, as it was cheaper to move the mill than to haul the logs.

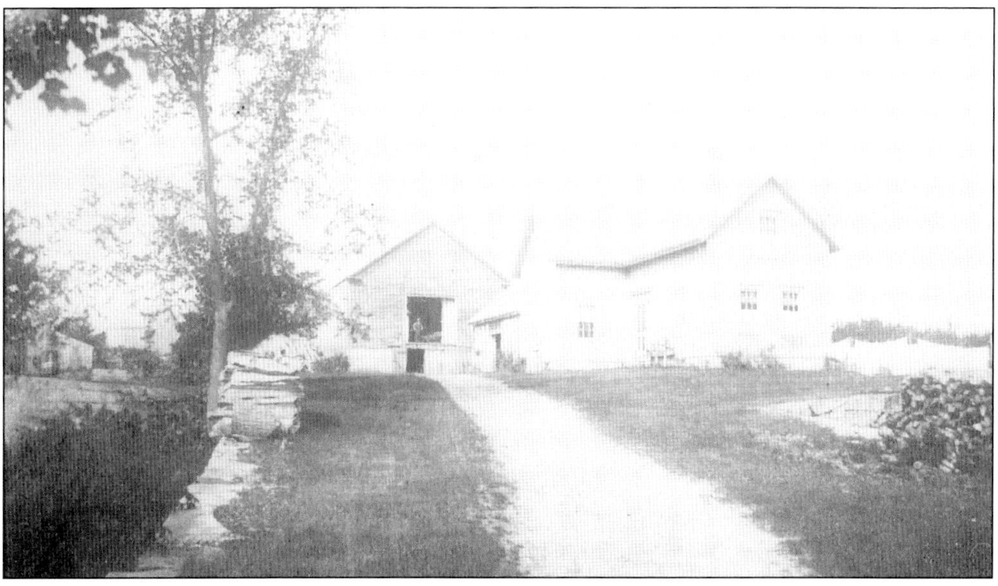

Samuel Noyes bought lot #51 from the Gray tax collector in 1784 and gave it to his daughter, Susanna Noyes Skillin. In 1822 the buildings went to Samuel Skillin. After the death of Samuel, it went to Mary Skillin, who passed it on to Hiram Skillin in 1848. Hiram built the house and barn that are there now. Additions to the building have been made in the following years. In 1895, Hiram's estate sold to Daniel S. and Annie M. (Foster) Cobb. Today the Cobb family still owns it.

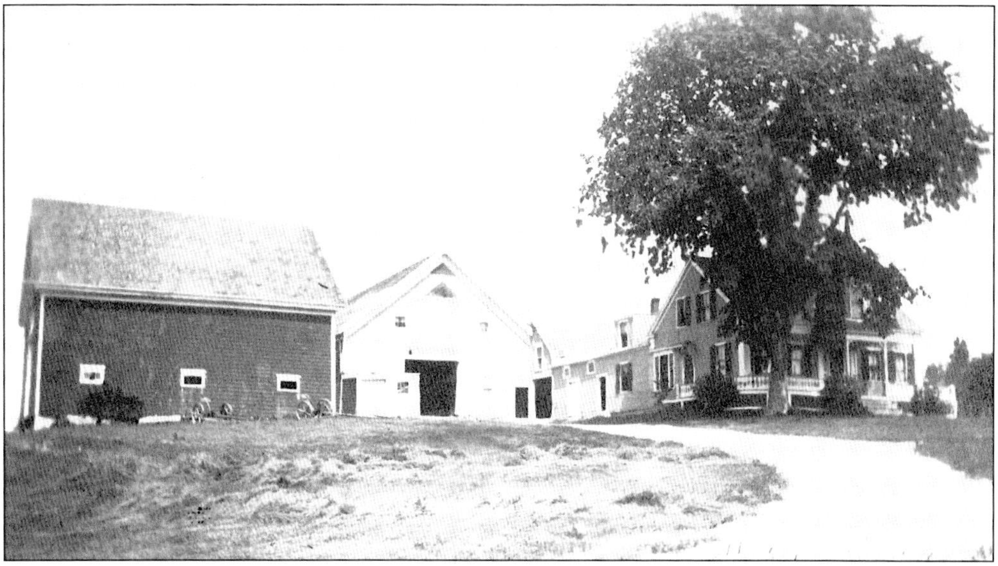

Springdale Farms includes several farms that were owned by George T. Merrill in the mid-1800s. In 1907 his son, George E. Merrill, purchased three farms adjoining the "home farm," increasing the acreage to more than 900. He hired men to help maintain the herd of purebred heifers and cows, sometimes numbering as many as 100. They grew all the feed to supply the herd and shipped the surplus by train to Boston. The farm is currently owned by Michael Wilson and is called the Wilsondale Farms. The prize-winning herd continues to grow.

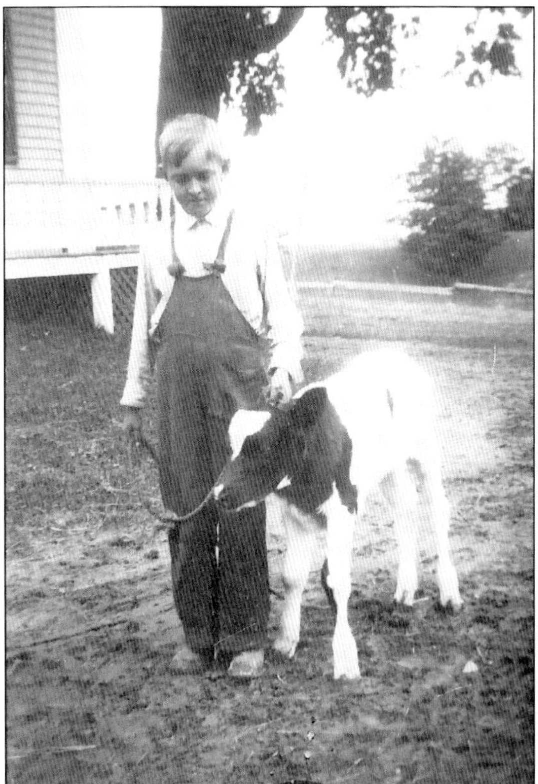

The Holstein calf beside ten-year-old Karl H. Merrill has roots that go back to the registered herd of Holstein cows first brought to the Springdale Farm by Karl's great-grandfather, George T. Merrill, who devoted the farm entirely to the raising and breeding of Holsteins. This young lad naturally grew into a thorough knowledge of the business, and under his guidance Springdale Farms produced one of the finest herds in the country. It is the oldest continuous registered herd of Holsteins in the U.S.

These members of the Merrill family are, from left to right, George Dwight , Karl Herbert, Mary Evelyn, and George Edwin Merrill. They all lived on the Springdale Farms and continued the hard work of farming. Cows were milked in the traditional fashion and milk was stored in 8- or 10-gallon cans. In 1916, milk was shipped to Boston at the handsome price of $1.90 per 10-gallon can. The family contributed greatly to the progress and prosperity of Gray, including serving as a teacher, a member of the state legislature, a selectman, and a trustee and deacon of the Congregational Church.

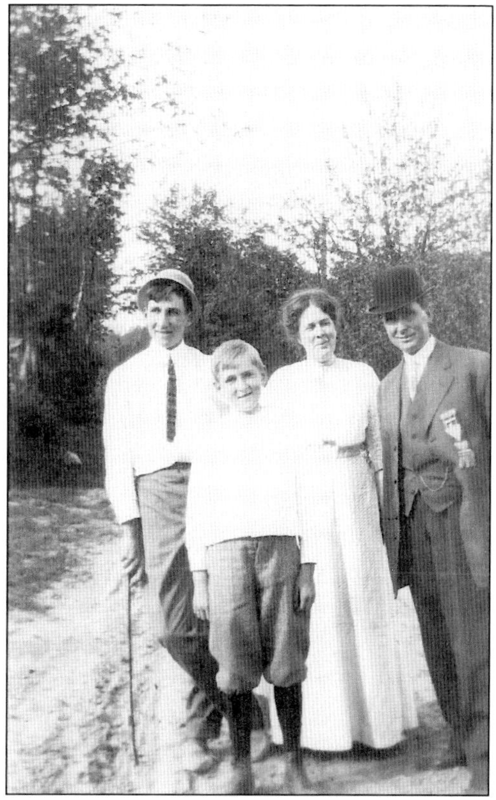

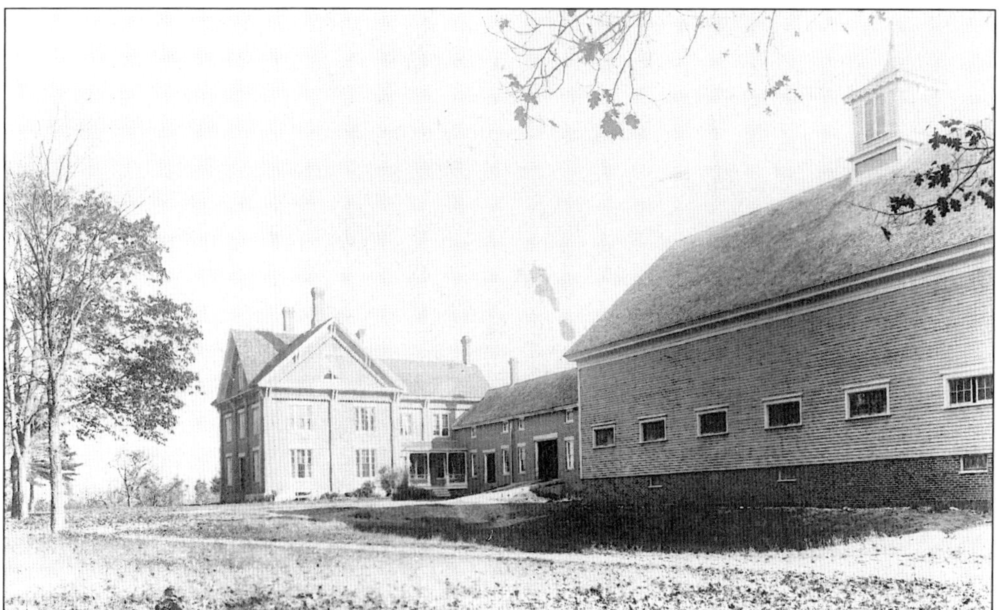

The brick Italianate-style Henry Goff House was built in the 1870s, and was located near the corner of Mayall Road and Depot Road in East Gray. Goff owned the largest brickyard in Gray; his house, Pennell Institute, and the Hancock Store were built with bricks from his brickyard, which was located below the bridge at Gray Depot by Royal River.

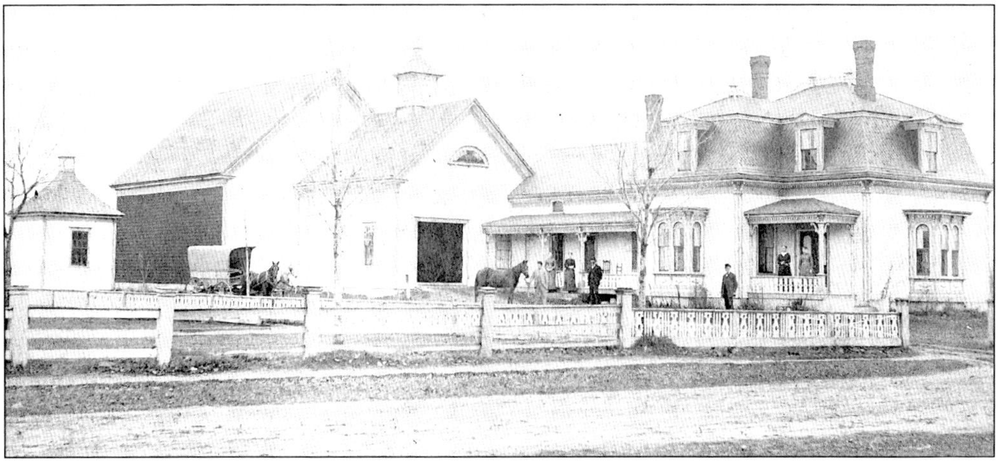

The Mansard-style farm of John T. Merrill was built by him in 1875. He was an organizer of the Gray Park Association and an active member until it closed. He and his wife, Frances H. Young of Gray, were both interested in music. In 1870 he organized the Gray Corner Band. His daughter taught music in the schools. He and his daughter gave freely of their talents, and many of Gray residents learned to appreciate music. At the rear of his property he built and ran a sawmill, a shingle mill, and a gristmill.

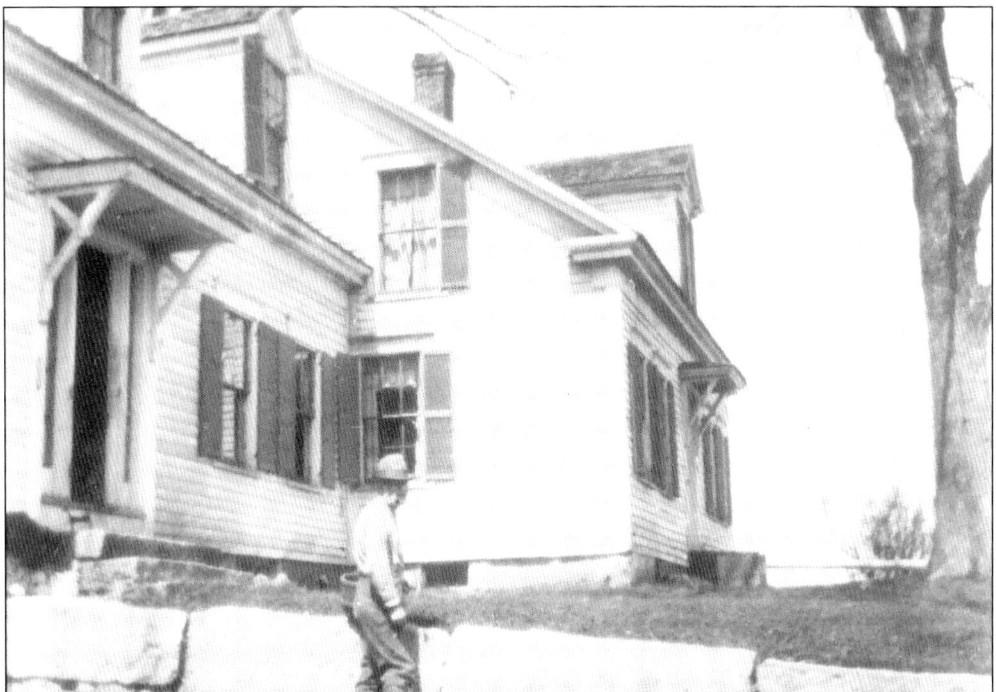

Pleasant View Farm had 200 acres of land and one quarter mile of shoreline on Little Sebago Lake. It stood on a hill overlooking Dutton Hill and the Windham area on lot #52. Probably built by Samuel Adams in 1799, the house and barn were connected by an enclosed walkway with a shed underneath that had to be opened to pass through to the lake. The grounds were landscaped with fruit trees. Other owners included Isaac Adams, John Adams, Albert Brackett (shown here in 1909), and the Knudsons and the Noyes.

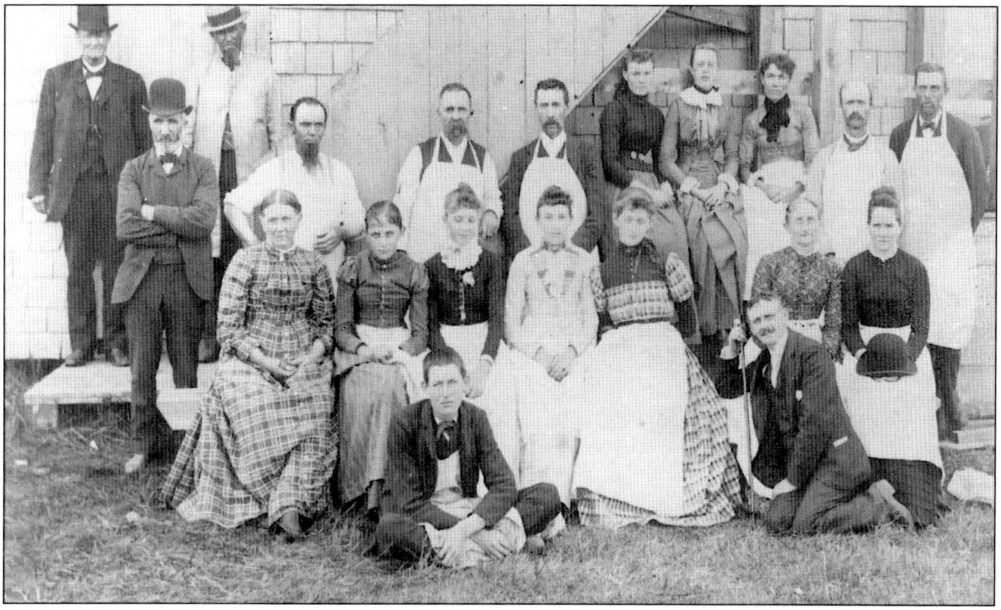

The canning factory was located on the south side of West Gray Road. Many farmers in Gray, including Frank Lowe, Eugene Lowe, and the Merrills, grew corn. The soil was well suited for growing corn, and it was considered one of Gray's most profitable crops. Corn seed was shipped by rail in large quantities to the Midwest. In 1887 Gray saw the opening of its first canning factory. Webb & Cummings was the first owner, followed by H.F. Webb & Company in 1891, and H.L Forhan in 1905. Forhan owned the factory until 1924.

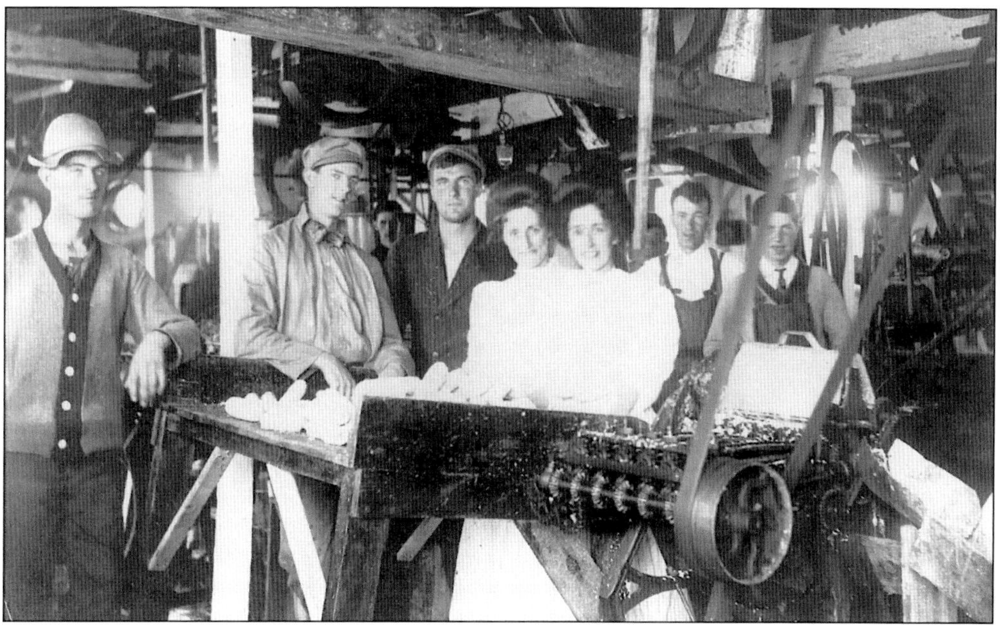

The fall was a busy time of year at the corn shop, which is shown here in September of 1909. Many people were employed here year-round, but canning season required a larger crew to help with husking the corn and operating the machinery. At one time Eugene Lowe managed the shop. In 1941 the Corn Shop was owned by Barber's Fruit Food, Inc.

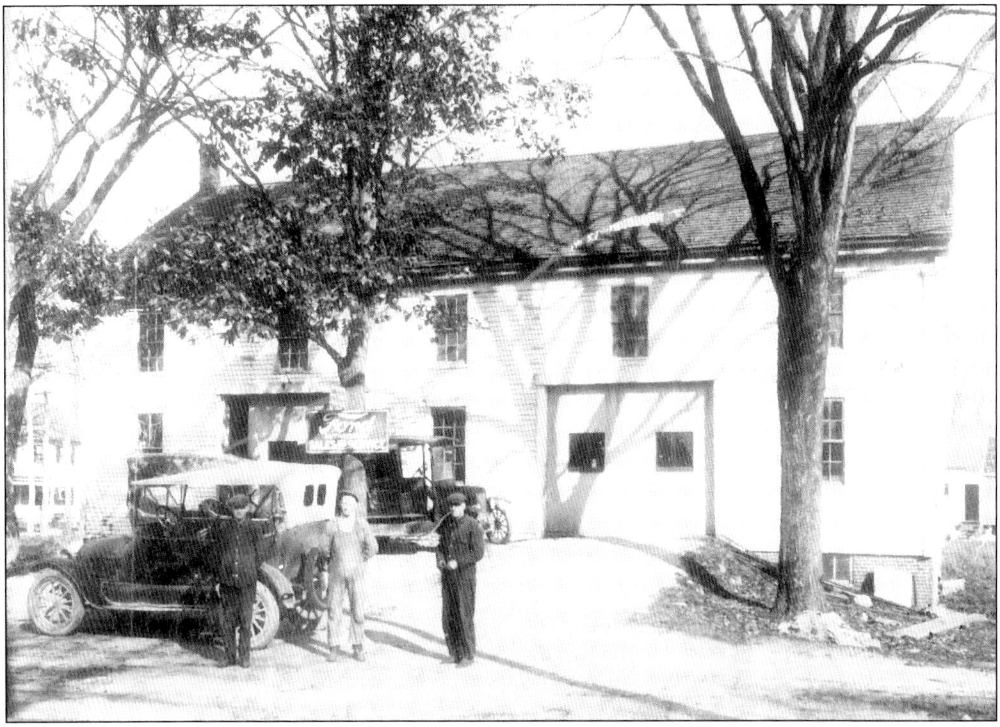

The Lawrence and Leighton Garage was established in 1920s by Perley Lawrence and Walter Leighton on the lot in back of the Elm House in the livery stable, on the north side of Brown Street. The Berry Garage and F.D. Sawyer Garage were two other garages in Gray Center at this same time.

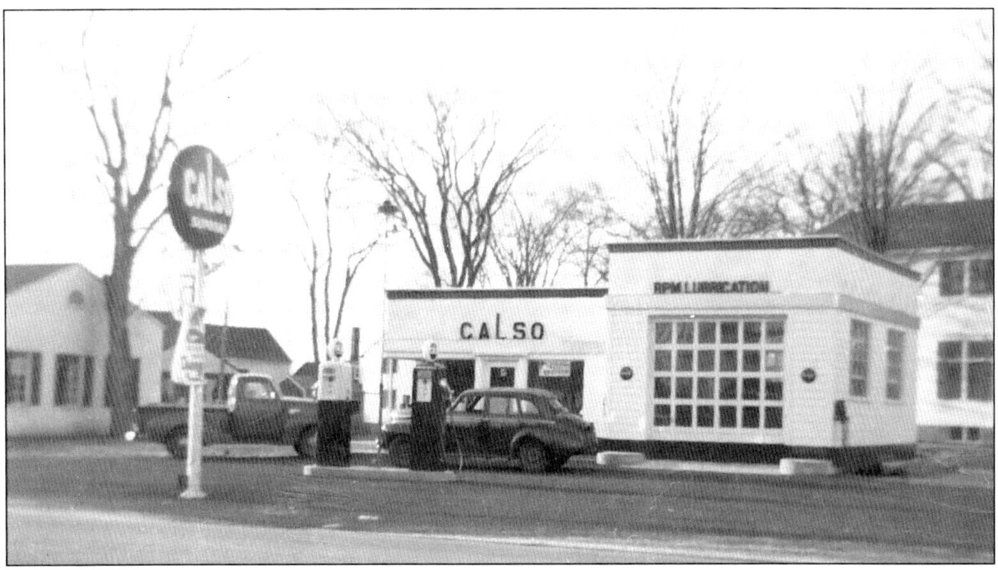

Who remembers this brand of gasoline? This Calso gas station was located on the west side of Main Street. It was just one of the many gas stations located on Main Street.

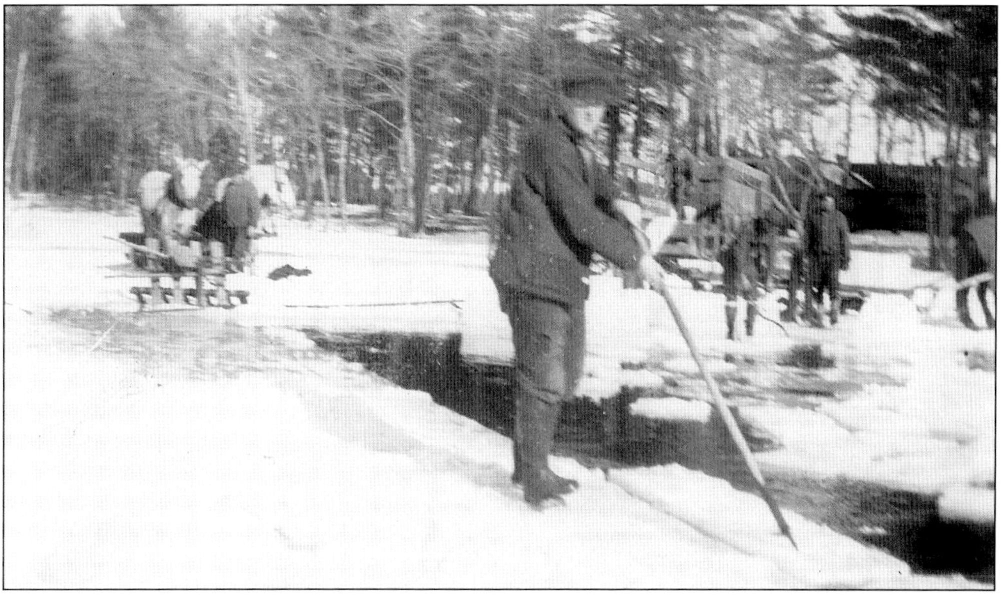

Ice that was harvested in the winter months lasted through the hot summer. Lester Jones and his helper are shown here getting their supply ready to sell to their customers. Ice for harvesting had to be about 18 inches thick, and clear—not snow ice. A special ice saw was used that had a tapered blade about 4 feet long. After the blocks were cut, they were pulled out using a pole with a pick on the end and put onto sleds using ice tongs. The ice was then covered with plenty of sawdust and stored in an ice shed.

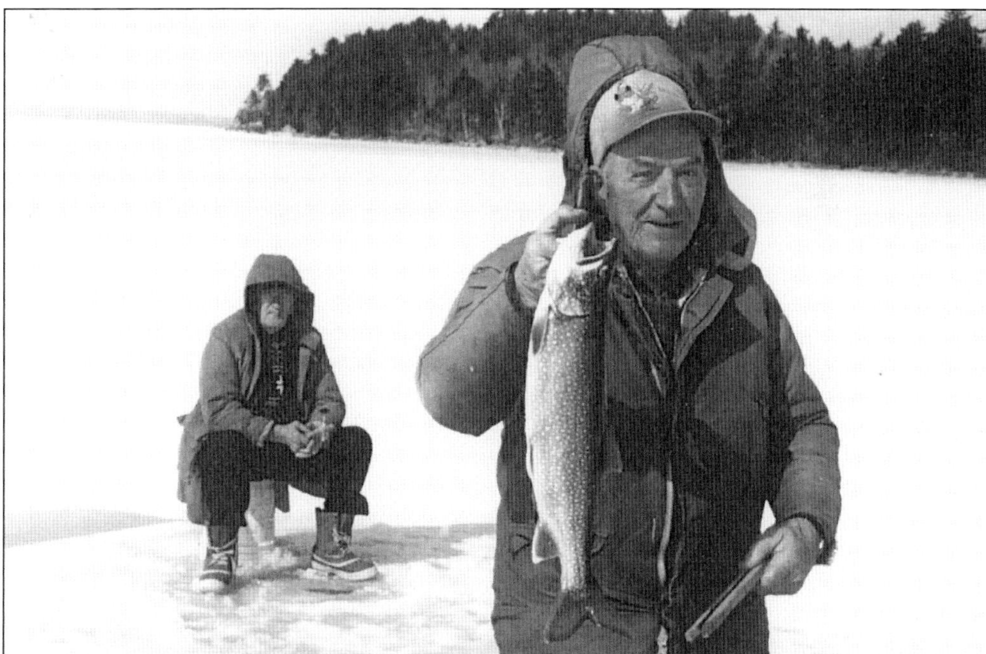

Ice fishing is a popular winter sport on the many lakes and ponds within the town limits. Pictured are Mr. Larry Walker with the fish and Mr. Frank Robinson.

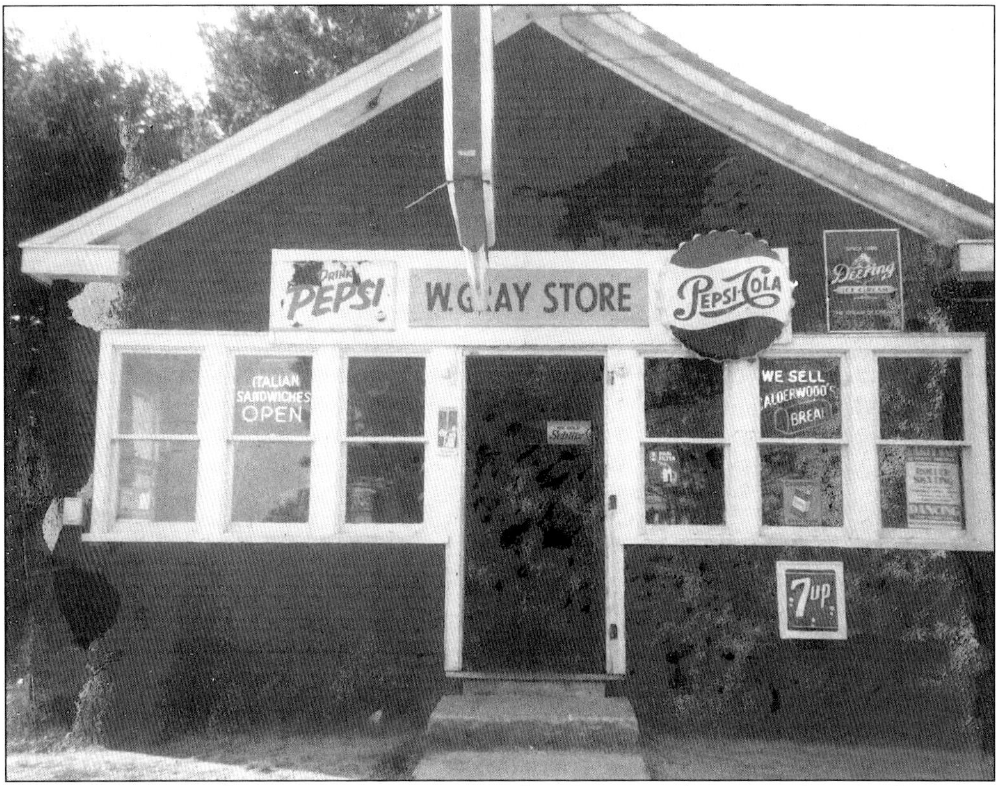

In the early 1950s, the West Gray Store opened on Route 115 in West Gray. Early owners were Ed and Josephine Robichaud, Bob Murphy, and Adeline and Irving Whitney. A local restaurant purchased the West Gray Store in 1962, and it has remained a restaurant ever since. The current restaurant is called The Colonial.

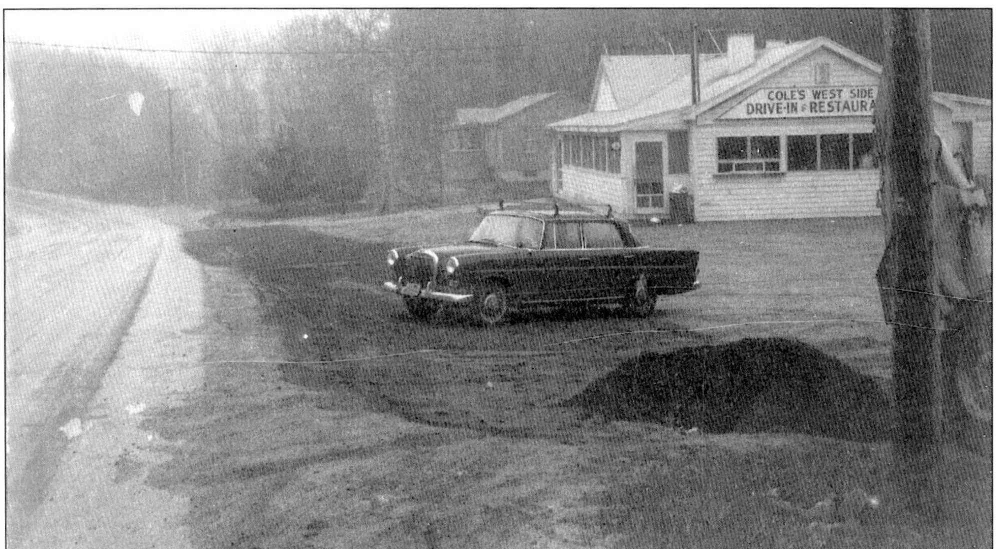

Cole's West Side Restaurant, shown here in 1963, featured a menu of home-style, primarily homemade, cooking. It remained at this location for approximately ten years.

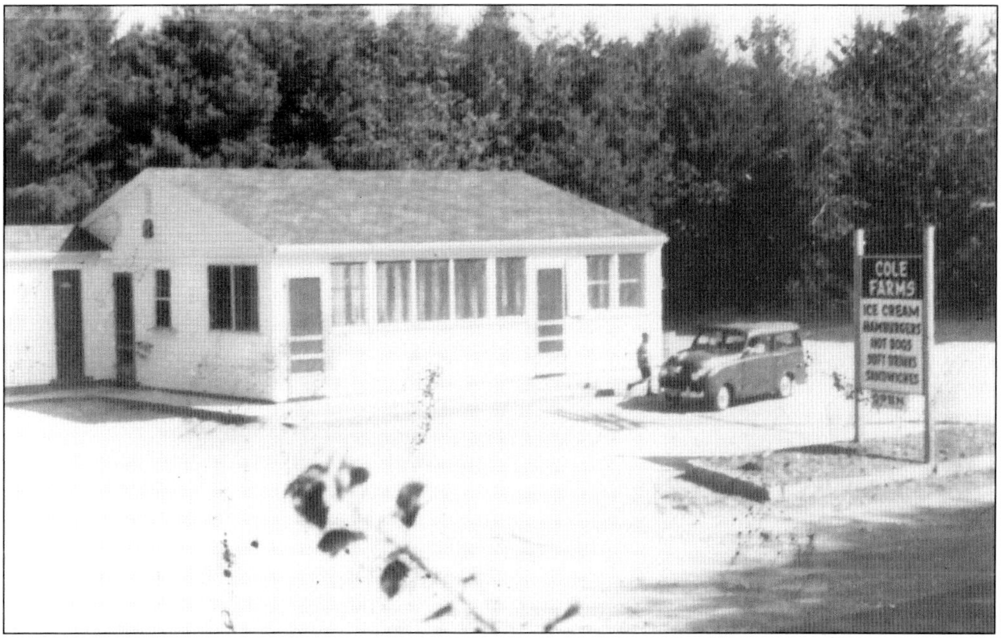

This 1952 photograph shows the original Cole Farm's Restaurant, located approximately one mile north of Gray Village. The small parking lot and 24-by-30-foot building were built on a former pasture. From that modest beginning a popular local restaurant, Cole Farms, emerged. Notice the Crosley station wagon.

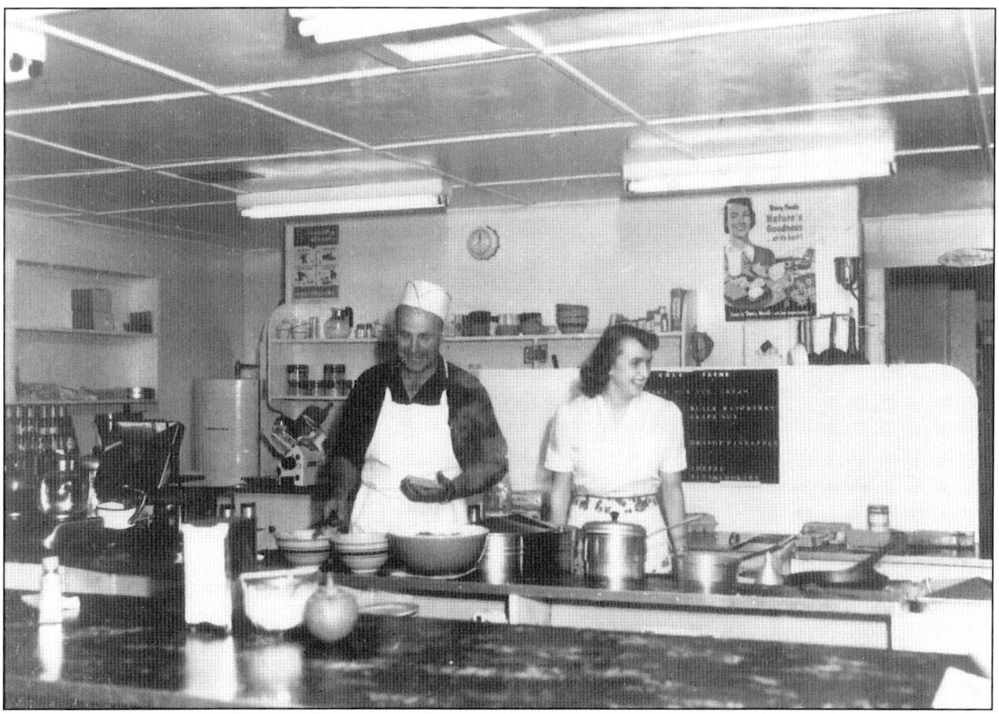

Co-owner Norman Cole stands behind the grill at Cole Farms. This is an early picture of "Chef" Norman and Mary Taylor, one of the first local high school girls to work at Cole's as a waitress.

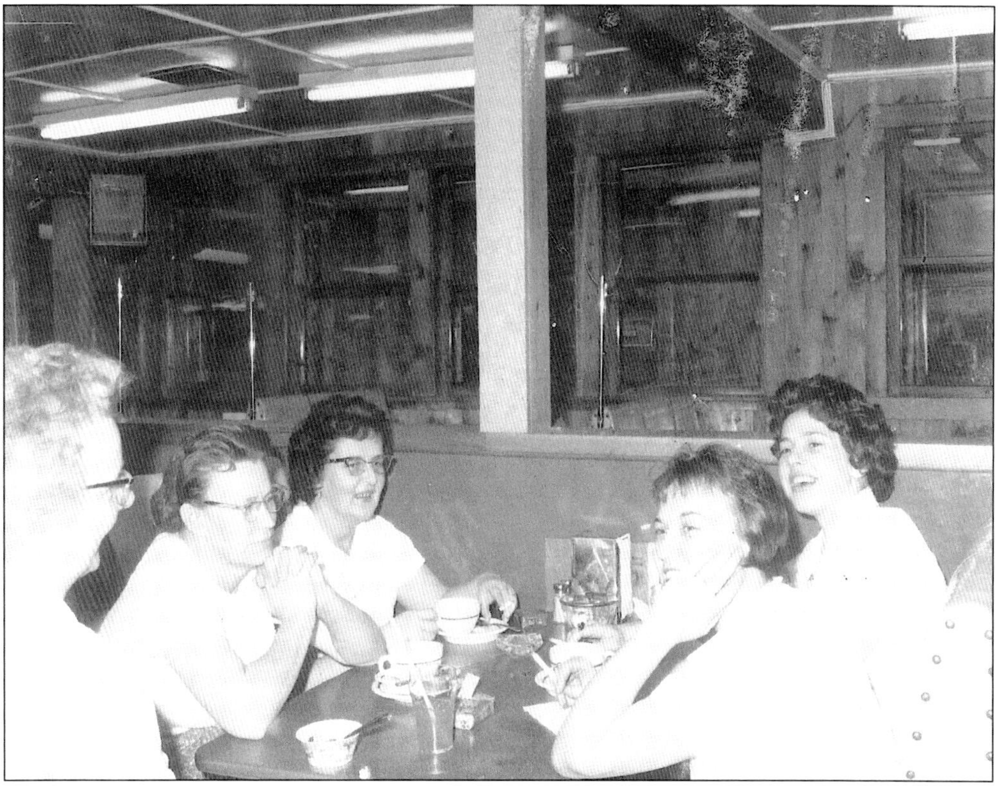

In 1962 a coffee break is enjoyed by, from left to right, waitresses Mrytle Verrill, Lucille McCann, Beverly Parker, Gloria Dahms, and Shirley Cole.

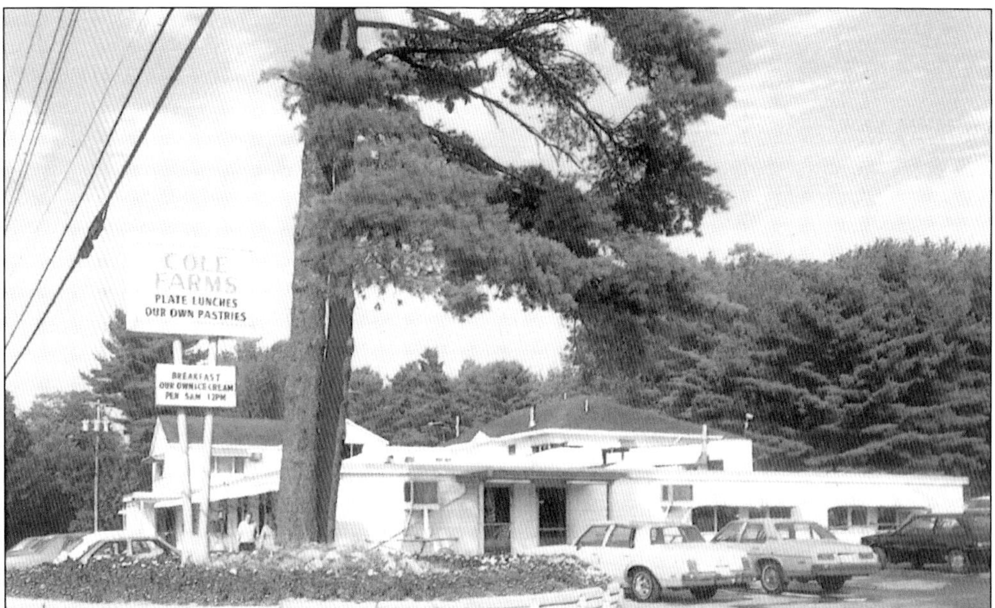

By 1984, Cole's had expanded to a 235-seat restaurant. It has since added a second story with additional seating, and a full third kitchen with banquet capabilities.

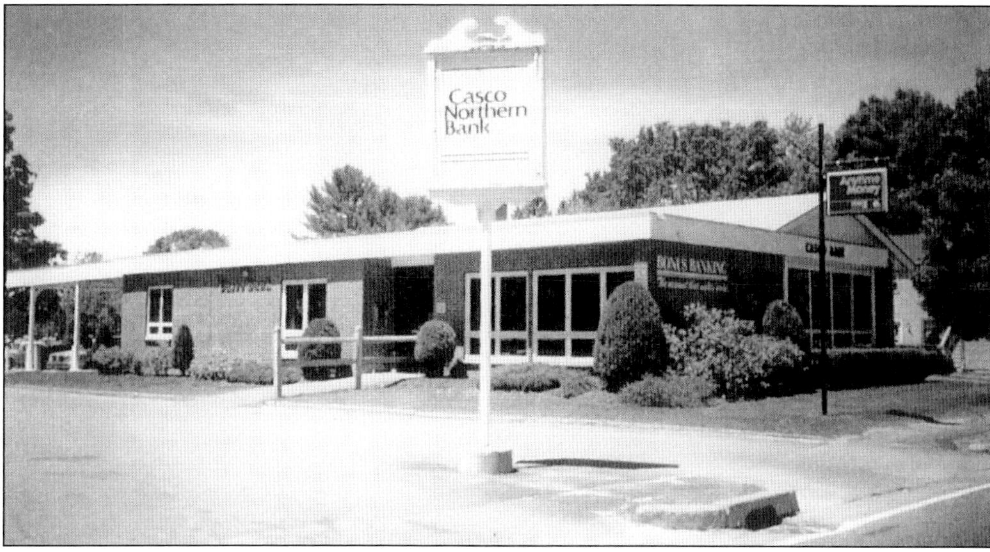

The First Auburn Trust Company opened in Gray on August 6, 1952. It merged with the Casco Bank and Trust in March 1, 1960, and moved to this location on Poland Spring Road in October of 1960. The Key Bank acquired the Casco Bank in February of 1995.

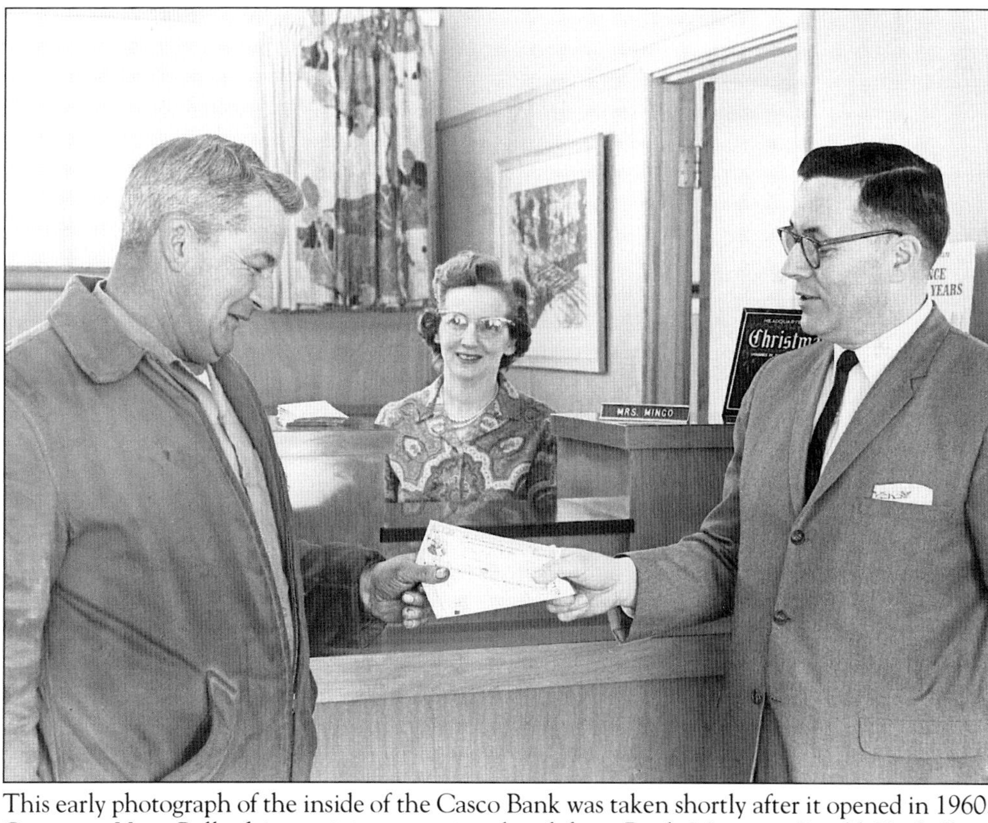

This early photograph of the inside of the Casco Bank was taken shortly after it opened in 1960. Customer Vern Pollard is receiving a savings bond from Bank Manager Gerald Kimball, as Teller Betty Mingo looks on.

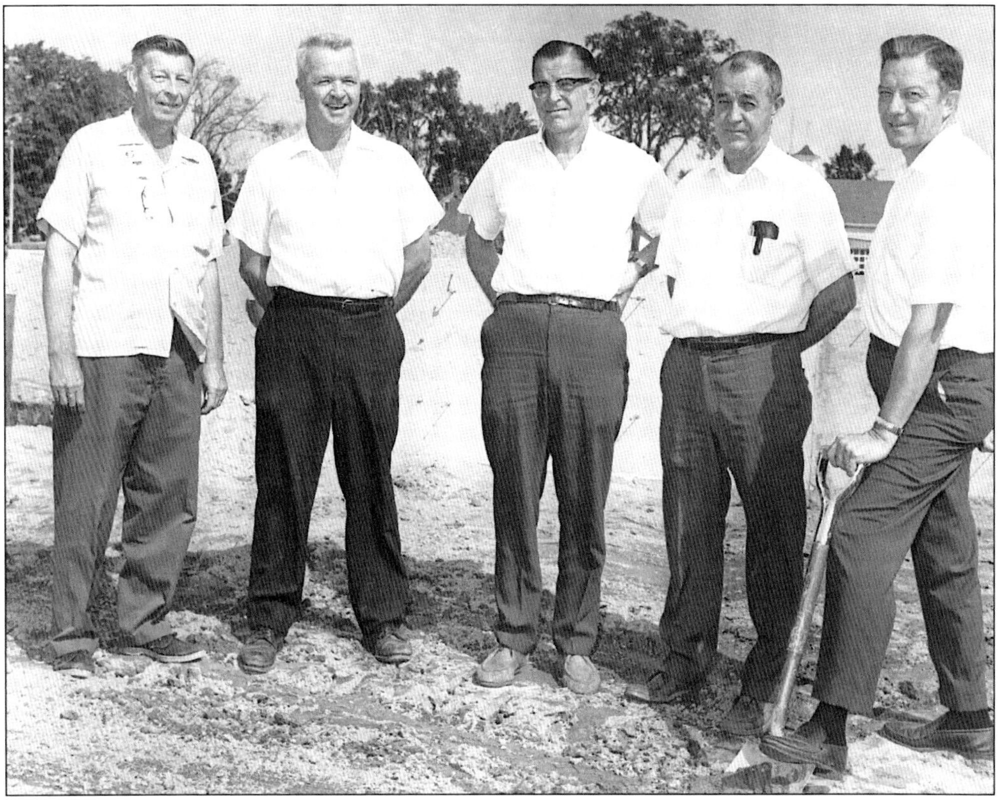

Groundbreaking ceremonies for the first shopping center in Gray took place in July of 1969. Those pictured are, from left to right, First Selectman Jim Morey, Pete Jordan, Stan Sampson, Don Cook, and Phil Cook. This modern shopping center was developed south of the village on the east side of Portland Road.

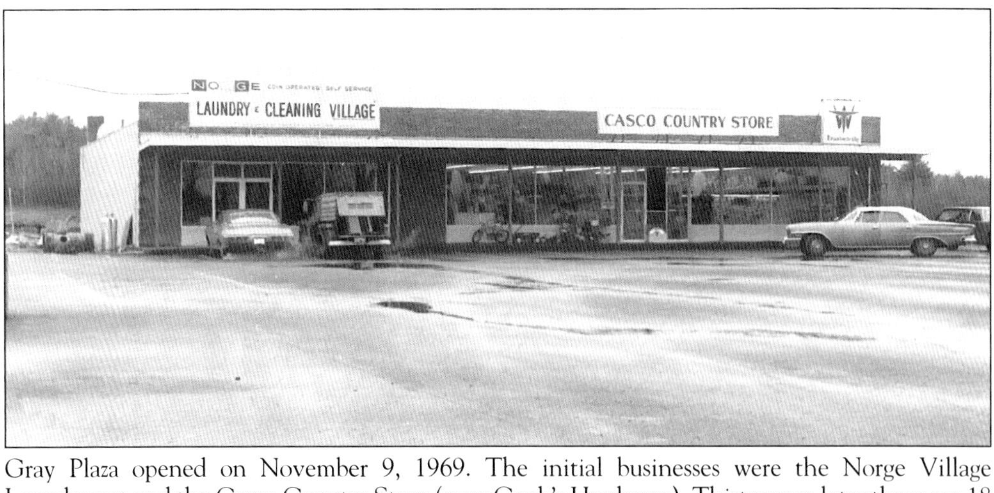

Gray Plaza opened on November 9, 1969. The initial businesses were the Norge Village Laundromat and the Casco Country Store (now Cook's Hardware). Thirty years later there are 18 businesses located in the plaza, providing employment for many people throughout the area.

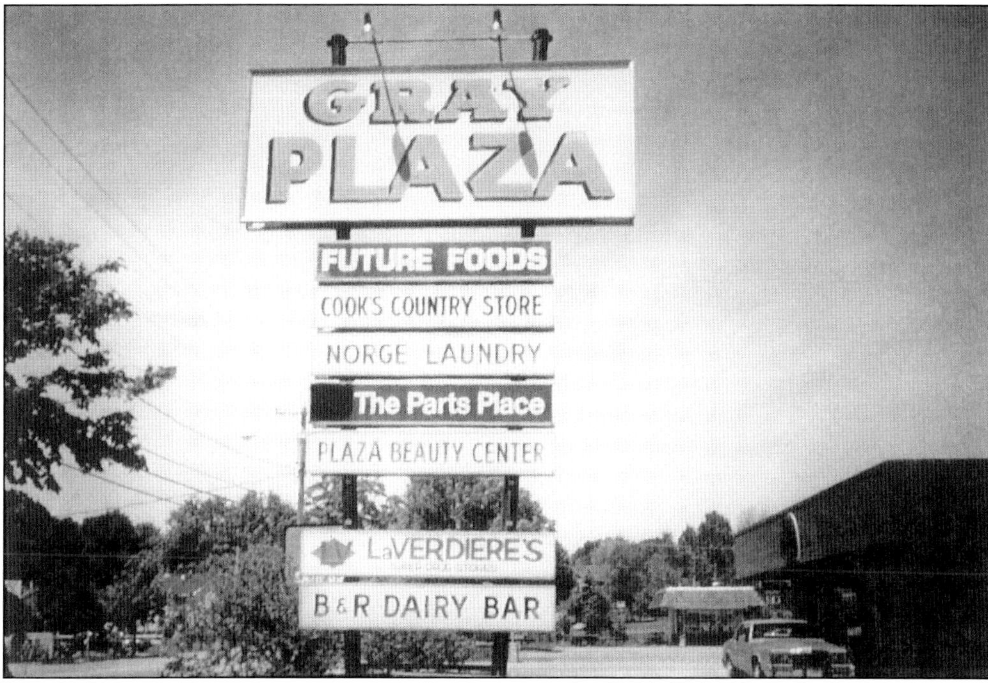

This sign, shown here in the 1980s, was located at the first Gray Plaza. How fast the town has grown, and with such fine services!

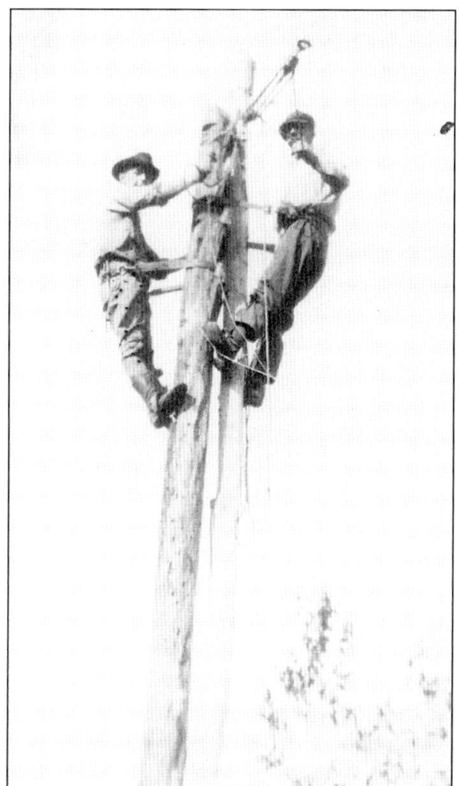

Linemen Victor and Bela Leach replace a broken telephone pole belonging to the Pine Tree Telephone Company in 1919. The first electrical community services came to Gray by 1877, when Maine Central Railroad brought telegraph service to the area. The Maine Central station, however, was located 3 miles from the center of town, which made getting and sending messages difficult. In 1880 a single wire was strung to Hall's Store at Gray Center, making it easier to get and send messages. Three telephone exchanges provided services in different areas in the early 1900s. Today, Pine Tree is the company that services Gray.

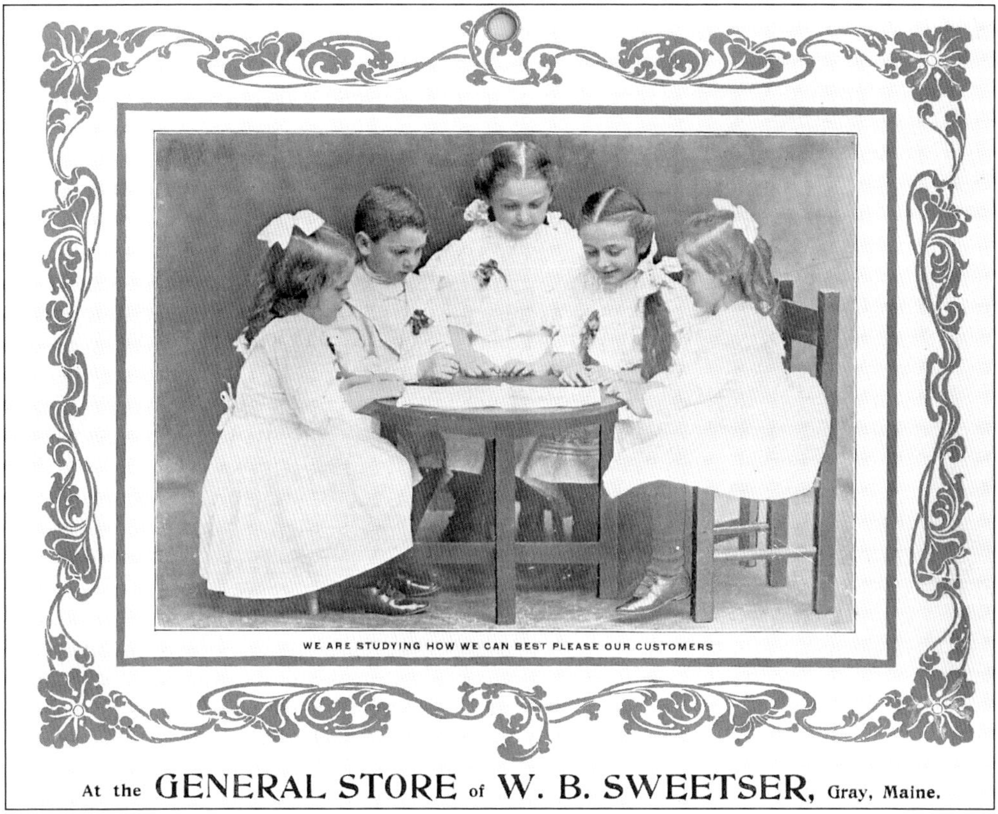

An advertisement for W.B. Sweetser's General Store was placed in a 1909 calendar. Pictured are the children of Will and Nora Sweetser, owners of the store. The little boy is Admiral Willard Sweetser, who now lives on Shaker Road. As the caption under the picture states, "We are studying how we can best please our customers."

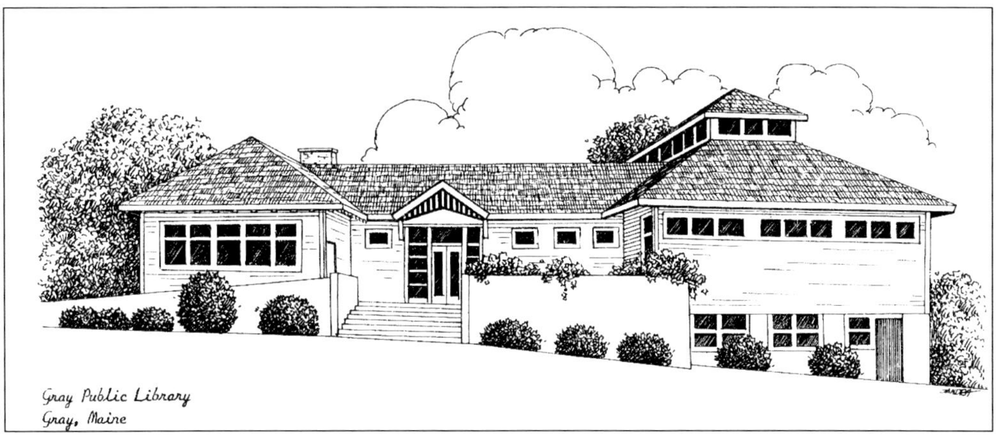

Today the Sweetser children would be able to study at the Gray Public Library at 5 Skillings Street, just off Greenleaf Street. (See p. 20 for an earlier library.) As the town grew in the past 90 years, so did the library outgrow its location several times. In 1977, it was moved to its present location at Hancock School, which was built in 1930. In 1989, the building was expanded to accommodate the collection of 15,000 volumes and over 36,000 items being circulated each year.

Seven

Those Who Served

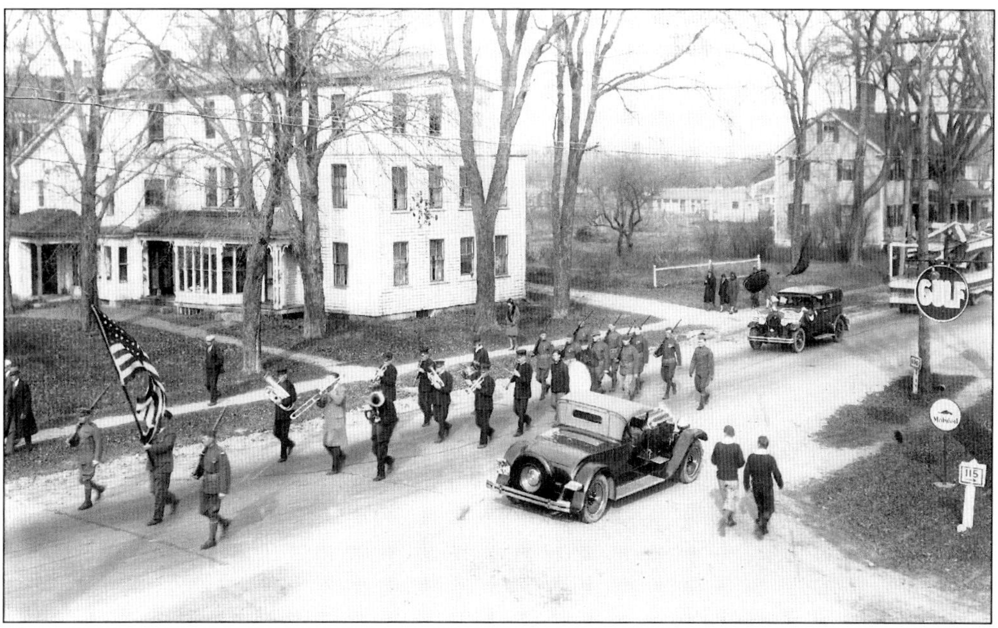

This Armistice Day parade in the 1930s was one of the many parades that the American Legion Post #86 sponsored. The parade is heading south on Main Street. The Osgood House is the large white building (see p. 17) on the left side of the picture. The Gulf sign is located in front of the Lawrence and Leighton Garage (see p. 92).

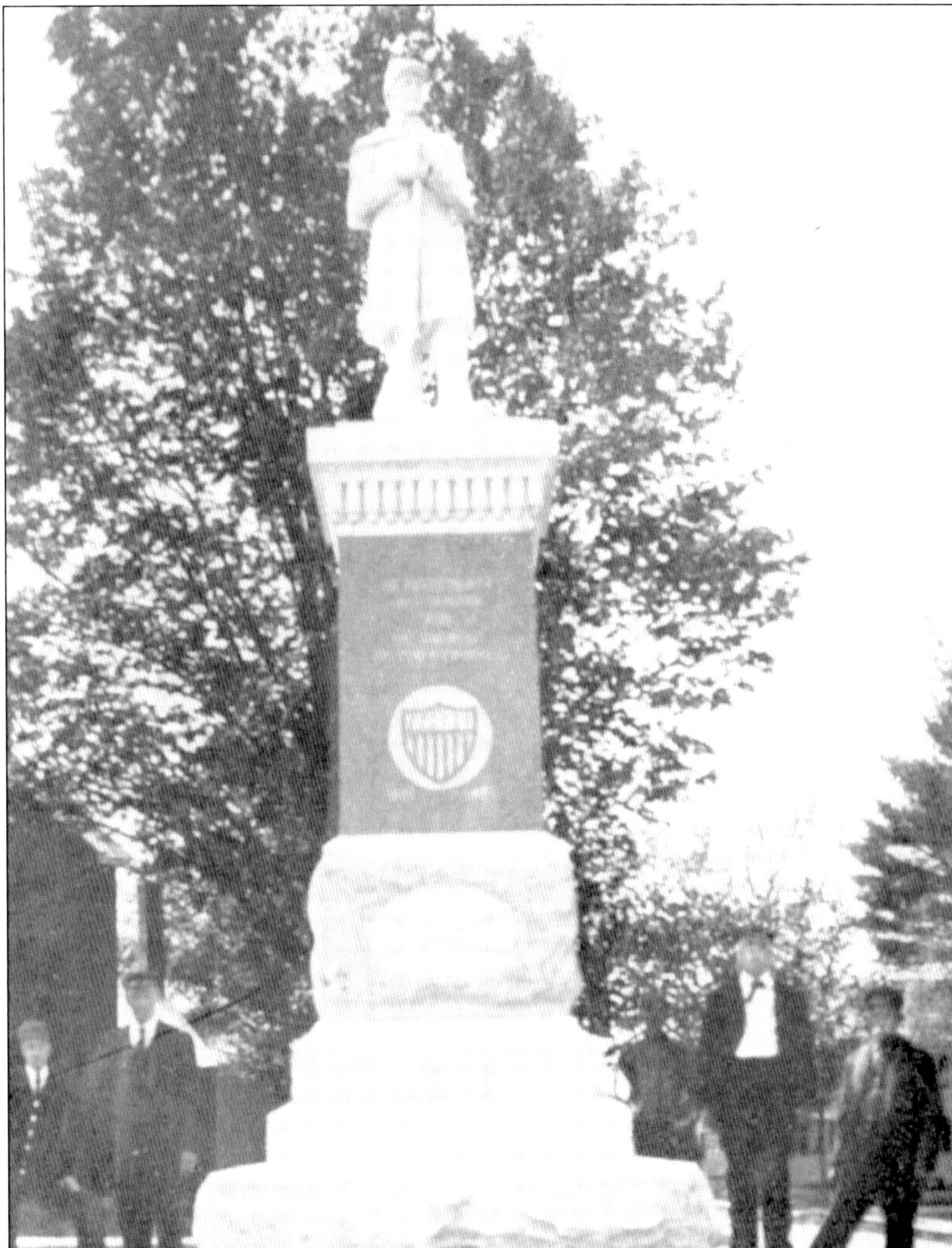

Dedication ceremonies were held June 20, 1911, for the Civil War memorial monument at Gray Corner. Three young girls, Elizabeth Douglass, Marguerite Morrill, and Mary Higgins, unveiled the new monument. The George F. Shepley Post, GAR, of Gray and its auxiliary, the George F. Shepley W.S.R.C. No 39, raised funds for the statue, and the cement foundation was put in place in the fall of 1910. A six-horse team hauled the larger parts of the monument from Auburn during the winter. The Centennial Elm tree, which had stood in this location since 1878, had to be removed. The monument has since been moved twice to its final location on the northwest corner of Routes 26, 100, and 4.

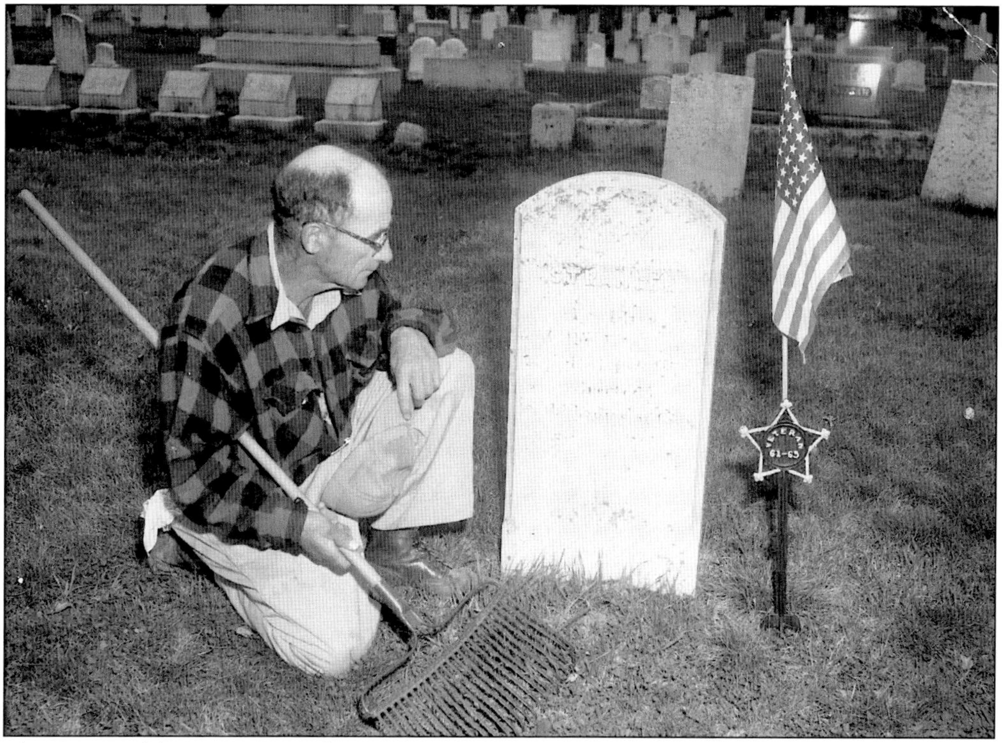

The Grave of the Stranger in the Gray Cemetery marks the resting place of an unknown Confederate soldier. Lt. Charles H. Colley of Gray was killed in the Battle of Cedar Mountain. However, when the casket arrived home, it contained the body of an unknown Confederate soldier. Unable to correct the mistake, the body was buried and a group of women from Gray arranged to have a stone placed on the Confederate soldier's grave. Shortly after, the body of Lt. Colley arrived in Gray and rests in the Colley family lot, not far from the stranger's grave. This picture was taken when Bill Verrill was a sexton of the Gray Cemetery.

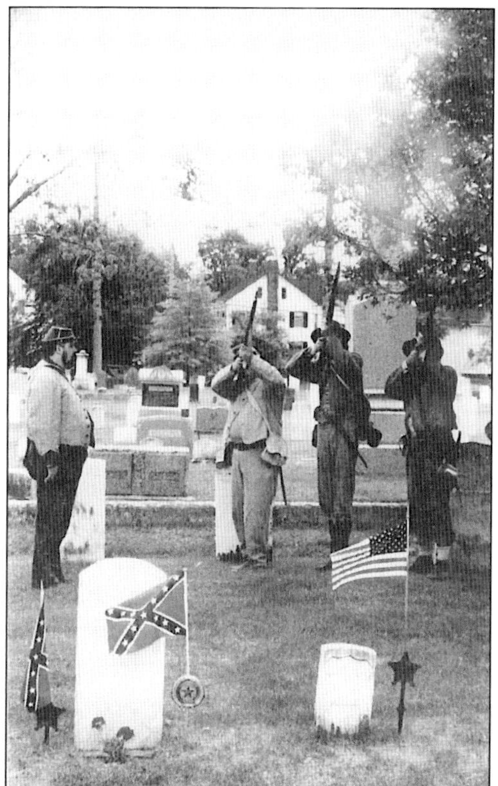

Each year, the town of Gray celebrates Memorial Day with a parade and ceremonies. Gray's unknown soldier is honored by Civil War reenactors with the dignity and respect due to a fallen soldier of the Confederacy. The inscription on his stone reads as follows: "STRANGER: A Soldier of the Late War: Died 1862: Erected by the Ladies of Gray."

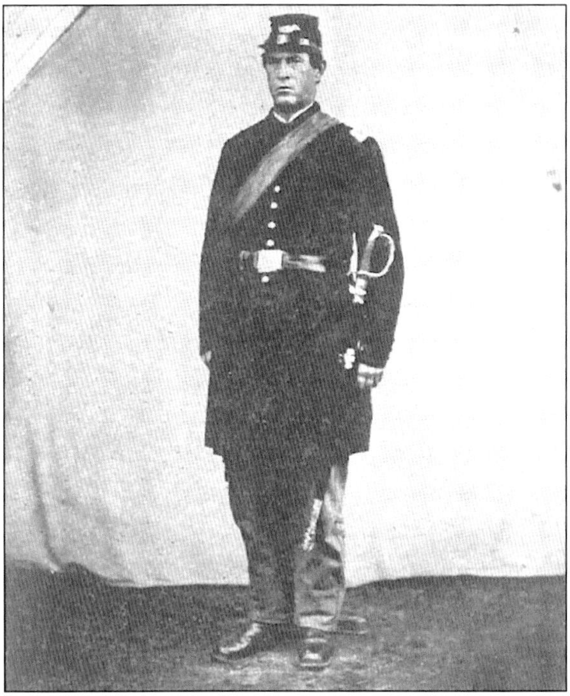

Charles H. Doughty (1822–1891) commanded Company C of the 25th Maine Infantry for a period during the Civil War. Gray sent more soldiers into the Union Army, in proportion to its population, than any other town in Maine. Over one-third of the male population over 18 years of age joined the Union ranks in the Civil War. After the close of the Civil War, Gray was the first town in Maine to pay its Civil War debts. By doing so Gray over-paid its obligations to the state, and the town eventually received a refund of $20,000.

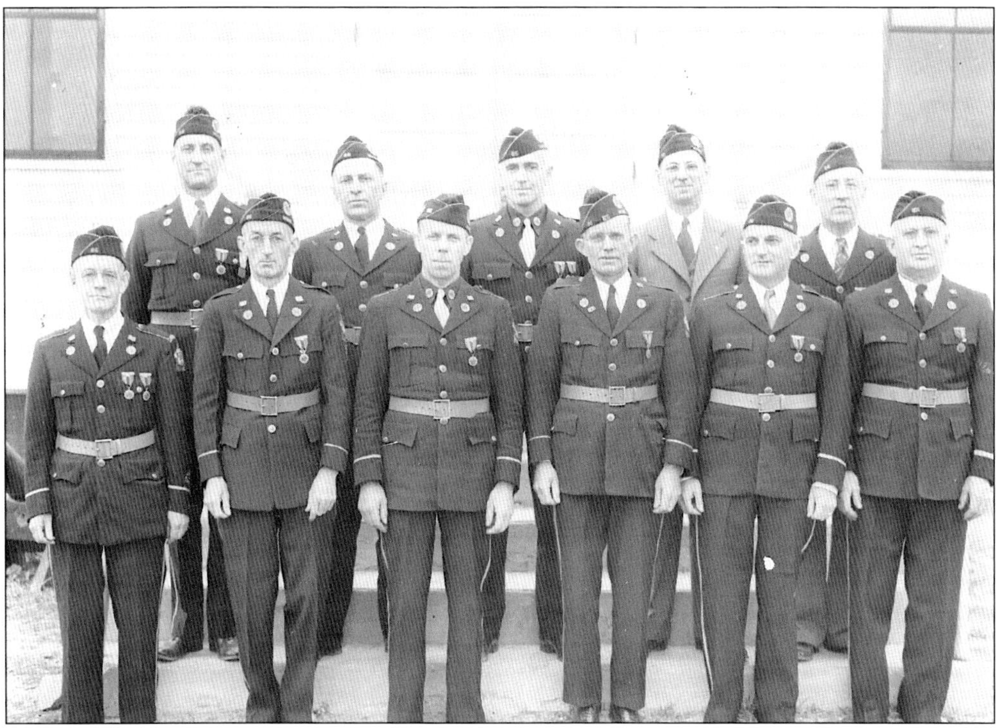

World War I Veterans stand in front of the American Legion Hall. All were members of Post #86. They are, from left to right, as follows: (front row) Arthur Duplisea, Joe Blais, George Maxwell, Earle Wilson, and Walter Leighton; (back row) George Hill, Earle Chase, Harold Ross, Fred Aikens, and Gerald Humphrey.

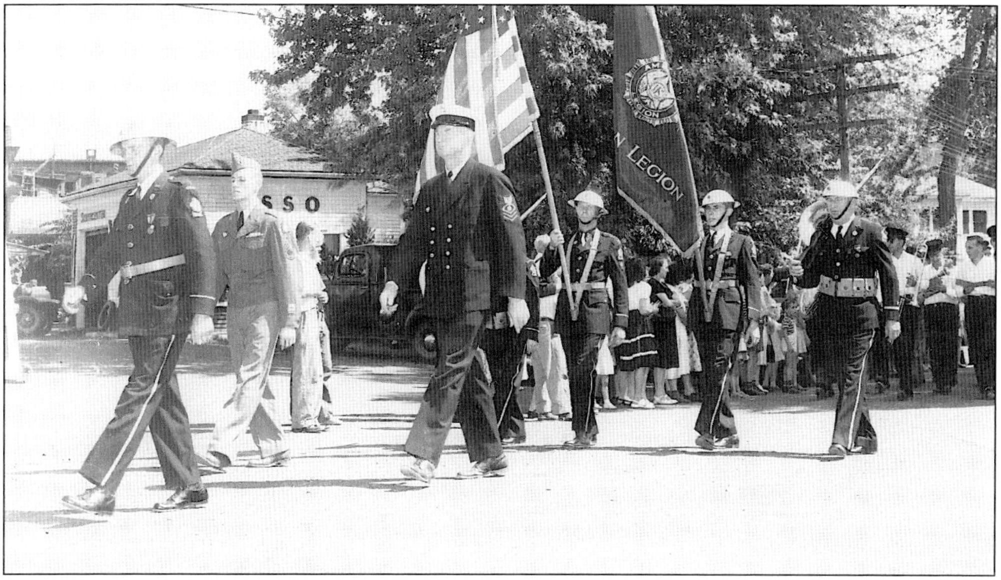

Everybody loves a parade! As town residents line Main Street and Greenleaf Street in 1940s, flags are held high during Memorial Day exercises in honor of Gray's veterans. George Maxwell was the grand marshall for this parade. In uniform are Almond Doggett, Joe Blais, Roger Blais, and Walter (Stub) Leighton.

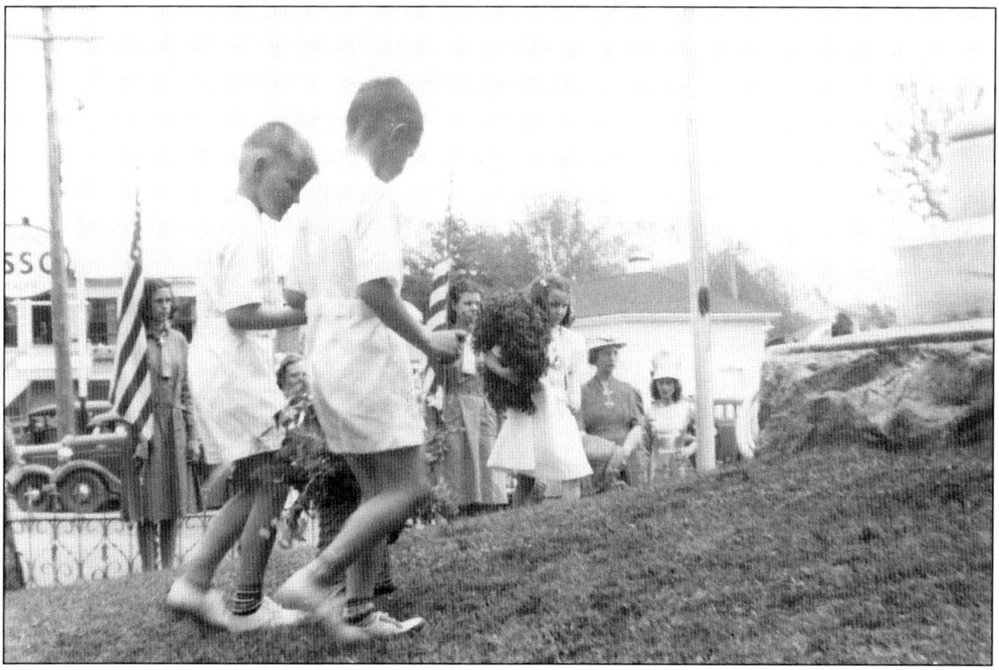

It is believed that Gray was the first town in the United States to hold a memorial service for her dead soldiers. The public service was held in the town hall in October 1865. Every Memorial Day a parade and services are held in honor of the veteran soldiers. A wreath is usually laid at the foot of the Civil War monument and at the Veterans Stone in honor of all veterans. In 1943, Neil Brown and Eugene Leach had the honors of putting the wreath on the monument.

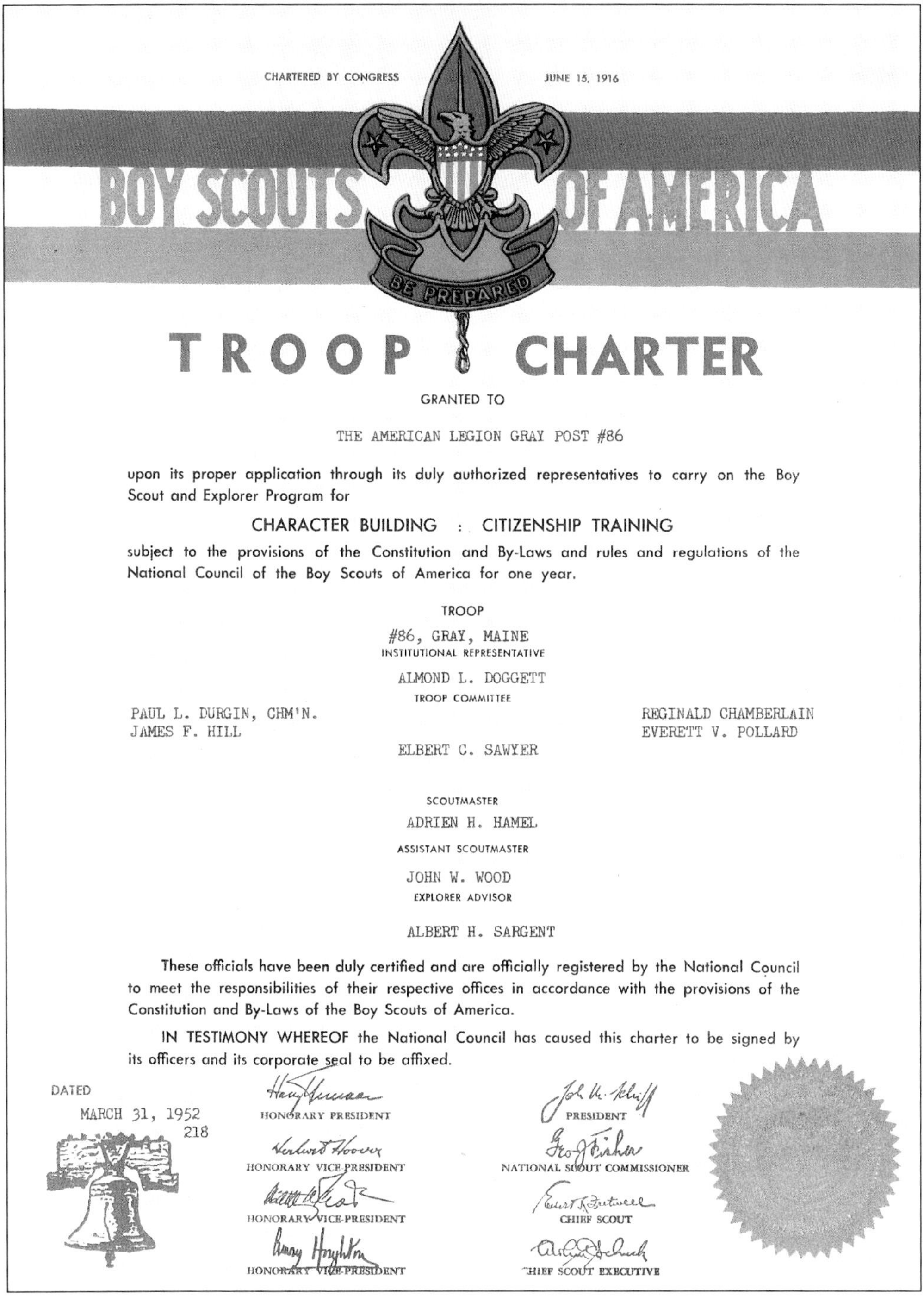

CHARTERED BY CONGRESS JUNE 15, 1916

BOY SCOUTS OF AMERICA

BE PREPARED

TROOP CHARTER

GRANTED TO

THE AMERICAN LEGION GRAY POST #86

upon its proper application through its duly authorized representatives to carry on the Boy Scout and Explorer Program for

CHARACTER BUILDING : CITIZENSHIP TRAINING

subject to the provisions of the Constitution and By-Laws and rules and regulations of the National Council of the Boy Scouts of America for one year.

TROOP

#86, GRAY, MAINE

INSTITUTIONAL REPRESENTATIVE

ALMOND L. DOGGETT

TROOP COMMITTEE

PAUL L. DURGIN, CHM'N.
JAMES F. HILL
ELBERT C. SAWYER
REGINALD CHAMBERLAIN
EVERETT V. POLLARD

SCOUTMASTER

ADRIEN H. HAMEL

ASSISTANT SCOUTMASTER

JOHN W. WOOD

EXPLORER ADVISOR

ALBERT H. SARGENT

These officials have been duly certified and are officially registered by the National Council to meet the responsibilities of their respective offices in accordance with the provisions of the Constitution and By-Laws of the Boy Scouts of America.

IN TESTIMONY WHEREOF the National Council has caused this charter to be signed by its officers and its corporate seal to be affixed.

DATED

MARCH 31, 1952
218

HONORARY PRESIDENT

HONORARY VICE-PRESIDENT

HONORARY VICE-PRESIDENT

HONORARY VICE-PRESIDENT

PRESIDENT

NATIONAL SCOUT COMMISSIONER

CHIEF SCOUT

CHIEF SCOUT EXECUTIVE

American Legion Gray Post #86 chartered Boy Scouts of America Troop #86 on March 31, 1952, a commitment that has been ongoing since then.

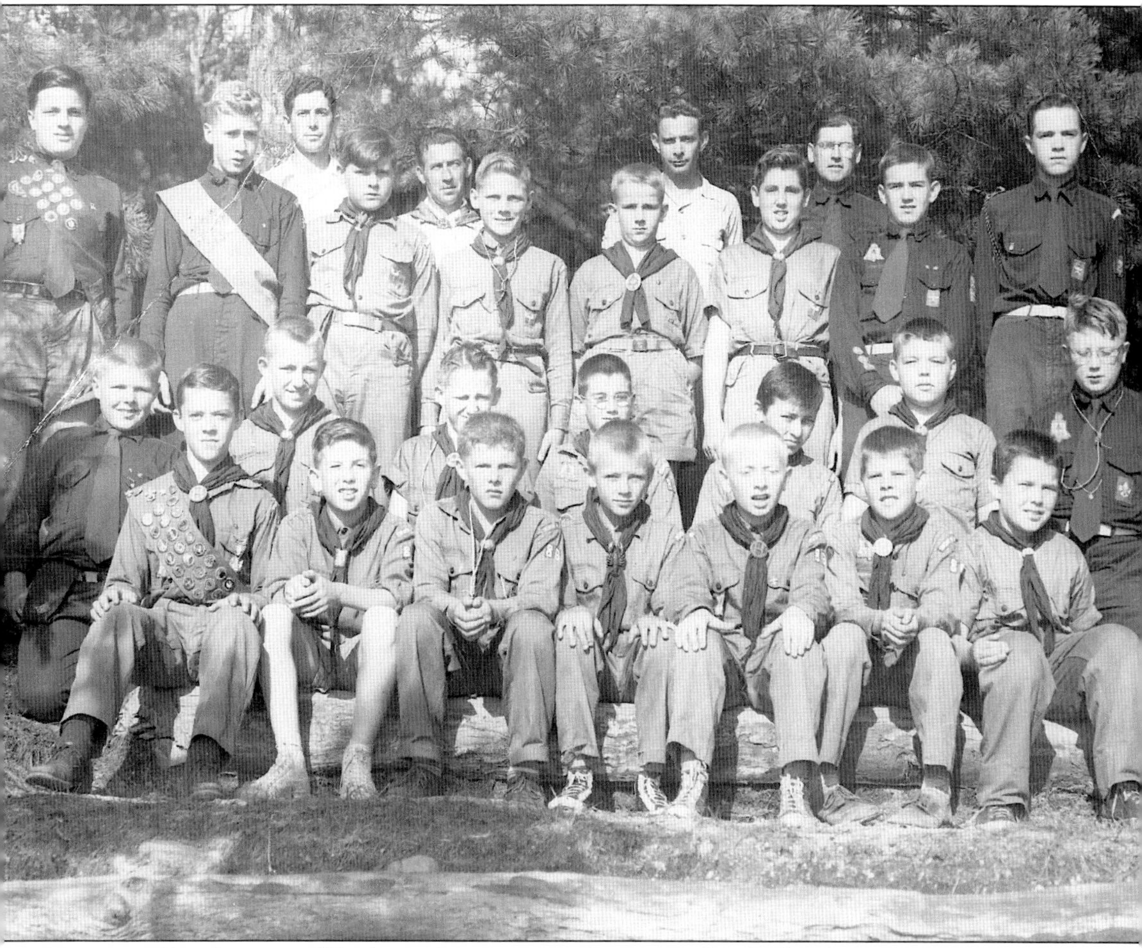

Troop #86 Boy Scouts and Explorers Scouts pose at Camp Hinds, which is located in Raymond, Maine, and serves as a camp for Boy Scouts. During the summer of 1953 the following boys, from left to right, attended camp: (front row) George Durgin, Stanley Liberty, Walter Smith, Ralph Gordon, Paul Doughty, Robert Morrison, and Dennis Durgin; (second row) Philip Smith, Harry Rand, Richard Rand, Steve Conley, Owen Nichols, Vaughan Crandell, and Norman Keene; (third row) Walter Hayes, David Herman, Donald Wallace, William Ayers, Richard Curtis, Brian Preble, David Conley, and Ronald Sawyer; (back row) Assistant Scoutmaster Robert Liberty, Scoutmaster Ray Hamel, Scout Leader Lafayette Wallace, and Scout Leader Martin Conley.

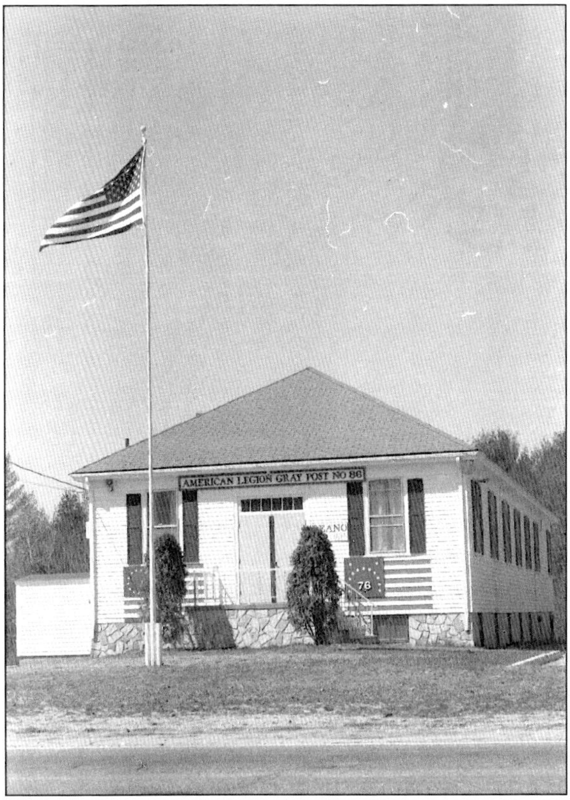

American Legion Post #86 was organized in 1919 and continues to be a very active organization in many worthwhile ways. Leonard B. Tripp was the leading person in establishing Gray Post #86, and he served as its first commander. In 1937, the American Legion Hall Post #86 was dedicated. The building is located on the west side of the Lewiston Road, just north of the village. An addition to the back of the hall and a ramp to allow handicapped people access have been added to the building.

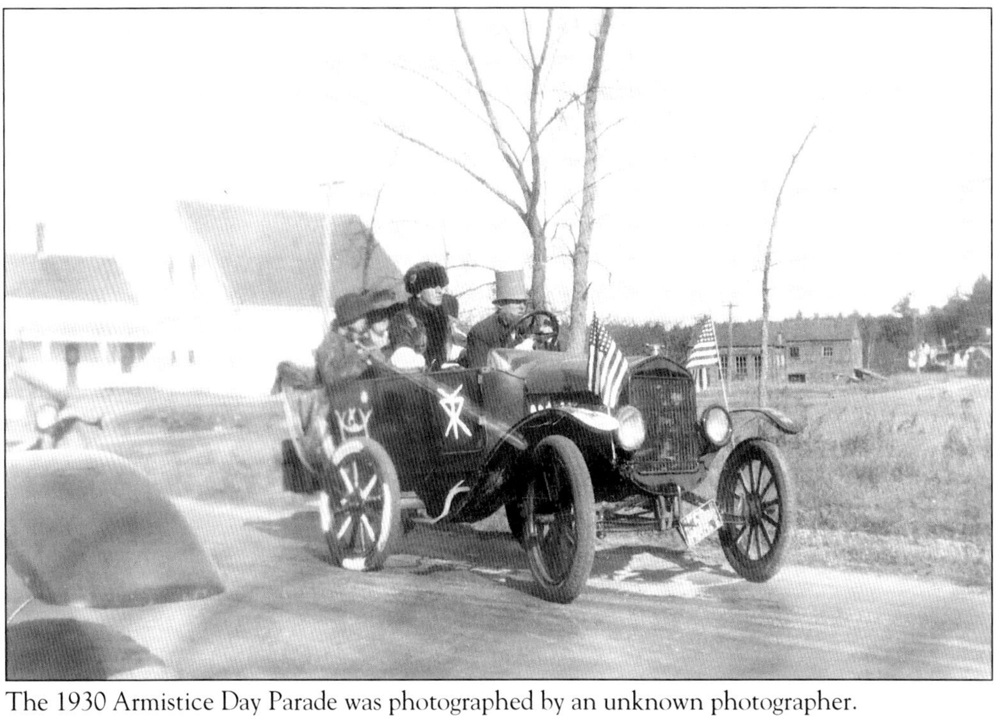

The 1930 Armistice Day Parade was photographed by an unknown photographer.

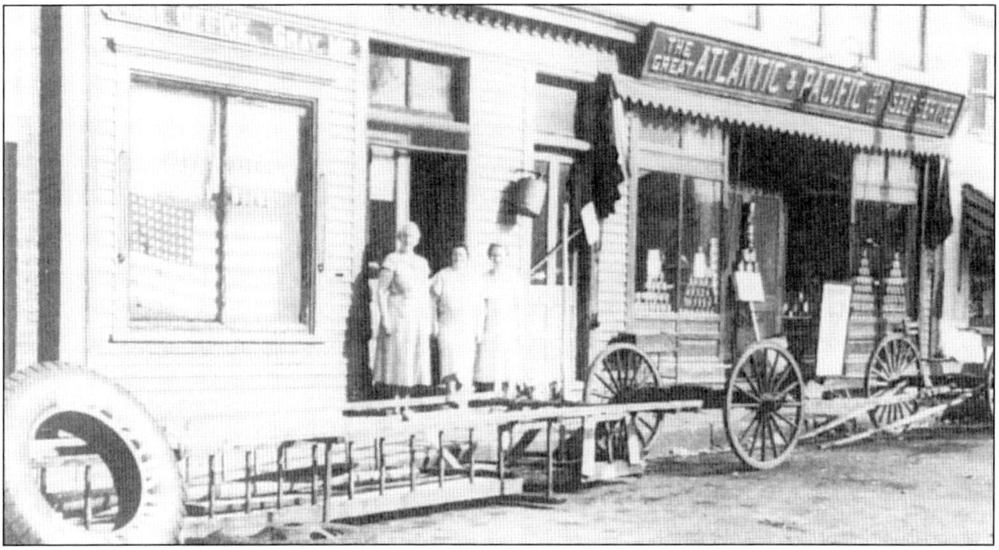

This picture shows the west side of Main Street on the Fourth of July, 1949.

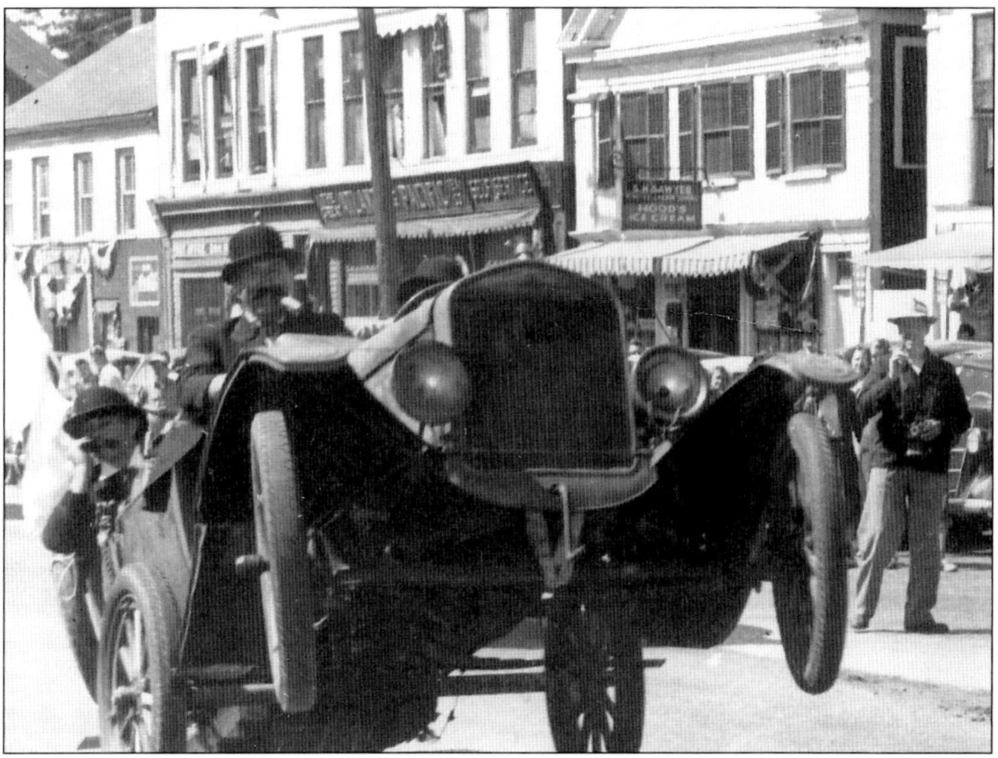

Leaping Lena, a five-wheel automobile shown here *c.* 1930s, was most always in the Old Home Day parade.

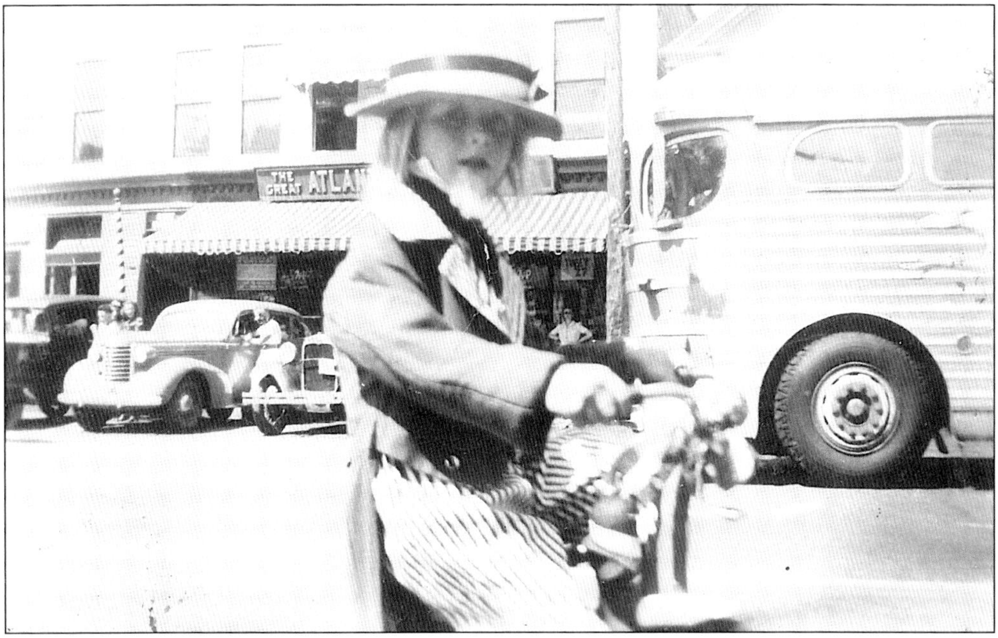

Uncle Sam (a.k.a. John Doughty) was the grand marshall of the Old Home Day parade in 1941. Notice the stores that are located on the west side of Main Street. There is even a barber pole. Susie Sawyer's drug store is located behind the Greyhound bus.

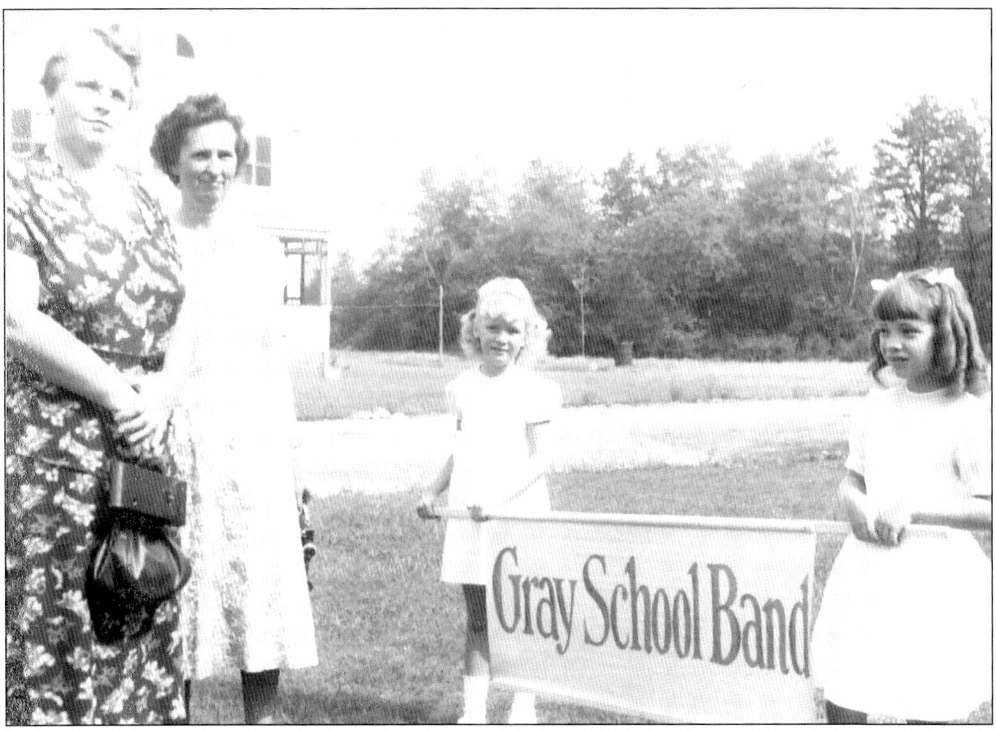

All ready for the parade are Betty Verrill and Carol Smith, holding the Gray School Band banner. It looks like Harriet Humphrey and Mae Beck are waiting for the drum roll.

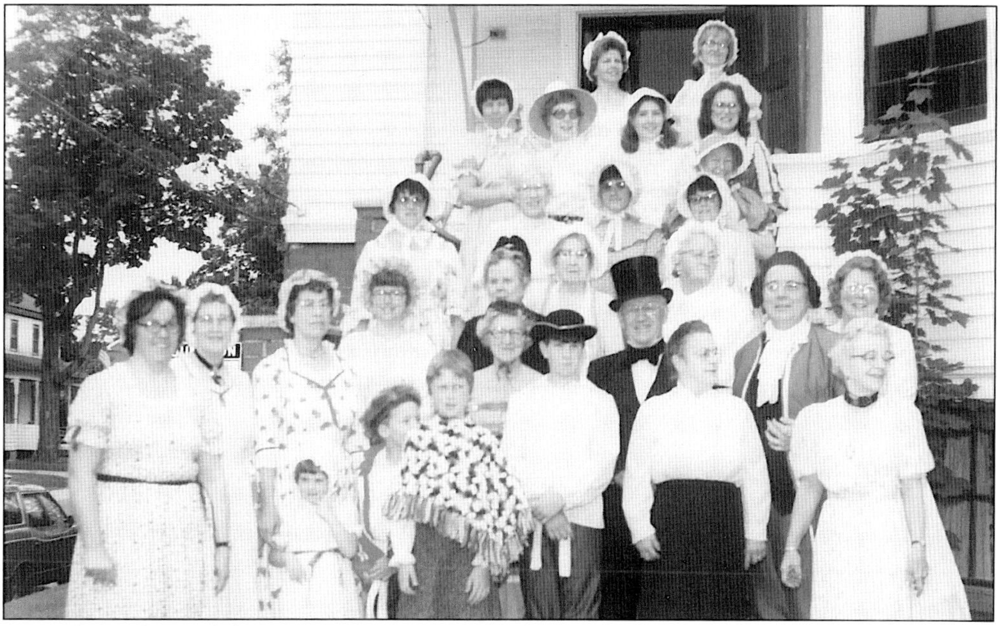

Several members of the First Congregational Church participated in period costume in the Bicentennial celebration. They are shown here on the front steps of the church following morning services.

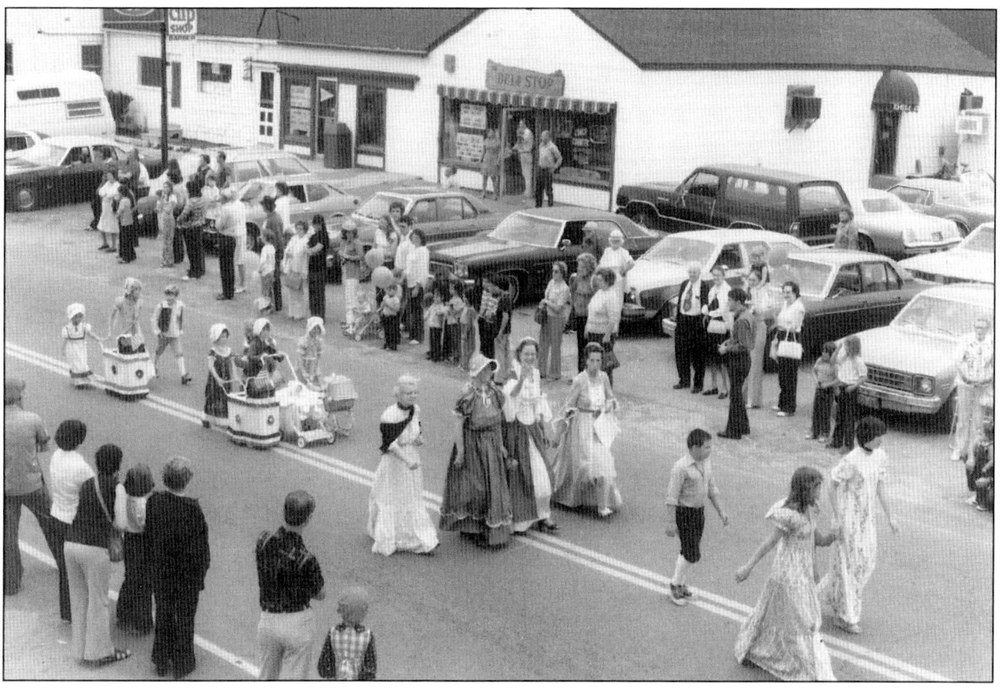

The Bicentennial parade, which took place on Main Street in June of 1976, is pictured on Main Street right in front of today's IGA Store. After it marched to Newbegin Hall, the celebration's concluding ceremonies began, which included cutting the cake, telling the history of the town, displaying a special handmade "Town of Gray" quilt, filling the time capsule, and presenting special awards.

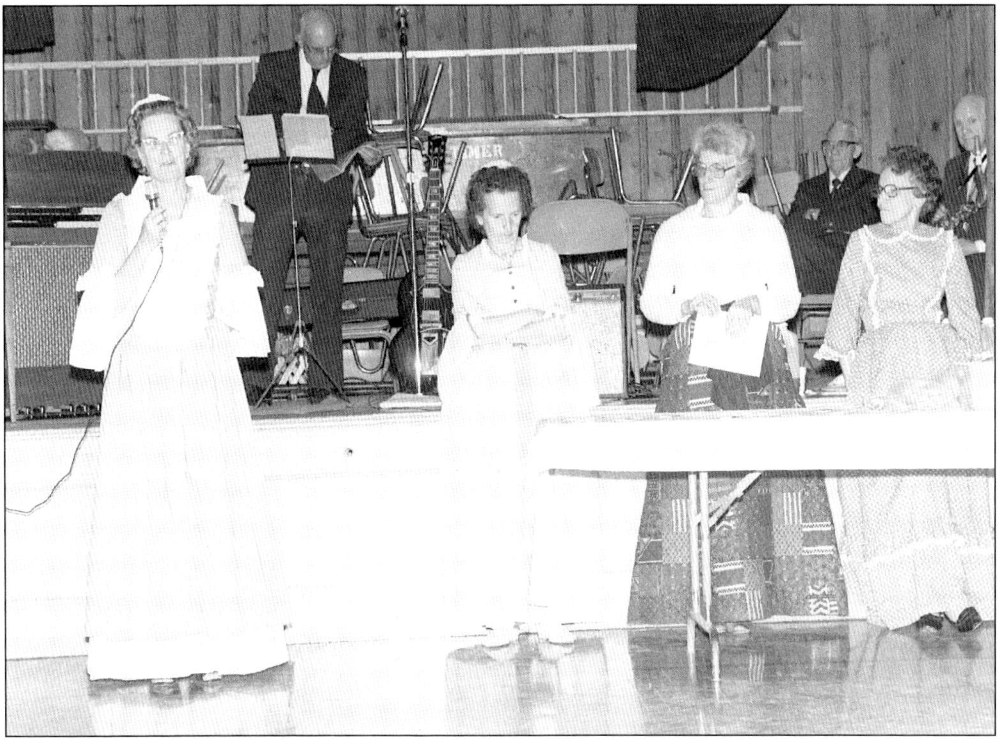

The 1976 Gray Bicentennial Committee consisted of Chairman Mae Beck, Dorothy Heseltine, Margaret Sawyer, and Wayne R. Holmquist. The Advisory Committee consisted of Frederick McCann, Ellen McCann, Albert Doughty, Daisy Doughty, Kenneth Sawyer, Evelyn Sawyer, and William Douglass.

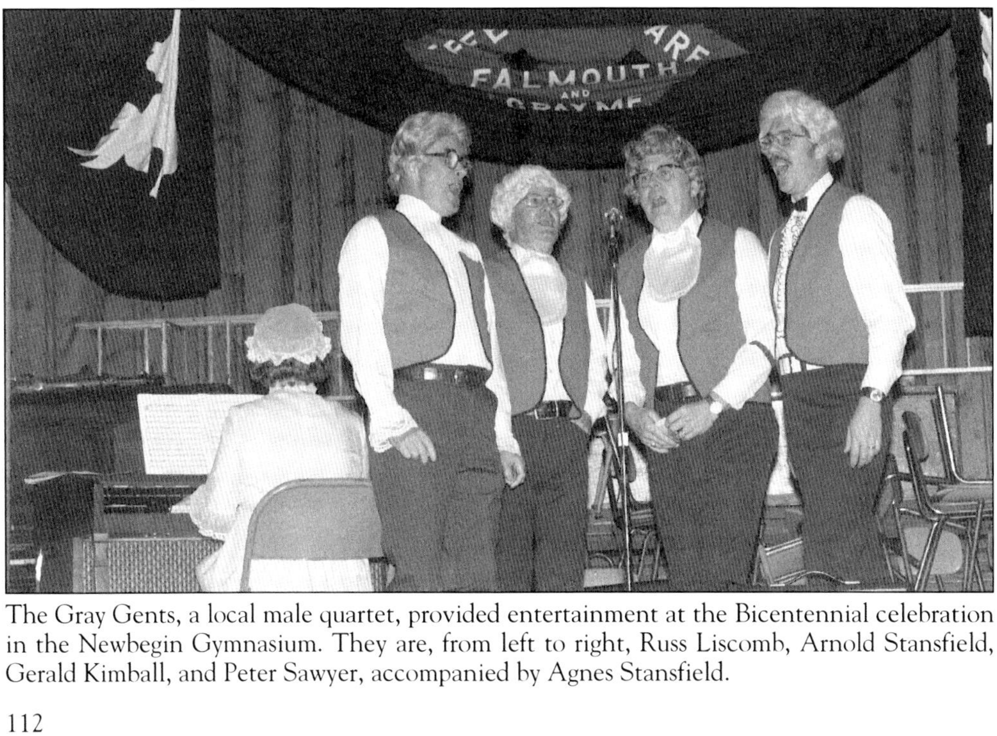

The Gray Gents, a local male quartet, provided entertainment at the Bicentennial celebration in the Newbegin Gymnasium. They are, from left to right, Russ Liscomb, Arnold Stansfield, Gerald Kimball, and Peter Sawyer, accompanied by Agnes Stansfield.

Eight

PEOPLE TO REMEMBER

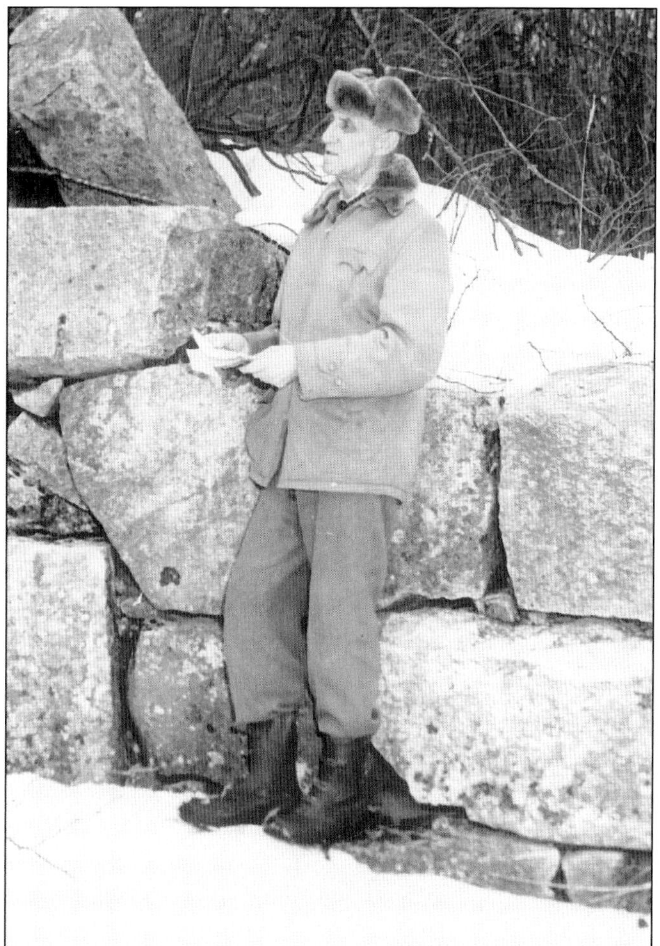

George T. Hill (1891–1978) was born in Gray, attended local schools, and graduated from Pennell Institute. He served in World War I and was employed as a mailman. Long before there was a Gray Historical Society, he began accumulating valuable information about the town, and was considered "the historian." All one had to do when information was needed about Gray was to ask George. He maintained inexhaustible files on every aspect of local history, and when the Gray Historical Society was formed in 1960, he was the origin and source upon which to rely. A master of anecdote, quick to see humor in any situation, George was also the author of *History, Record, and Recollections of Gray, Maine*, which covers Gray history from 1735 to the early 1900s.

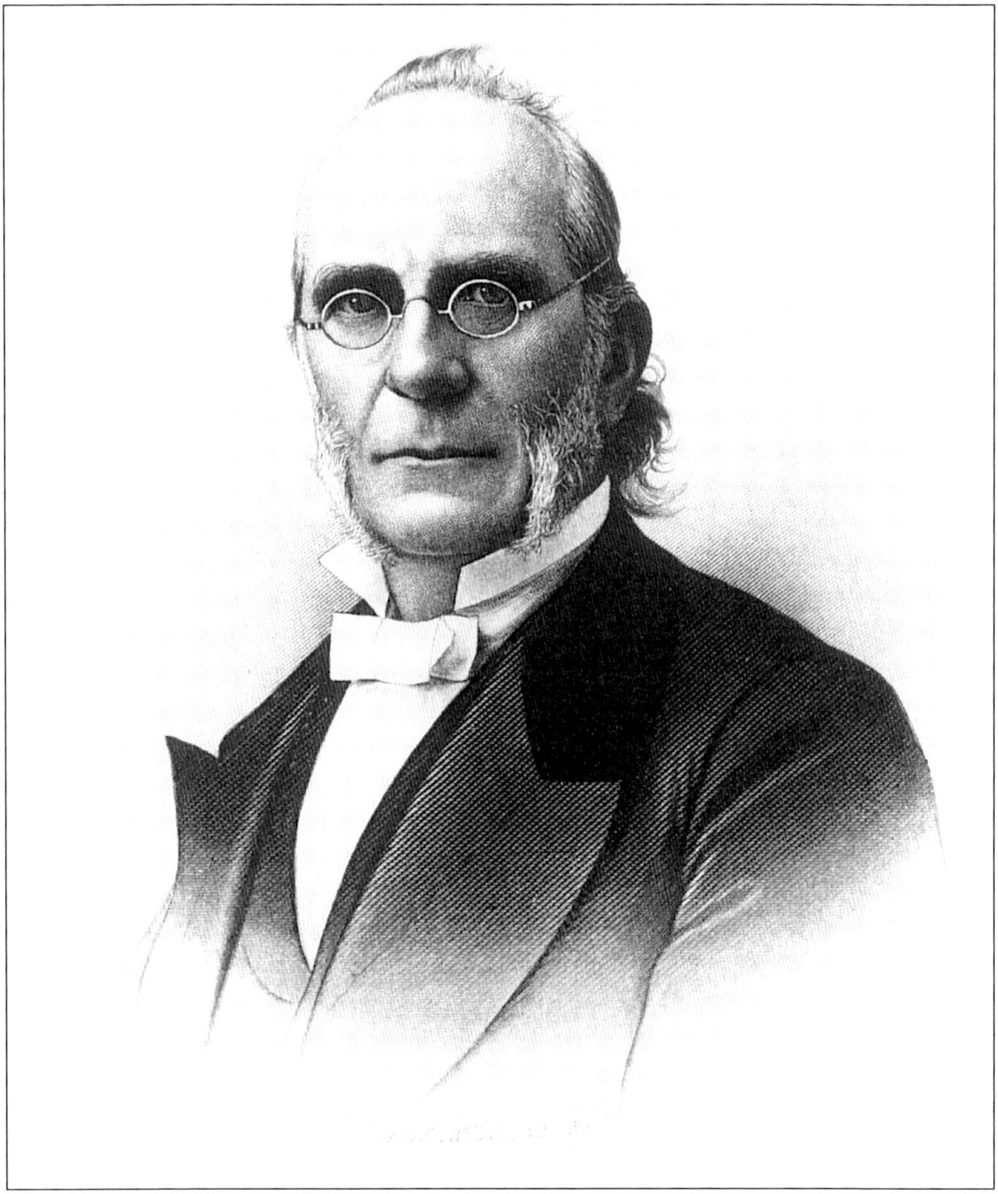

Samuel Mayall II, the son of the founder of Mayall Woolen Mills, was born June 21, 1816. He and his brother John served as Maine state senators, and Samuel II later became a member of Congress. He was an active abolitionist, a friend of Lincoln, and a Whig who helped establish the new Republican party. When he returned to Gray he opened the Mayall Woolen Bank of Gray at the town's center. Behind it, in the Gray Village Cemetery, he had the Mayall family monument erected.

When the financial panic of 1856 erupted, Samuel left to join his younger brother, James Herschel Mayall, in the newly emerging city of St. Paul, Minnesota. It is said that they saved St. Paul in that crisis, perhaps partly due to their use of bank notes issued by the Mayall Woolen Bank of Gray. The two brothers became influential businessmen in the St. Paul area, and earned a place of distinction in St. Paul's history. Samuel II served in the Civil War, then spent the rest of his life in Minnesota.

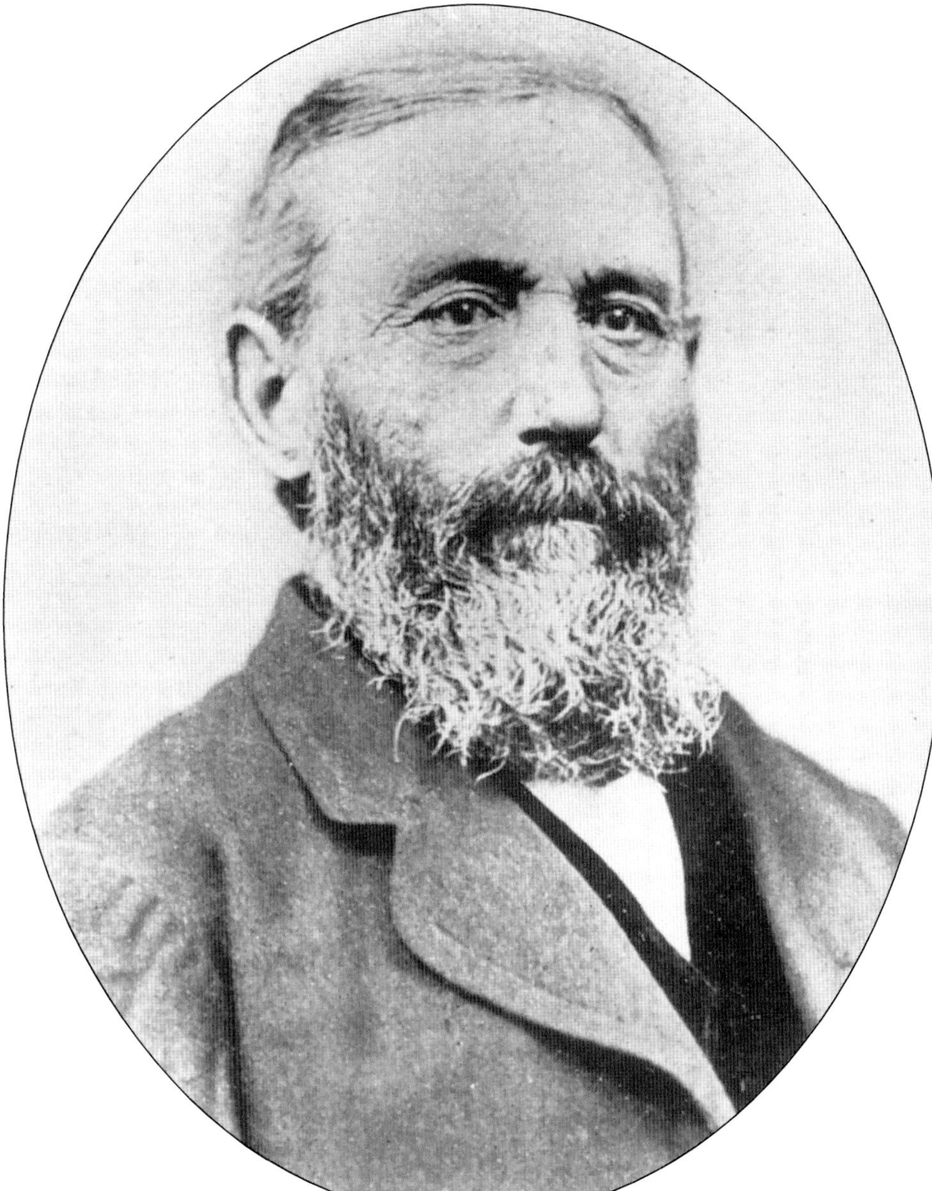

Henry Pennell was born on January 6, 1803, in Danville, Maine. He was adopted by Stephen and Rebecca Pennell, who lived at the South Gray end of the Dutton Hill Road. Henry was educated in the schools of Gray, which at that time provided a very meager education. He started in business as a butcher, later becoming a cattle drover, buying and selling cattle and sheep. He married Mary Susan Weston of Gray on November 19, 1832. Mr. and Mrs. Pennell adopted a daughter, Susan A. Humphrey, a niece of Mrs. Pennell. Henry enlisted in the Army during the Civil War and was mustered out with the rank of major. Returning to Gray, he dealt in real estate and mortgages, was sheriff of Cumberland County (1857–58), and served in the state senate (1872–73). He built the main building of Pennell Institute in 1876. After Mrs. Pennell died in 1881, Henry moved to Portland, Maine, and lived there until his death in 1884. In his will he left Pennell Institute, with a trust fund for its support, to the town of Gray.

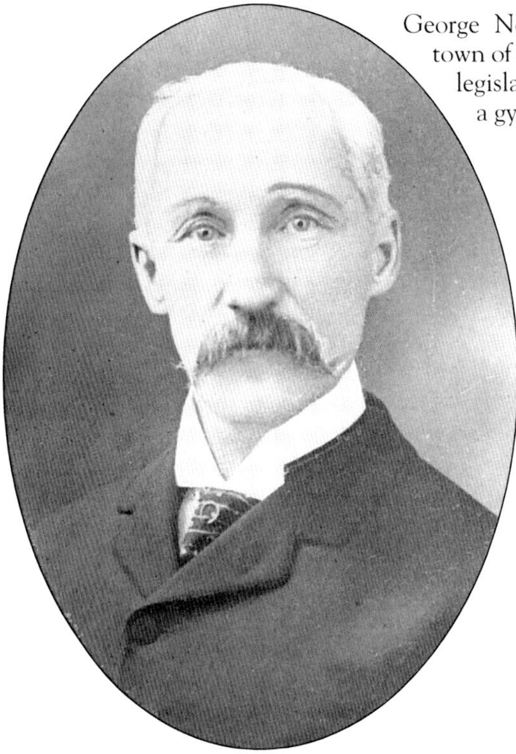

George Newbegin (1848–1936) was treasurer of the town of Gray in 1909 and a representative to the state legislature in 1905. In his will he left money to have a gymnasium built.

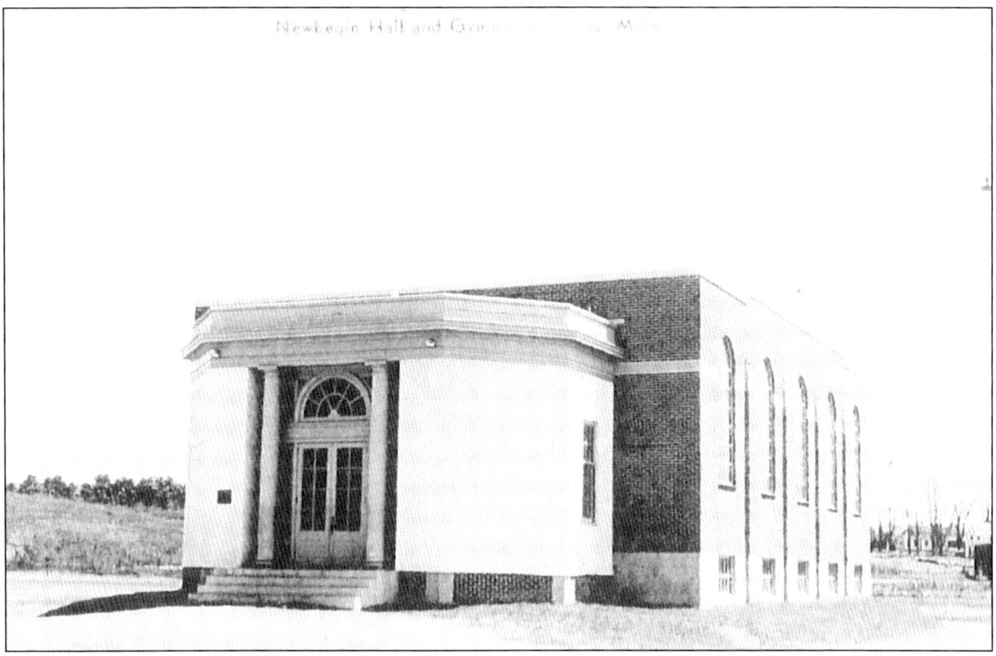

Newbegin Gymnasium was built in 1937 with money given by George Newbegin. It was located on the Pennell Institute grounds. Perley Sawyer and Pennell Alumni gave the land for the building. Today, Newbegin is utilized for a wide variety of sports and community events. It is the center for the parks and recreation department.

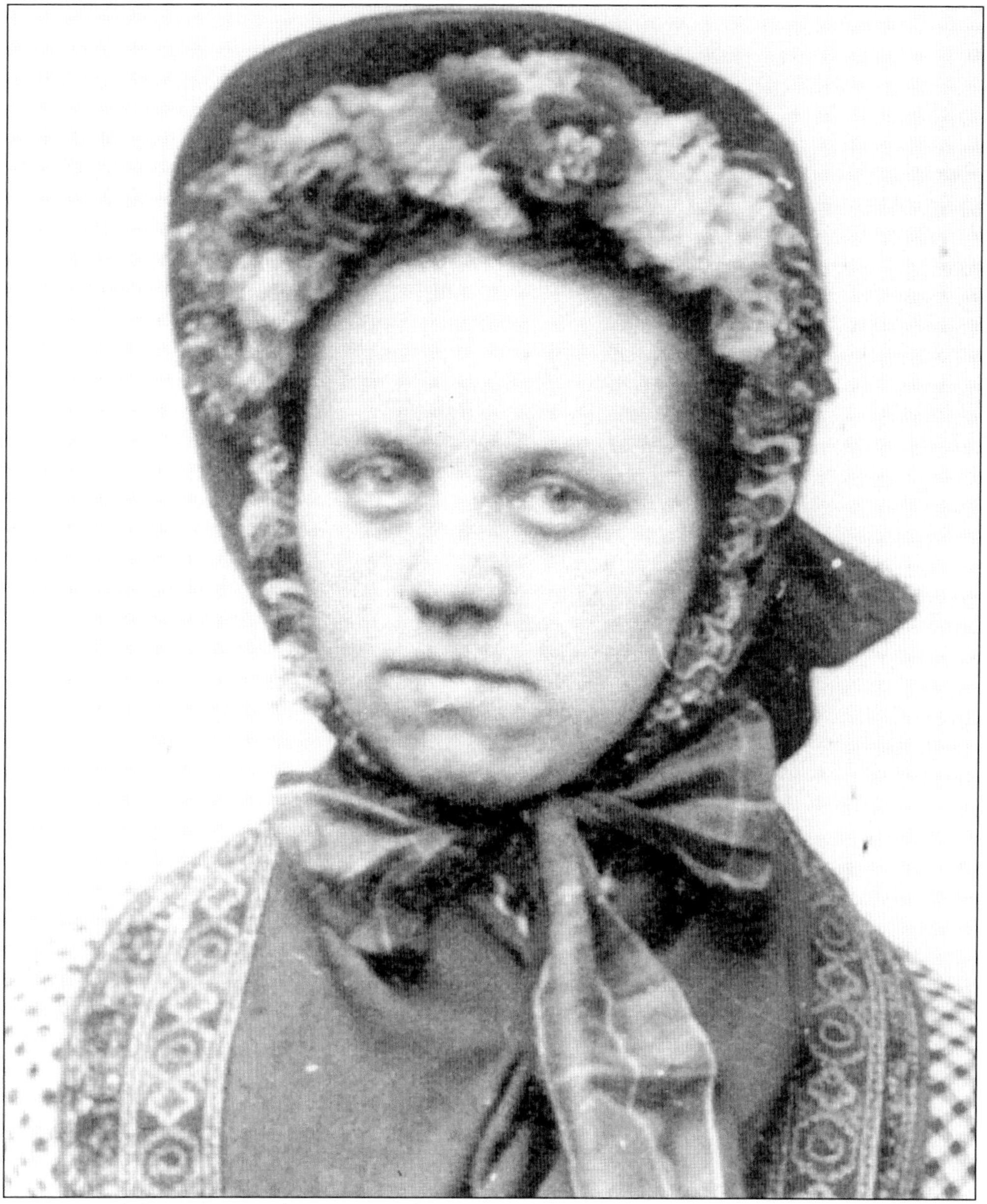

Young Sarah Jane Foster of Gray was a heroine of the post-Civil War period. The daughter of Moses B. and Eliza A. Benson Foster, she was born October 12, 1839, and was raised in Gray. Their home stood beside the Old Brick School on Church Street, now Shaker Road. In 1865, under the auspices of the Free Will Baptist Home Mission Society, she left for West Virginia, where she became a dedicated teacher and friend of the newly freed men and boys. Facing many difficulties, she continued this work in Charleston, S.C. in 1867 and 1868 with the American Missionary Association. Sarah was also a writer and poet whose work was published in newspapers and magazines. Her career was cut short in June 1868 at the age of 28, when she returned to Gray with a fatal case of yellow fever. Some of her diaries, letters, stories, and poems are contained in the book *Sarah Jane Foster, Teacher of the Freedmen*, edited by Wayne E. Reilly, published by the University Press of Virginia in 1990. (Photograph courtesy Wayne E. Reilly.)

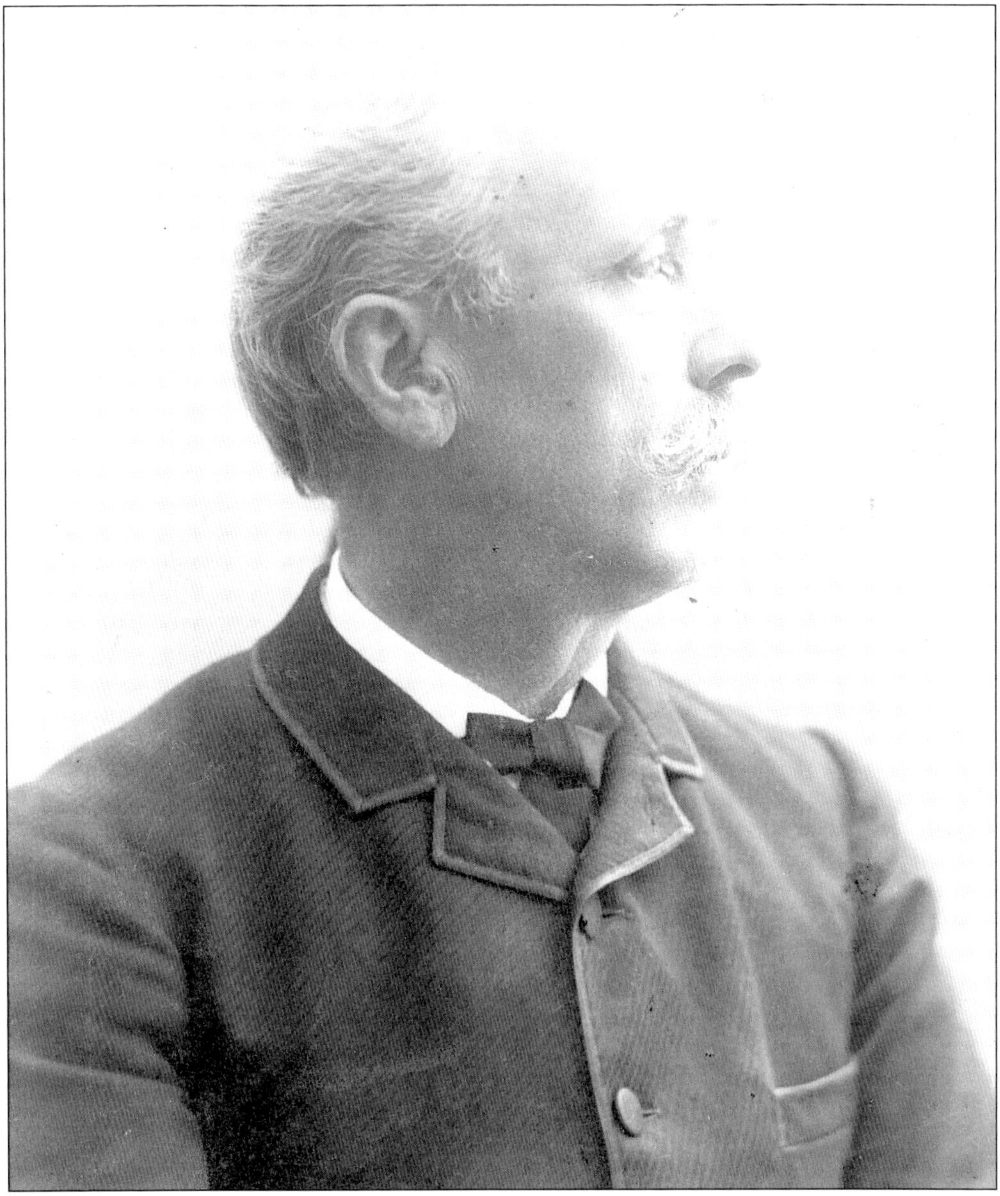

Major John D. Anderson was born in the early to mid-1800s, the son of Abraham and Lucy (Smith) Anderson. He attended Gorham Academy and Yarmouth Institute prior to entering Bowdoin College, where he graduated in 1859. He taught school in Georgia and Wisconsin before enlisting in the 1st Wisconsin Battery and serving as a first lieutenant in the Cumberland Gap and Ohio River Campaigns. He was in the 32nd Maine Infantry and was wounded in the Burnside Mine assault. After the war he returned to Gray, where he taught school, practiced law, and sold insurance. In March of 1869 he married Anna S. Thayer of Gray, and they had six children. From 1873 until he died in 1924, he was an attorney, a representative to the state legislature, a U.S. pension agent for Maine, treasurer of the eastern branch of the Soldier's Home at Togus, Maine, and a lawyer and town official in Gray. He was also active in the GAR and was its state department commander in 1890. Major John Anderson also served as town moderator for more than 25 years.

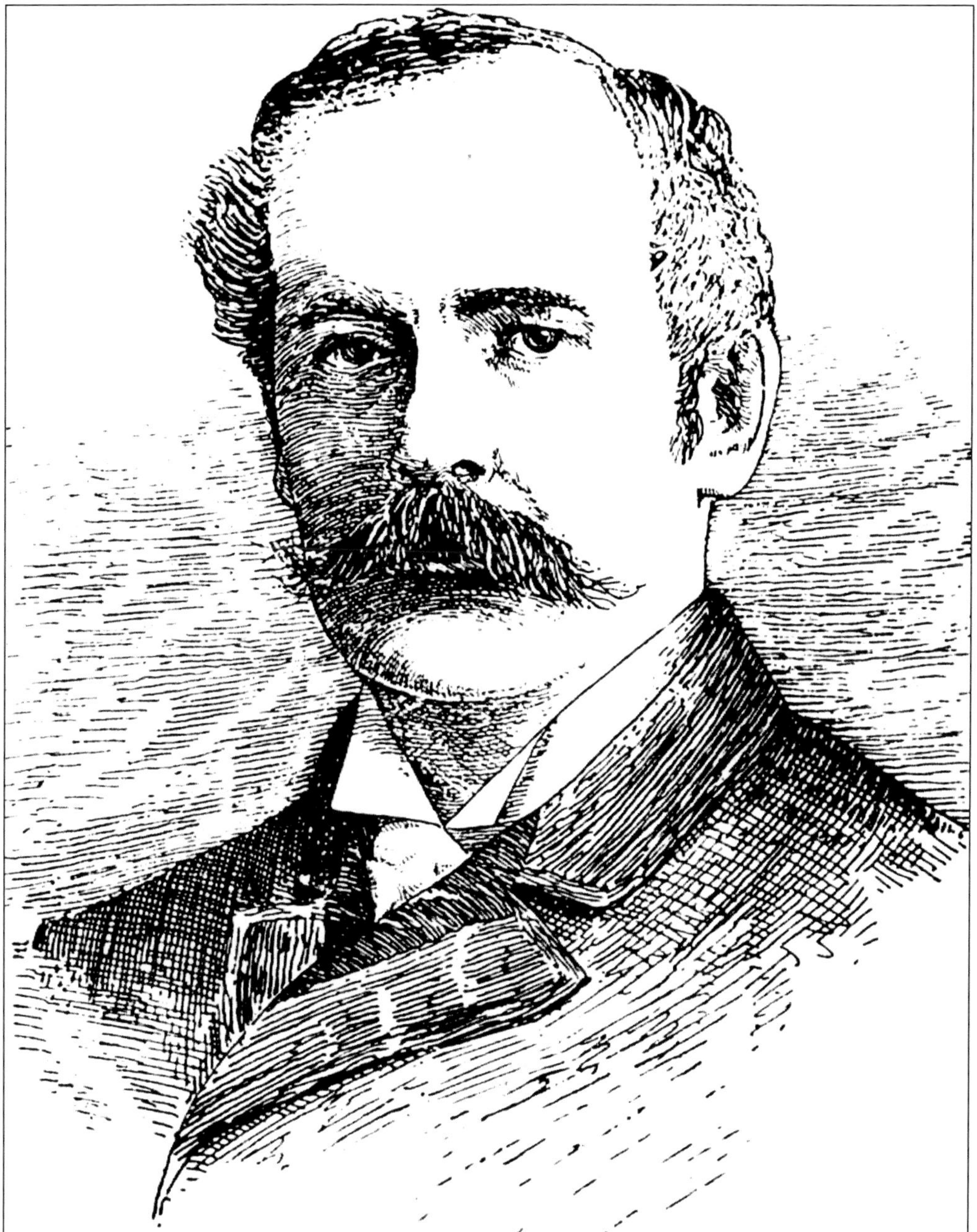

Artist N.W. Scott Leighton was born in 1847 in Auburn, Maine, but his parents, Nicholas and Deborah Whitney Leighton, soon settled in Gray, where he grew up. As a boy he showed a passion for horses and a largely unappreciated talent for drawing. With money earned from horse trading, he persisted and at age 17 moved to Portland, where he studied painting under the city's leading landscape painter of the time, Harrison Bird Brown. Leighton eventually moved to Boston, and his portraits of race horses became very popular, as horses were still an important part of the daily scene at the time. His home became a gathering place for horse enthusiasts. Leighton's animal pictures were reproduced by several firms, but he became most widely known for the *Currier & Ives* lithographs of his work.

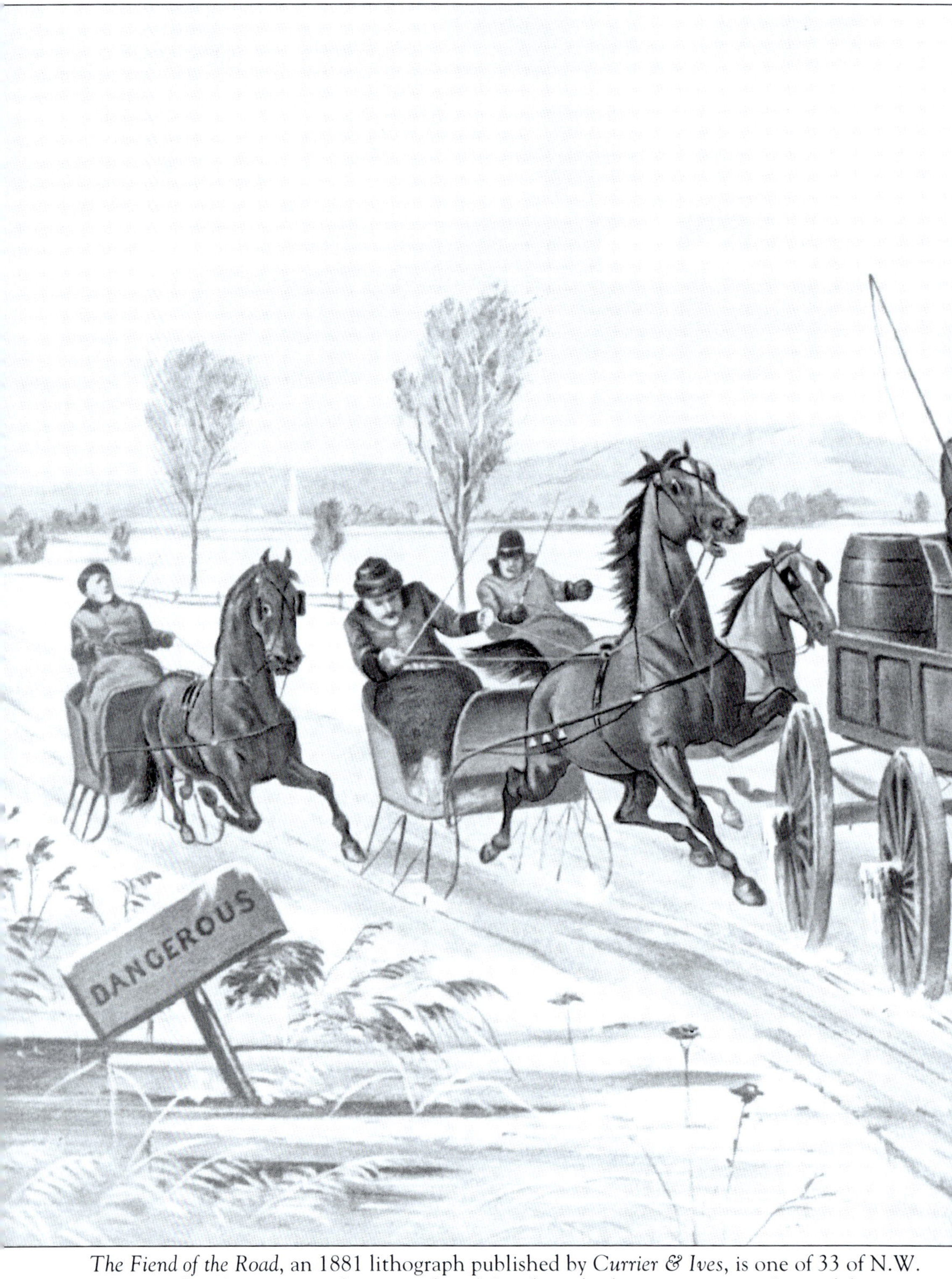

The Fiend of the Road, an 1881 lithograph published by *Currier & Ives*, is one of 33 of N.W. Scott Leighton's paintings they reproduced. Leighton built a reputation as "one of the most

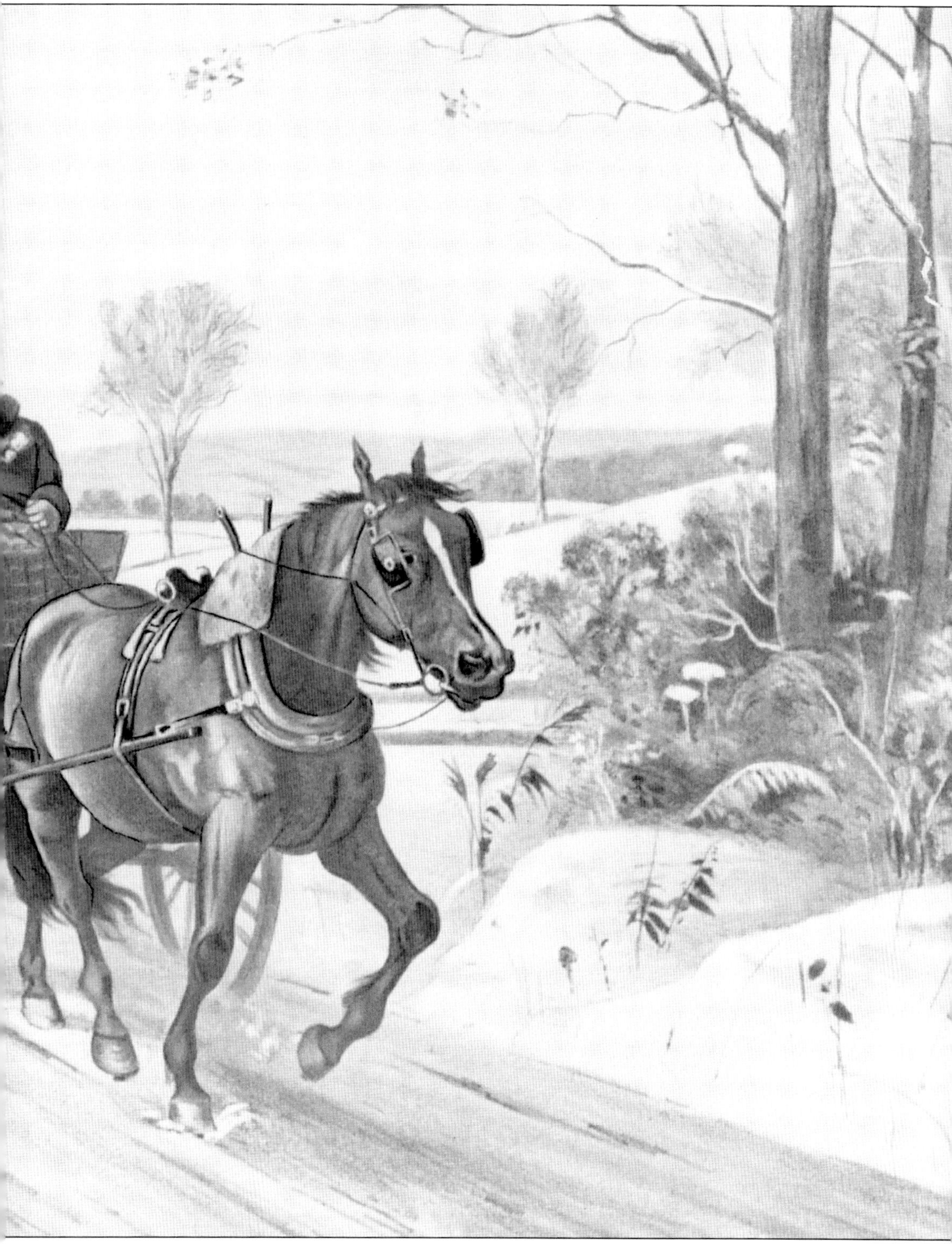

famous animal painters of the day," as stated in his obituary in the *The Boston Transcript* of January 18, 1898.

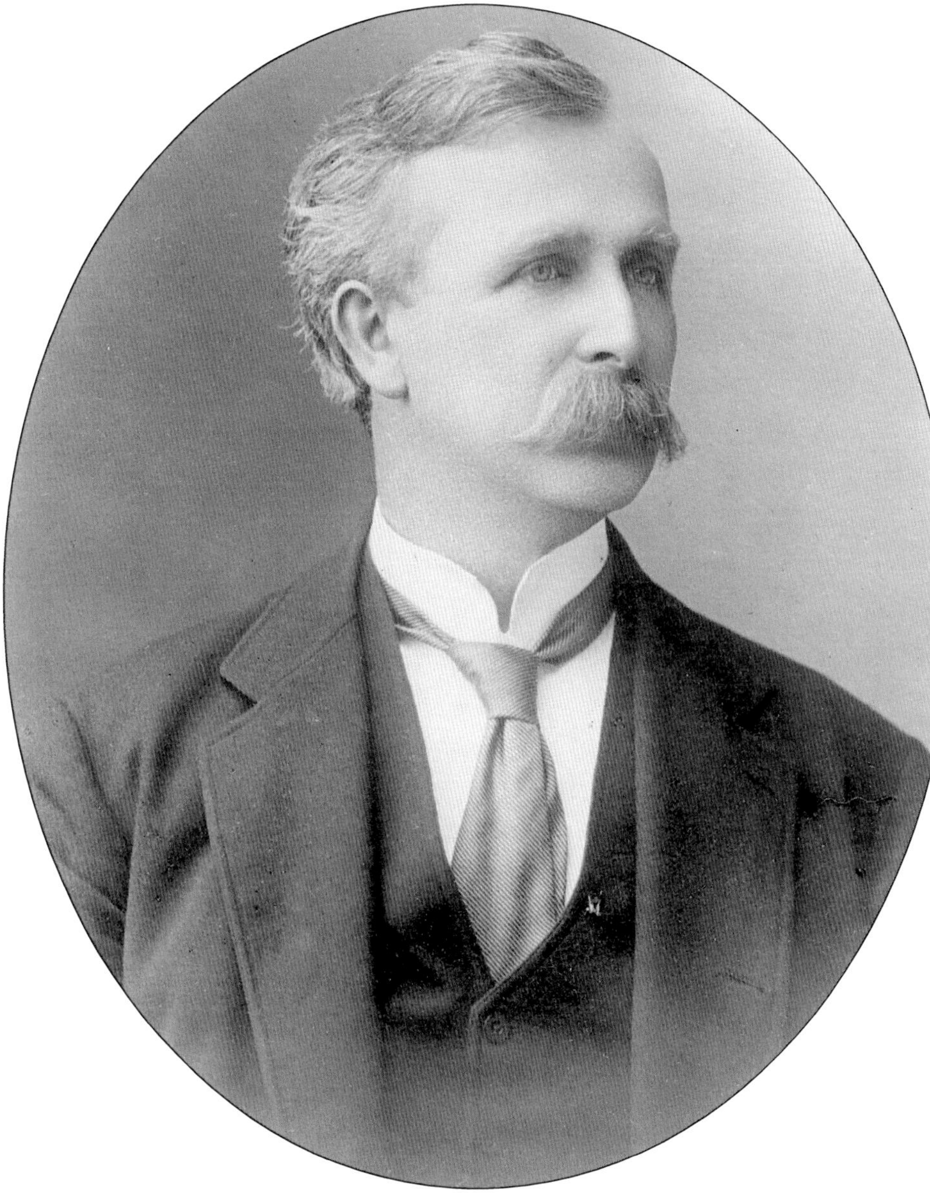

Andrew F. Johnson (1854–1943), a native of Nova Scotia, came to Gray as a youth and for some time was associated with the Smith and Leslie Company, which manufactured sleighs and carriages. He joined the staff of the Technical School for Carriage and Automobile Draftsmen and Mechanics in New York, and was the principal for 26 years when the school was in the Midwest. Many of the 2,500 men he trained became involved in the nation's aircraft and tank plants, and several became giants in the automobile industry. He trained the three famed Fisher Brothers, Fred, Alfred, and Edward, who designed automotive bodies for General Motors.

In 1927 a banquet was held in his honor in recognition of his generosity, his high standards, and the influence he had had on his students' lives. He was presented with a maroon 1927 Pontiac 4-door sedan. Since he didn't drive, his students expected he would sell the car, but Mr. Johnson could not sell a gift so lovingly given to him. When he died in 1943 the car was still virtually new, but it did have four flat tires.

James W. Russell (1921–1945), a native of Gray and the valedictorian of his class, lost his life in the service of his country during World War II. The new school built in 1948 in Gray Park was dedicated as a memorial to him.

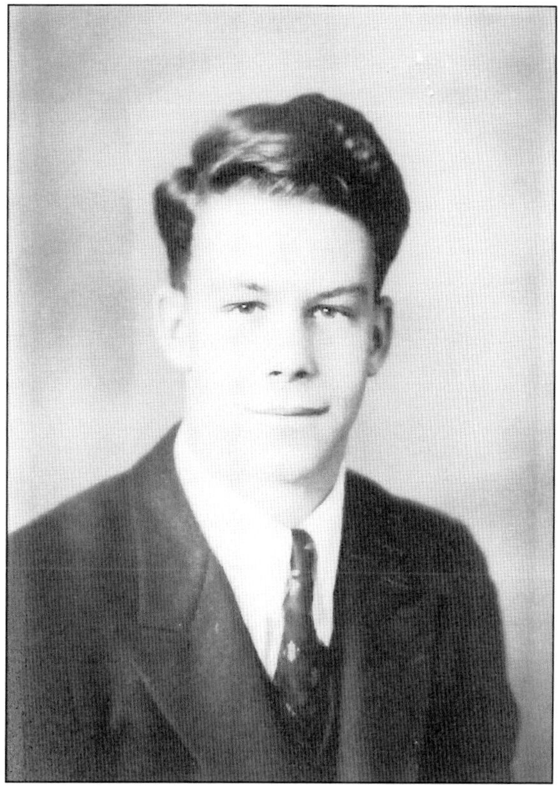

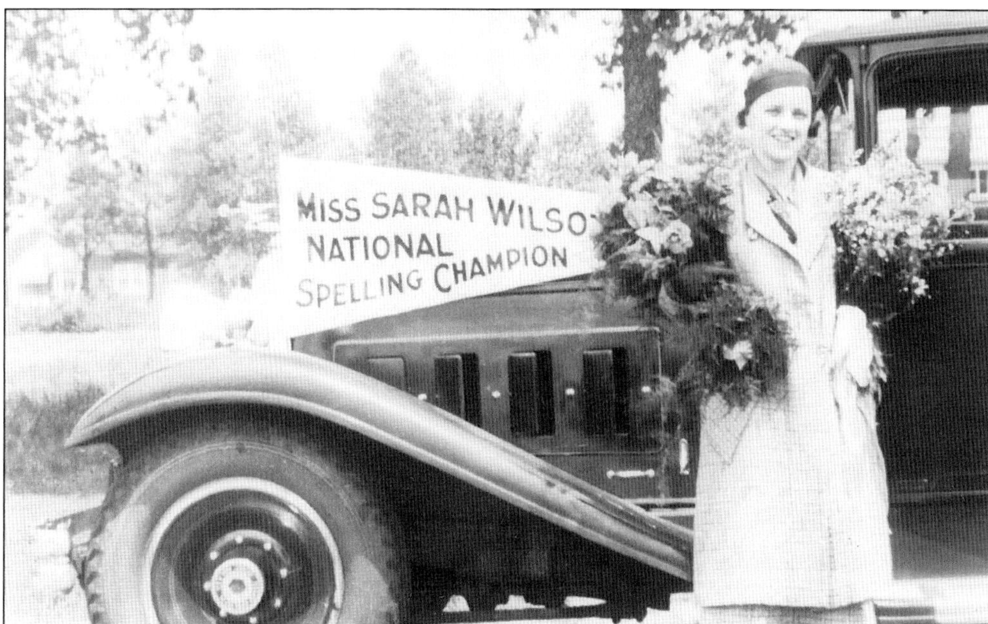

In 1934 Sarah A. Wilson, an eighth grader at the Hancock Junior High School, won the National Spelling Bee in Washington, D.C., making her the first contestant from Maine (as well as New England) to win the honor. Sarah became an attorney in Washington, D.C., and was employed by the Internal Revenue Service. She died in 1998.

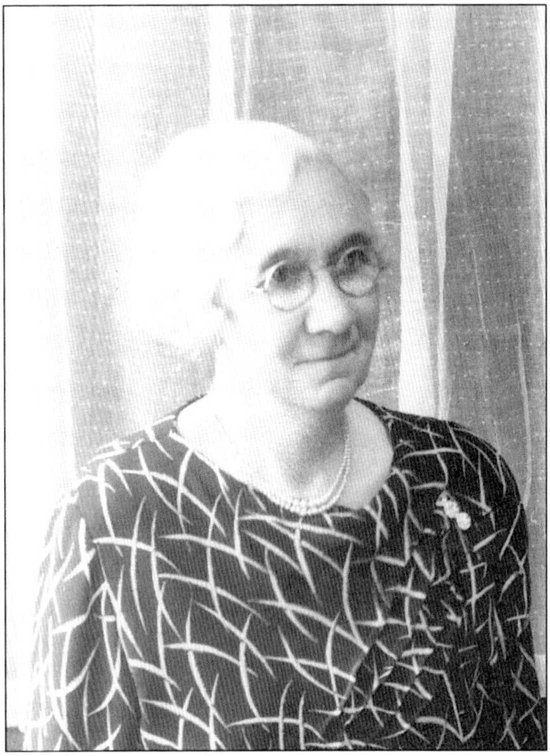

Mrs. Inez Yeaton moved to Gray in 1908, and in 1936 she became the first woman tax collector. The following quote about the town meeting of March 2, 1936, appeared in a local newspaper: "For the first time in its history, Gray today elected a woman as tax collector, Mrs. Inez Yeaton being chosen for that office. The town meeting was favored with a record attendance." She died in 1940.

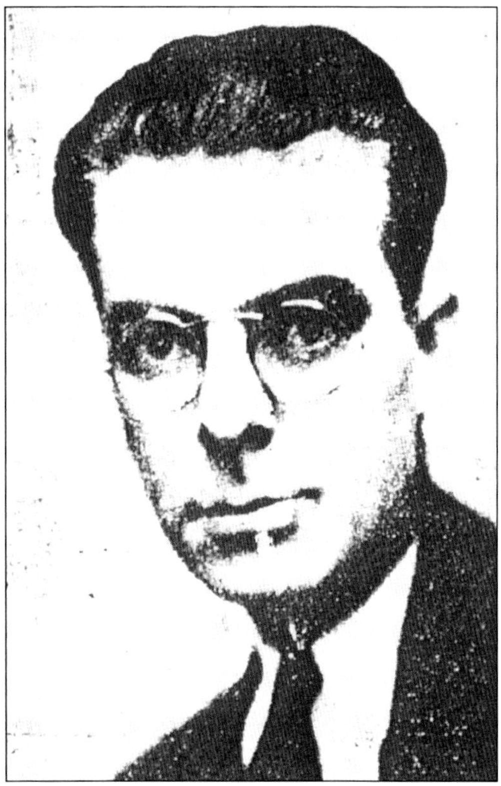

The Shadow knows Gray! Walter Gibson, a Gray resident in the 1940s, lived at 26 Shaker Road. Under the pseudonym Maxwell Grant, he wrote about 300 Shadow stories for the radio, novels, and comics, penning 120,000 words a month on average. He also wrote about another 112 stories and novels, under the names of Andy Adams, Douglas Brown, Ishi Black, and Harry Hershf. His wife, Litzka, also wrote many books under the name of Leona Lehman. A good friend of Harry Houdini and others, Grant often gave magic shows in town.

In the 1960s, Ralph S. Sawyer, a Gray native, became the head of the electrical systems branch of the flight systems division of the Manned Spacecraft Center of the National Aeronautics and Space Administration in Houston, Texas. His job was to perfect the tracking and data systems that would relay information from within the Project Apollo spacecraft. An early NASA scientist who pioneered space flight as well as moon landings, he received his early training from Pennell Institute, here in Gray, Maine, and graduated from Tufts College in Massachusetts. He now lives in Texas.

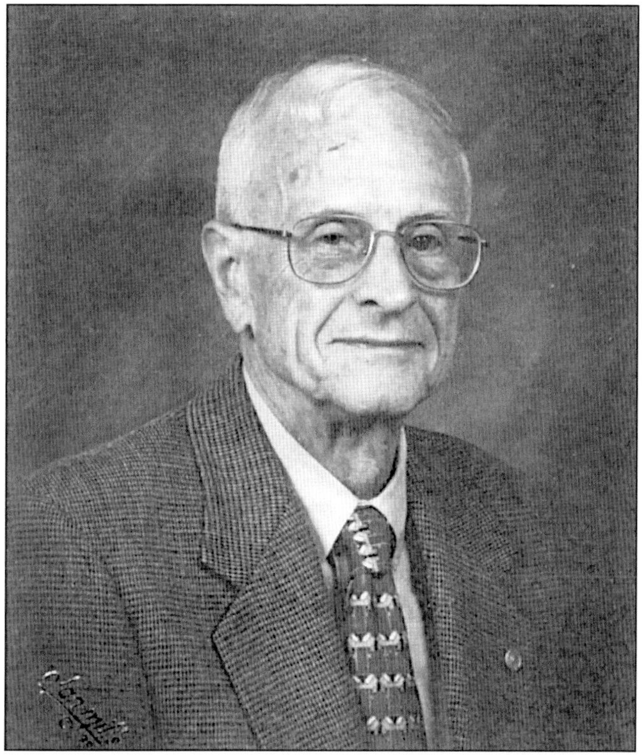

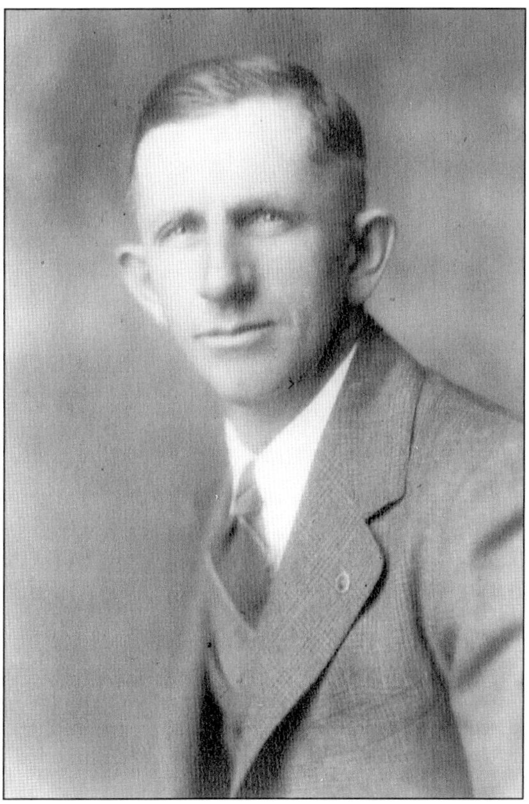

The Doughty family has long been a part of Gray's history. John T. Doughty (1898–1976) was the son of Henry C. Doughty and Jennie Merrill. His grandfather was Captain Charles H. Doughty. John served the town in many ways: as the town treasurer (1936–46), a justice of the peace (1944), a contractor and carpenter for many years, a bus driver, a member of the House of Representatives (1941–43), and as a selectman on the town council. Some of the buildings he built included the Russell School (1948), the Lawrence and Leighton Garage, and the houses of Kenneth Sawyer, Lin Libby, and Horace Grant, to name a few. He married Louise Chipman and they had three children, John Jr., Ruth, and Paul. Ruth and her family continue to live in Gray.

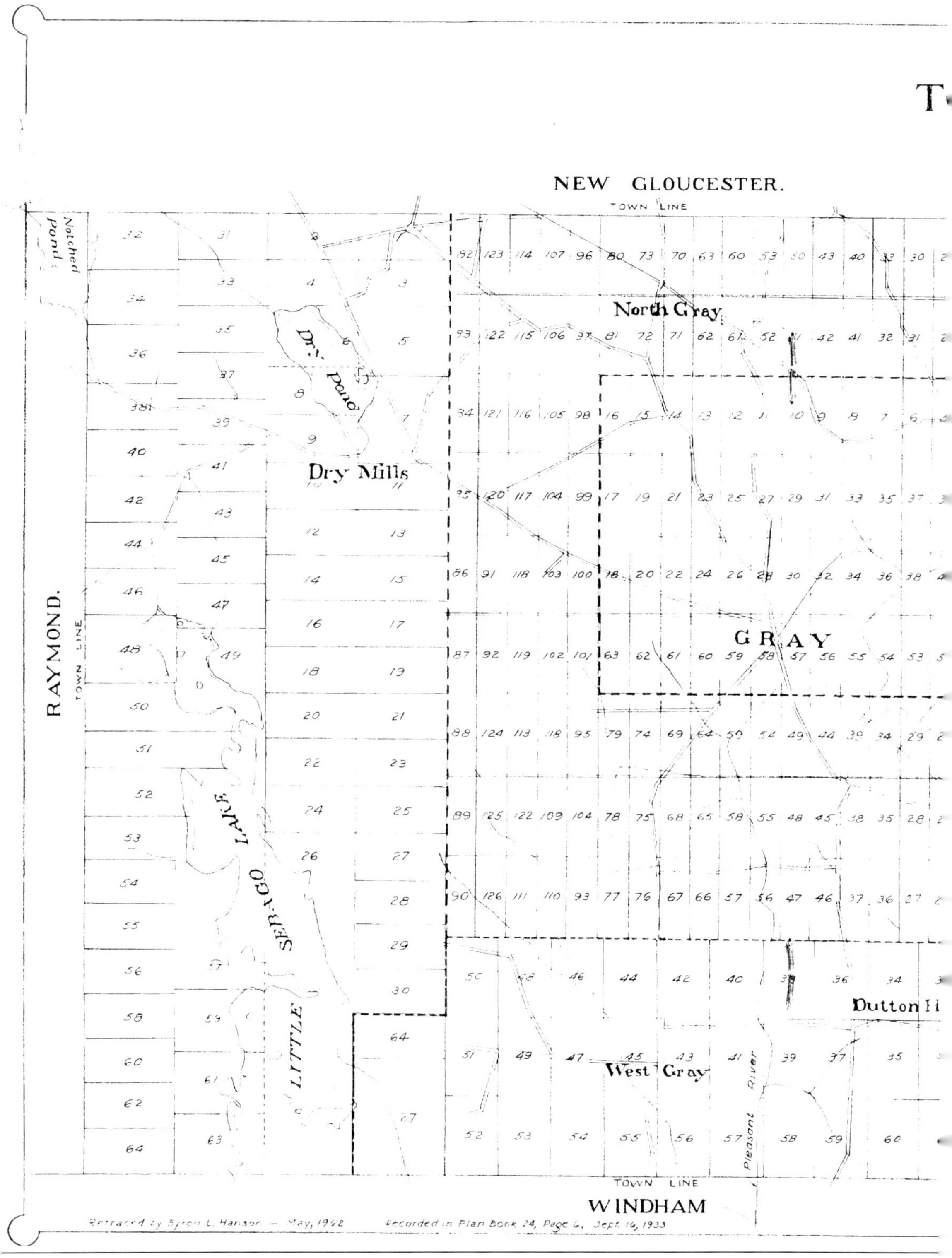
NEW GLOUCESTER.
TOWN LINE
Notched Pond
Dry Pond
Dry Mills
North Gray
GRAY
RAYMOND.
TOWN LINE
LAKE
SEBAGO
LITTLE
West Gray
Dutton H
Pleasant River
TOWN LINE
WINDHAM
Retraced by Byron L. Hanson — May, 1962
Recorded in Plan Book 24, Page 6, Sept. 16, 1933

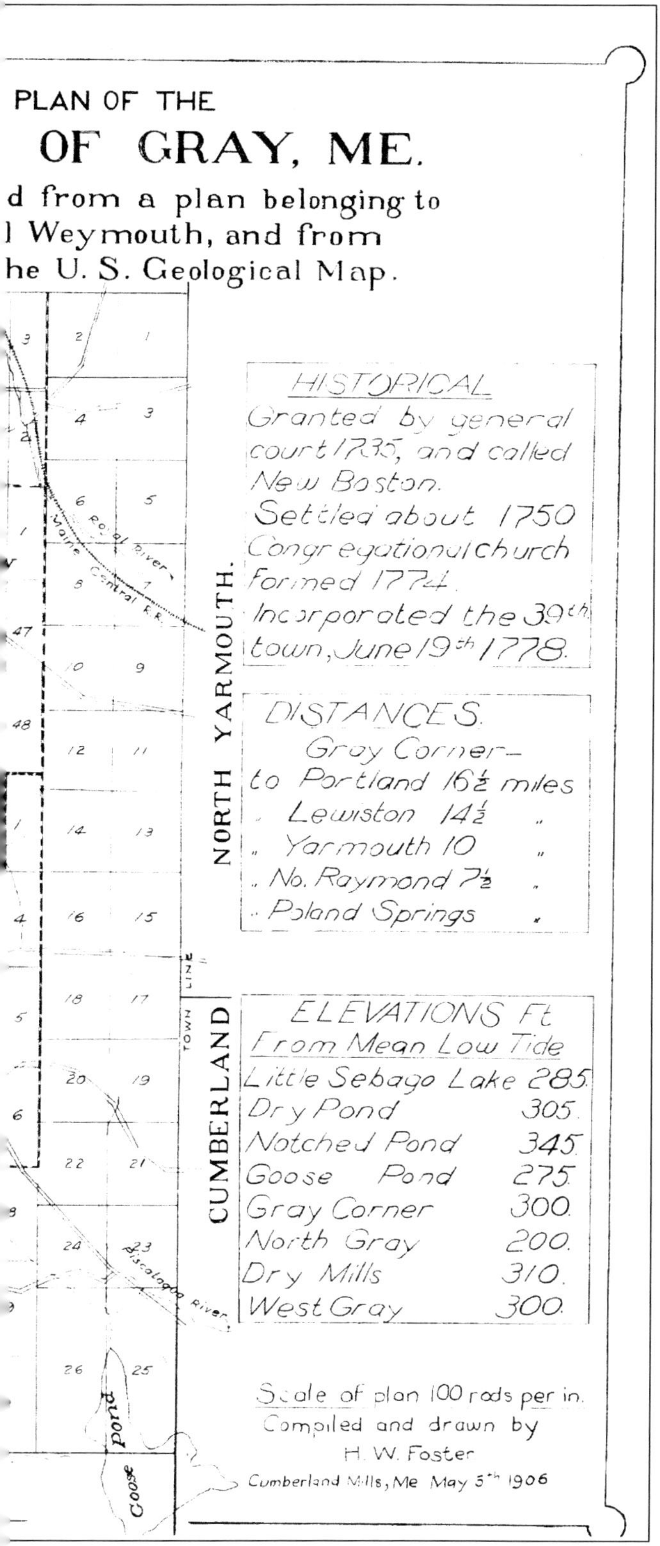

This map of Gray shows the plan for the town.

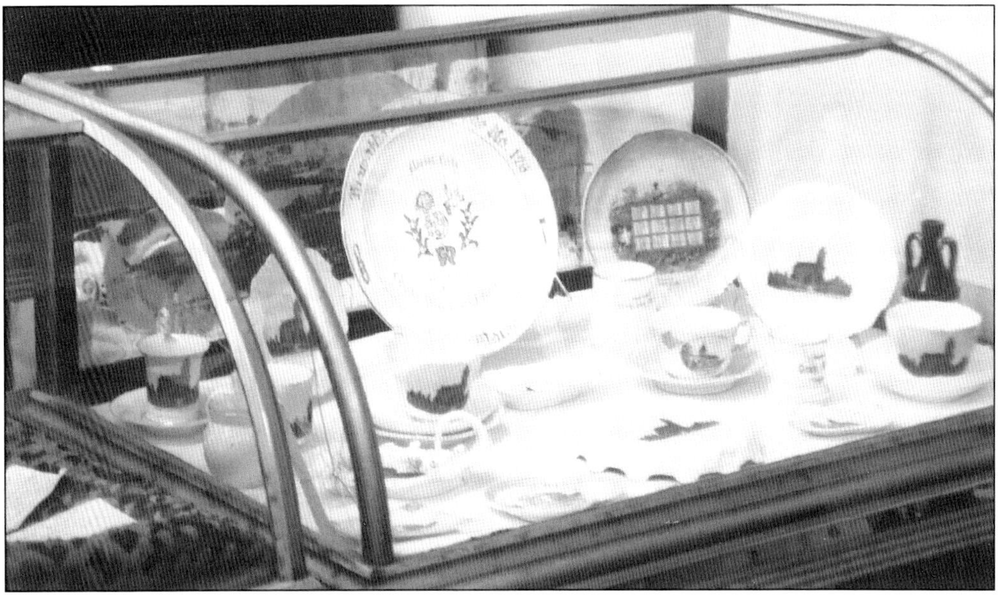

This is one of the many displays at the Gray Historical Society Museum.

Acknowledgments

On behalf of the compiler and the Gray Historical Society we are indebted to those who have donated the raw material for this book: pictures and personal stories. These contributions, obtainable from no other source, significantly increase the value of this pictorial. The majority of the photographs came from the Gray Historical Society's collection of items that have so generously been donated over the years. Also, a significant source of information was the book *History, Records, and Recollections of Gray, Maine* by George Hill and Willard M. Sweetser.

The compiler would also like to acknowledge the following contributors and sources: the *Portland Press Herald*, for information found in many old newspaper clippings in our collection of scrapbooks; Wayne Reilly, author of *Sarah Jane Foster, Teacher of the Freedmen*, who loaned Sarah's photo; permission to use the picture of Samuel Mayall came from the Minnesota Historical Society; the Gray Town Reports from the Gray Public Library; and the pamphlet "Gray, Maine: Past and Present," published by the Gray Historical Society in 1978.

The following contributors of personal pictures, stories, and help were instrumental to the completion of this work: John Welch, Jean Szendrei, Margaret Sawyer, Lucille Stampon, Judy Huff, Diane Fields, Jim Gillies, Norma Liberty, Bill Hinds, Ray and Barbara Clark, Earle Wilson, Nancy McMinn, Phil Cook, Mary Taylor, Monsignor Robert Lavoie, Ted and Ruth Pierce, John Doughty Jr., Hubert Cobb, Cora Skilling, Ann Cobb, Karen Taylor, George and Bea Muzzy, Teresa Pickens, Bob and Ruth Clark, Cindy Skilling Trinward, Glenice Wilkinson, Edith Bell, Gloria Jordan, Albert Vining, Librarian Melanie Coombs, Dean Bennett, Galen Morrison, Howard and Shelley Black, Helen Davis, Don and Fran Hutchings, Miriam Bisbee, Kenneth Knapp, Agnes and Arnold Stansfield, Sheryl Wilbur, Beverly Prince, Edra Wilkinson, Pamela Wilkinson, and Brad Pollard. My greatest thanks must go to Warren Knapp.

The time spent compiling this pictorial history will hopefully give current and future residents a look at Gray's past. To all those mentioned above and those errantly omitted, who have provided information, opinions, and help compiling this work, go my deepest thanks.

—Louise M Knapp